UNLEARNING THE LANGUAGE OF CONQUEST

UNLEARNING THE LANGUAGE

OF CONQUEST

*(Deceptions that influence war and peace, civil liberties, public
education, religion and spirituality, democratic ideals, the
environment, law, literature, film, and happiness)*

*Scholars
Expose
Anti-
Indianism
in America*

EDITED BY
WAHINKPE TOPA (FOUR ARROWS)
AKA DON TRENT JACOBS

UNIVERSITY OF TEXAS PRESS
Austin

Requests for permission to reproduce material from this work should
be sent to:
  Permissions
  University of Texas Press
  P.O. Box 7819
  Austin, TX 78713-7819
  www.utexas.edu/utpress/about/bpermission.html

∞ The paper used in this book meets the minimum requirements of
ANSI/NISO Z39.48-1992 (R1997) (Permanence of Paper).

LIBRARY OF CONGRESS CATALOGING-IN-PUBLICATION DATA

Unlearning the language of conquest : scholars expose anti- Indianism in
America : deceptions that influence war and peace, civil liberties, public
education, religion and spirituality, democratic ideals, the environment,
law, literature, film, and happiness / edited by Wahinkpe Topa (Four
Arrows), aka Don Trent Jacobs. — 1st ed.
     p.   cm.
  Includes bibliographical references and index.
  ISBN-13: 978-0-292-70654-5 (cl. : alk. paper)

  ISBN-13: 978-0-292-71326-0 (pbk. : alk. paper)

     1. Indians of North America—Public opinion.   2. Indians of North
America—History.   3. Indians in popular culture—United States.
4. Public opinion—United States.   5. United States—Ethnic
relations.   6. United States—Race relations.   I. Jacobs, Donald
Trent, 1946–
  E98.P99U55   2006
  305.897′073—dc22   2005035367

This is no mere matter for the philosophy classroom. We face the possible or probable extinction of life on our planet. If we can, we must grasp the bias and limitation of the "West's" worldview, powered by a hegemony that makes us oblivious to the wisdom of the people of America's First Nations.

—BRUCE WILSHIRE

The traditional Native People hold the key to the reversal of the processes in Western Civilization which hold the promise of unimaginable future suffering and destruction.

—"A BASIC CALL TO CONSCIOUSNESS," THE HAUDENOSAUNEE ADDRESS TO THE WESTERN WORLD, PRESENTED TO THE UNITED NATIONS IN GENEVA, SWITZERLAND, AUTUMN 1977

To Chief Seathl's Vision

This we know. The earth does not belong to man. Man belongs to the earth. Whatever befalls the earth befalls the sons of the earth. Whatever happens to the beasts soon happens to man. If men spit upon the ground, they spit upon themselves. All things are connected like the blood that unites one family. Whatever befalls the earth befalls the sons of the earth. Man did not weave the web of life. He is merely a strand in it.

—CHIEF SEATTLE'S STATEMENT OF 1854,
EDITED BY PROFESSOR TED PERRY

And

In memory of Vine Deloria Jr. (1933–2005). May his courage, spirit, and wisdom be remembered, and may his belief that we can and must unlearn the language of conquest—for the sake of all our futures—be realized in time.

CONTENTS

EDITOR'S NOTE ON CHIEF SEATHL'S SPEECH

Seathl, more commonly known as Seattle, made a now-famous speech in January of 1854, in his native tongue, Lushotseed. A Dr. Henry Smith took notes and created his version for the *Seattle Sunday Star* thirty years later. Several more adaptations followed and then, in the 1960s, William Arrowsmith, a literature professor at the University of Texas, wrote an edited version to make it sound more like he thought the original would have sounded. He read this version in 1970 at the first Earth Day celebration. Later, another University of Texas professor, a playwright named Ted Perry, under contract with the Southern Baptist Radio and Television Commission, edited and embellished Arrowsmith's version and used it to narrate a film on ecology called *Home*. The producer of the film, John Stevens, revised the speech further, apparently without Perry's knowledge, and his version was published in several major periodicals that subsequently led to various adaptations being published throughout the world.

Amazingly, all of these modifications and adaptations never lost the core essence of Seathl's vision. In fact, the changes, additions, and edits might even have fulfilled Seathl's desire for the red and white nations to work as partners for a better world. Thus the nurturing and dissemination of his speech by both Indian and non-Indian people may be as meaningful as the original speech itself. Ultimately "Chief Seattle's Speech" has offered an eloquent, emblematic, and enlightened expression of native wisdom. It expresses Chief Seattle's ultimate aim of shaking off the consciousness of the new civilization that came to exercise dominance over the Earth. Although the power of the speech has not sufficiently stopped the gruesome overrunning of Indigenous People* that continues today, it has nevertheless withstood the test of time and continues to prepare us for a return to a wisdom and sensibleness that might save us from the dire straits in which we find ourselves.

NOTE

*The United Nations Working Group for the Decade of the World's Indigenous People adopted this terminology, using capital letters as a gesture of respect in the same way one might refer to an English or German person. Throughout this text, the authors use various words to describe First Nations groups sharing similar worldviews.

ACKNOWLEDGMENTS

I would like to express appreciation to the scholars who have contributed to this book; to the University of Texas Press editorial staff, who were as committed to our message as they were to creating an excellent final edition; to Rick Two Dogs and my Medicine Horse Sun Dance brothers and sisters, who sometimes laugh at my attempt to analyze things and try to change the "white man's" ways but who always remind me of the greatness of the "Old Ways."

UNLEARNING THE LANGUAGE OF CONQUEST

Grandfather, don't you know me?
Grandfather, look what I have done to our world.
Mother earth is on her knees.
I don't understand the language you speak Grandfather.
I want my Pepsi, Levi's and Porsche too.
I don't have time to dance in the old way Grandfather.
Grandfather?
Grandfather why are you crying?
Grandfather, don't you know me?

— EXTRACTED FROM "GRANDFATHER CRIES," BY
CHARLES PHILLIP WHITE

COLUMBINE AND RED LAKE

On March 20, 2005, a seventeen-year-old Ojibwa boy from the Red Lake Indian Reservation (in Minnesota near the Canadian border) murdered his grandfather, his grandfather's friend, five students at Red Lake High School, a security guard, and a teacher. As of this writing, seven other students are hospitalized. The event has been billed in newspapers as the worst school shooting since the Columbine tragedy in 1999.

There are similarities between the two events. Both involved high school boys who, after killing others, shot and killed themselves. Both were young men who contemplated certain neo-Nazi assumptions about social systems. They had similar psychological profiles and similar preoccupations with media violence.[1] Both had been taking antidepressant drugs. Such similarities are perhaps helpful to note in terms of understanding how to recognize and maybe prevent some of the precursors that may have moved these boys to such horror. Children, whether white, black, brown, red, or yellow, are fundamentally the same and may be susceptible to the same kinds of influences.

There are also differences between the Red Lake and Columbine cases. Noting the most significant ones may serve to set the stage for this text. The contributing authors herein have attempted to reveal with their unique presentations how culture has distorted the truth about the "the Red Road" (a phrase many Indigenous People use to convey a way of living in harmony with others). Perhaps their purpose will be enhanced if the reader understands the Red Lake tragedy in relation to the perspectives of this prologue. Then Red Lake may serve as a "red flag," a warning about what may continue to happen in this world if the messages in this book are ignored.

"Using" the Red Lake tragedy in this context is a sensitive undertaking. Prayers, not politics, define the response of most Indigenous People to such a happening. Prayers, however, require focus. They also benefit from increasing numbers of people participating with this focus in mind. In an age where deception keeps so many people unaware of what things need prayers and actions, Red Lake offers an opportunity to make people more aware. This is especially true since what has been happening there and on other "Indian"[2] reservations will not likely be fully covered by the media.

In spite of this sensitivity, a number of Indigenous People have already begun to vocalize about the political ramifications of Red Lake. On October 25, 2005, a *Washington Post* article entitled "Native Americans Criticize Bush's Silence"[3] reported that a number of Indigenous People were contrasting Bush's recent preemption of his vacation to speak publicly about the Terri Schiavo case (regarding the brain-damaged Florida woman caught in a legal battle over whether her feeding tube should be reinserted) with his failure to give Red Lake at least equal attention. The *Post* piece seems to have prompted a response, if only a cursory one. Shortly after it appeared, Bush called Buck Jourdain, chair of the Chippewa tribe, from his home in Crawford, Texas, and "offered his prayers" and "pledged continuing federal support."[4]

There are a number of likely reasons why Red Lake has not received the attention that Columbine did, such as Red Lake's relative remoteness, the protectiveness of the tribe, or even the fact that school shootings are just not as newsworthy anymore. However, there may also be more compelling reasons—reasons that might relate to the language of conquest. Might Bush's silence about the shootings be intentionally designed to prevent a larger national and international discussion about things best left out of the spotlight? Is this why other political leaders and the media are giving the Red Lake story significantly less attention than they gave Columbine? Is there something disingenuous about Bush's pledge to Jourdain about "continuing federal support?" How might Red Lake's history and traditional ways of seeing the world be a threat to those in power? Many people did not care for Michael Moore pointing out the connection between the Columbine shootings and the fact that Littleton's main industry is making bombs.[5] They might be especially upset to have someone discuss certain "connections" regarding Red Lake.

Within twenty-four hours after the Columbine High School shooting in Littleton, Colorado, many of the nation's most prominent politicians had made public statements. Then governor George W. Bush immediately ordered flags in Texas to be lowered to half-staff in memory of the shooting victims at Columbine. He talked about his heart being broken. He said he wished love could be legislated and that love needs to happen at home. Within days he was supporting legislation that would jail juveniles caught carrying weapons until a judge could review their case (something that since has happened all too frequently to "Indian" juveniles whether they were carrying guns or not).

Alan Keyes spoke about the loss of morality threatening young people and suggested that if schools let God on campus, children would not have to seek God when such evil occurs. John McCain told the press that children should have a basic right to learn in an environment devoid of fear and violence. Lamar Alexander spoke of Columbine as a wake-up call for all Americans to build stronger families. Pat Buchanan pondered why violence and suicide seemed to be accepted as valid expressions of resentment and said Americans had glimpsed the last stop on the train to hell.[6] Dan Quayle wondered what could have possessed young people to do something so horrific and expressed the hope that Columbine would not be used as an excuse to take away guns. Newt Gingrich used the event as a platform to attack liberals.

Such comments that first day were just the beginning of a ground swell that would make the Columbine shootings "the single most important news event that happened in the nation or the world in 1999."[7] Nine out of ten Americans followed the shootings very closely. Hurricane Floyd and the destruction it wreaked on the mid-Atlantic was a distant second to Columbine. Most significantly, the tragedy became emblematic for the religious right. For example, later in the year, the U.S. House of Representatives voted 248 to 180 to allow states to post the Ten Commandments in public schools.[8] Georgia Congressman Bob Barr helped pass the bill with his statement on the House floor claiming that the Columbine killings would not have happened if the Ten Commandments had been posted in each classroom.[9] Georgia became one of the first states to take advantage of the law, passing a subsequent amendment to its Quality Basic Education Act requiring local school systems to "post in every public school classroom and in the main entryway in every public school a durable and permanent copy of the Ten Commandments as a condition for receiving state funds" (House Bill 1207). Later legislation allowed faith-based groups to apply for public funding. The increasing influence of the Christian right and its financial supporters led to larger and larger numbers of legislators and judges supporting Christian fundamentalist platforms. These in turn led to more restrictions and penalties on juvenile behavior, in and out of schools, to the authoritarian and punitive No Child Left Behind Act, and to an unprecedented attack on the environment.

Bill Moyers eloquently made the connection between the religious right and this attack on environmental policy. On receiving Harvard Medical School's Global Environmental Citizen Award, Moyers referred to the relationship between the post–Columbine era's destructive environmental policies and the growing Christian fundamentalism movement:

> For the first time in our history, ideology and theology hold a monopoly of power in Washington. Theology asserts propositions that cannot be proven true; ideologues hold stoutly to a worldview despite being contradicted by what is reality . . . So what does this mean for public policy and the environment? Go to Grist to read a remarkable work of reporting by the journalist Glenn Scherer—"The road to environmental apocalypse." Read it and you will see how millions of Christian fundamentalists may believe that environmental destruction is not only to be disregarded but actually welcomed—even hastened—as a sign of the coming apocalypse. As Grist makes clear, we're not talking about a handful of fringe lawmakers who hold or are beholden to these beliefs. Nearly half the U.S. Congress before the recent election—231 legislators in total—more since the election—are backed by the religious right. Forty-five senators and 186 members of the 108th Congress earned 80–100 percent approval ratings from the three most influential Christian right advocacy groups.
>
> I once agreed that people will protect the natural environment when they realize its importance to their health and to the health and lives of their children. Now I am not so sure . . . I read that the administrator of the U.S. Environmental Protection Agency has declared the election a mandate for President Bush on the environment. This for

an administration that wants to rewrite the Clean Air Act, the Clean Water Act and the Endangered Species Act, as well as the National Environmental Policy Act that requires the government to judge beforehand if actions might damage natural resources.[10]

So, what does this religious right, anti-environment, post-Columbine phenomenon have to do with Red Lake, the seventeen-year-old shooter, and the language of conquest? One can only speculate, of course, but one must indeed reflect on the possibilities, as difficult as it may be to do so. Does right-wing extremism or religious fundamentalism or even radical opposition to Christian fundamentalism play a role in the Red Lake situation and/or among Indigenous people worldwide? Similarly, should people discuss tendencies among American Indians and Indigenous Aboriginals that could make them susceptible to far-right ideologies? "Some adherents of the white-supremacist Christian Identity movement are known to argue that Indians are Aryans, while others voice admiration for Native Americans who insist on marrying only within their tribal notions."[11] Discussions about efforts to suppress authentic traditional Indigenous ways and intrusions from either Christian fundamentalists or white supremacists should, more than ever, be on the table.

As Moyers pointed out, there seems to be a connection between fundamentalist notions and a negative approach to ecological issues. The environment is a crucial issue for Indigenous People and may have been for the Red Lake shooter as well. It is likely that he had radical beliefs about protecting the environment. Maybe this is one reason he fell prey to the Libertarian National Socialist Green Party—he hoped to do something about the attack on the environment by the United States and wanted to fight back somehow. According to his own statements posted on the web, he respected Adolf Hitler because "I guess I've always carried a natural admiration for Hitler and his ideals, and his courage to take on larger nations."[12] Consider this statement in light of the environmental policy of the group that was becoming his beacon. The LNSGP made fighting the government in order to protect the environment a main tenant of its platform.[13]

Nature is our point of origin into this world and the order that still regulates the world around us, including many aspects of our own behavior . . . It is wise to recognize the universal wisdom of natural design and to embrace it as it is both superior to and more pragmatic than anything we have created. Further, as an object of function and for lack of a better word, art, nature is uncomparable and remains an inspiration to us all . . . Nature as an ideal and actuality is the best centering for any political viewpoint. IT ensures that first, we do not wipe ourselves out by disregarding our environment; second that we learn early on to appreciate beauty and function and larger systems; third, that we find inspiration in studying the largest and most complex form of creativity yet shown to us. Hell, we could go on all day. If you don't think nature is worth saving from greed, pollution, min-malls, highways, strip shopping centers, plastic trash, toxic waste and endless parking lots, what's wrong with *you?*[14]

Besides concerns about cultism and environmental disaster, the Red Lake shootings also offer the chance for deeper discussions about Indigenous identity. The shooter identified himself as "Native American."[15] He was apparently proud of his Indigenous heritage and angry that his friends only gave lip service to this heritage. What might the Red Lake tragedy reveal about conflicts between the ancient, traditional way of seeing the world and the fragmented worldviews that exist on the reservation? Consider what he says in one of his postings on the National Socialist website:

For example, if I asked your average teenager on this reservation: "Are you proud to be Native?" the answer I would get is, "hell yeah dawg." Now for some reason, I would find myself asking "if you're so proud to be Native, then why do you walk, talk, act and dress like an African American?" But I always refrain from doing so . . . Most of the Natives I know have been poisoned by what they were taught in school . . . But you are right about us Natives having a lot of pride in our heritage. I own my share of "Native Pride" shirts and sweaters, and I see many more in school, yet they are still outnumbered by your basic Rap culture paraphernalia.[16]

What if his pride, as distorted as it may have been, was sincerely about the value of his Indigenous heritage and how he felt Christianity had attacked it? After all, only three of the nine shooting victims had Ojibwa funerals. The other six victims, including the shooter, were buried with Christian rituals.[17] Maybe the boy's pride, not self-hatred, as many have claimed,[18] was one reason he was so interested in LSNGP, which has this to say about religion:

Christianity, as an offspring of Judaism, bears with it the same victimhood morality which aspires to place selfless suffering above all else while enforcing the righteousness of suffering in barter and other power transactions, rendering those who use logic and force impotent against the emotional reactions of masochists. Christian identity movements are wrapped in the same paradox as that with which the regime of Adolf Hitler collided in its whirlpool of fanaticism; the leviathan that is created must be exorcised, and the slavery to a collective will of the state perpetuates the mental confusion of humanity while directing all energy toward a disguised path leading to a future of the same. For this reason Christianity is on par with our thoughts about Judaism and other essentially elitist and delusional attempts to explain away the need to appreciate and understand life.[19]

It should go without saying that it would be very wrong to suggest that the killing of innocent people might in any way be justified, or that such a radical opposition to religion in general is anything but unhealthy and, in fact, not in line with the Indigenous philosophy that embraces all ways that people choose to honor the "great mysterious." To ignore realities about how aberrations of religion and how cults can create antagonisms, even insane actions, is also wrong. Just as a gun is dangerous in the hands of an unbalanced person, so a legitimate concern in the mind of a confused, depressed, angry, drugged, but otherwise intelligent and thoughtful teenager can also be harmful, especially if he or she is led down a slippery slope by a well-organized group that says on its website: "All of life is sacred to us. We want to protect it, regardless of the cost in individual lives, including ours."[20] (This was an answer to a question posed on the LNSGP website: "Every life is sacred to me. How can you advocate ideas that restrict the freedom of many and possibly will get them killed?")

Where does such insanity intersect with eco-violence and religious or cult fundamentalism? There are a number of research projects indicating that they do intersect. For example, two studies in Ohio and Michigan found that between one fourth and nearly one half of women who killed their children had religious-themed delusions.[21] Such studies are vital considering the staggering degree of mental illness in the United States. A recent study by the World Health Organization revealed that America has a much higher percentage of its population suffering from clinically diagnosed mental disorders than any other country in the world, and it leads in almost every type of mental disorder related to anxiety, mood, impulse, and substance issues, affecting an "underestimated 27% of the population."[22] What correlations can be made with other trends in the United States?[23] How might Red Lake represent a forecast of both the problems and the solutions that relate to mental health for all Americans?

How might the truth about Indigenous ways of seeing the world impact this rate of emotional illness?

Of course, we cannot forget that, aside from clinical insanity per se, church doctrine legitimized the domination of Indigenous cultures throughout history.[24] Was, in some way, this young teenager fighting back, blind and confused and on drugs, wrong as can be, but fighting back nonetheless, as many activists have done over the years?

Before leaving the arena of religiosity and identity as it relates to the Red Road–Red Lake–Red Flag trilogy, it is worth quoting from Wub-e-ke-niew, author of *We Have the Right to Exist: A Translation of Aboriginal Indigenous Thought*, if only to do so in light of what the young man who randomly killed his fellow students might also have been thinking at some level of his psyche. Wub-e-ke-niew, a traditional elder from Red Lake, writes from his Ahnishinahbaeotjibway (the original Red Lake Ojibwa/Chippewa term for "We, the People") perspective that comes not from "American Indians," whom he says represent a Euro-American colonial mythology, but from "Aboriginal Indigenous" people who understand a nonhierarchical, nondualistic reality. In his chapter on religion, he talks about his spiritual tradition and how it differs from what prevails on the Red Lake reservation. Specifically, he explains that what the "Indians" call the "Great Spirit" and "what Christians call 'God,' do not exist in our religion, and neither does the Devil. These concepts come from the good-and-evil dichotomy of their believers' European, Catholic roots. The fragmentation of peoples' world-view into pairs of opposites with emotionally-laden connotations is part of Lislakh[25] hierarchical society."[26] He continues:

> Now, under the Euro-American and "Indian" religion and economic system, everything is destroyed. All the lakes and streams are polluted, and the water is undrinkable . . . We have said in English, "all life is sacred," although a more accurate translation would be "all life transcends Western Civilization's dichotomy between sacred and profane." . . . Because of this culturally-imposed blocking of information which is threatening to the hierarchy, I would be greatly surprised if even one percent of the people who read this understand what I am writing. I am not questioning that the people who are reading this are intelligent. I am simply observing that the boxes of compartmentalized thinking into which the heirs of Western Civilization are forced by their culture, are extremely difficult to escape. . . .

At St. Mary's Catholic Mission at Red Lake, the staff wanted to bring us into their imaginary world, and simultaneously protect themselves from experiencing our world . . . The institutions of mainstream Lislakh society (at Red Lake) are saturated with violence, and living the totality of one's life non-violently within their context is not always easy . . . The Lislakh paradigm of world conquest comes directly from their religions. They absolve themselves from responsibility be retreating into the abstract, and recently by saying "church and state are separate," but the very first chapter in the Judeo-Christian Bible includes the political admonition: "and God said unto them, Be fruitful, and multiply, and replenish the earth and subdue it: and have dominion over the first of the sea, and over the fowl of the air, and over every living thing that moveth upon the earth."

CONTINUING FEDERAL SUPPORT?

Besides not wanting to talk about possible issues concerning the infiltration of right-wing groups into the culture of the Red Lake Reservation, there may be other reasons politicians are not using this catastrophe as a platform. Interestingly, Bush's statement about offering "continuing federal support" may have stimulated a rebuttal the administration does not want to hear. The following is a very brief overview of what could easily be enough material to create another book. In short, the statement coming from this president is a classic example of the kind of deceptions this text's authors expose.

Continuing federal support? Just this month, after Congress completed the first phase of its 2006 budget, Bush's plan reduced funding to the Bureau of Indian Affairs by $108.2 million, including a cut of $90 million—or 33 percent—for school construction. Bush also wants to cut $107 million from the Native American Housing Block Grants Program and $46 million from the Indian Housing Loan Guarantee Fund. Bush has further proposed taking away $85 million from the budget for building new health care facilities.[27] Funding for programs associated with promises to help reduce poverty have fallen short, according to a recent report entitled "A Quiet Crisis: Federal Funding and Unmet Needs in Indian Country," by the U.S. Commission on Civil Rights.[28] The study reveals that "federal funding directed to Native Americans through programs at these agencies has not been sufficient to address the basic and very urgent needs of indigenous peoples." This is not the place to recount the sad details of the "quiet" and "urgent" crises. A brief reading of the 55-page report will reveal these truths all too clearly in vital areas such as education, agriculture, food, health care, housing, justice, and the environment.

What may be more relevant to the context of this discussion is the relationship between such poverty and the kind of psychopathology that may have contributed to the Red Lake killings. A single research experiment may suffice in helping to connect some dots. A representative population of 1,420 rural children aged nine to thirteen at intake were given annual psychiatric assessments for eight years. One quarter of the sample were American Indian and the remaining were mostly white. Halfway through the study, a casino opening on the reservation gave the Indian group an income supplement that ultimately moved about 14 percent of the study families out of poverty. The results of the study, published in the *Journal of the American Medical Association,* showed that before the casino opened, poor and ex-poor children had more psychiatric symptoms than the never-poor children. After the opening, the "less-poor" children still had issues relating to anxiety and depression, but improved with regard to conduct and oppositional disorders.[29]

My own interpretation of this study, keeping in mind many other studies on related topics, is this: Poverty is indeed a significant contribution to violent behaviors and yet coming out of poverty alone, without an improved sense of self, is not enough to diminish depression and anxiety. A sound, healthful way of seeing the world and one's place in it is paramount.

The reader can make his or her own conclusions about how this and other studies might shed some light on what the Red Lake shootings were all about, but it seems that Bush's earlier Columbine remarks about an absence of love in the home may not suffice. Today the sixteen-year-old son of Tribal Chairman Floyd Buck Jourdain, considered by everyone to be a good, loving father, was arrested in connection with the shootings. It is very possible that he may be tried as an adult, according to federal laws and policies pertaining specifically to Red Lake. Apparently the young Jourdain, a cousin to the shooter, had exchanged what might turn out to be conspiracy-oriented emails with him:

A government official briefed on the investigation told AP that prosecutors were contemplating charging Jourdain as an adult with conspiracy to commit murder. The official spoke only on condition of anonymity because the investigation is ongoing. Authorities began to suspect that Weise may not have plotted the attack by himself after examining his computer and e-mails he exchanged with Jourdain, this official said. More arrests are possible, said this official and the law enforcement official. The law enforcement official said FBI behavioral analysts who were brought into the case also doubted that Weise acted alone, based on personality traits they identified.[30]

At this point there is no telling how this new turn of events might wind up. Whatever happens, Red Lake should not fall prey to rhetoric about "family values" or the absence of love in the home. The people of Red Lake, like most Indigenous People, love their children and their neighbors' children.[31] The love, however, like the hope that has seen Indigenous People through many tragedies throughout history, hovers precariously close to despair. (According to a recent survey in Red Lake, 80 percent of the ninth-grade girls say they want to go to college, and 81 percent have considered suicide.[32])

One can only hope that the recent arrest of Buck Jourdain's son will not somehow develop into further violence on the reservation. In light of the reservation's historical tensions all the way up to present times, one cannot be so sure:

- 1842—The first mission is established at Red Lake.
- 1851—U.S. purchases 5 million acres of land for $230,000 to be paid over twenty years without interest.
- 1858—A Catholic mission is opened at Red Lake by Rev. Father Lawrence Lautischar. He occupies a portion of the house owned by Joseph Jourdain, a French trader.
- 1864—The Ojibwa send a "delegation" to Washington to amend the Treaty of 1863; they cede 8 million more acres.
- 1877—The Episcopal Mission is founded at Red Lake.
- 1879—The Red Lake and Leech Lake Agencies are consolidated with the White Earth Agency in April.
- 1884—Courts of Indian offenses are established on several reservations, including Red Lake.
- 1889—A commission is authorized by an act of Congress approved on January 14 to negotiate a treaty with all the Ojibwa bands in Minnesota with respect to removal and the ceding of all surplus lands not needed for allotments. The Indians complain to the commission of unfulfilled promises by the government in past treaties, plead for mills and cattle, and ask that their boundaries be surveyed in accordance with past treaties. The loss of their crop the year before has made food scarce, and help is needed. Food sources, including rice beds, habitat for game, and other sources, are destroyed and people go hungry.

- 1889—Three million more acres are ceded to the U.S. government.
- 1892—An executive order on November 21 sets aside certain lands as an addition to the diminished Red Lake Reservation on three sections for the purpose of clearing boundaries.
- 1902—In an agreement with the adult male Indians of the Red Lake Reservation, 256,152 acres of land are given within Red Lake County to the U.S. Government for $1 million. Of this amount, $250,000 is to be paid in fifteen annual installments.
- 1904—By an act of April 8, the Minneapolis–Red Lake and Manitoba Railway Company is authorized to select 320 acres from land on the Red Lake Reservation.[33]

Jump to:

- 1979—There is a bloody uprising over a contentious tribal-council vote that results in riots, fires, and the shooting deaths of two teens. The tribe sues the federal government because it claims the FBI improperly withdrew its officers and allowed the siege to continue. (This is just five years after the infamous and bloody siege at Wounded Knee on the Pine Ridge Reservation, also involving the FBI.)
- 1986—A chief judge on the reservation is shot to death in connection with a dispute related to the Bureau of Indian Affairs.
- 2002—Red Lake is involved in a suit against the U.S. Bureau of Land Management in regard to mismanagement of the forest. (Lumber is a principal industry of the Red Lake Band. A number of people in Red Lake believe that the U.S. government continues to exploit their forests, profiting white-owned corporations and giving kickbacks to corrupt tribal members.)[34]
- 2002—Forensic auditors of the Red Lake Gaming Enterprises releases financial reports by the newly elected tribal treasurer verifying that no one has been at the financial controls for at least the past four years.[35]
- 2002—Senator Paul Wellstone and his wife Sheila, perhaps the last of the true supporters of the Red Lake people with this degree of power, die in a mysterious plane crash.[36]
- 2003—An affiliate tribe accuses local police of covering up a wrongful shooting of a young tribal member.[37]
- 2004—Fifty-page study of the Red Lake Chippewa Tribal Court finds inadequate record-keeping, no Court Rules procedures, no proper accounting for monies collected for fines, inadequate facilities, fifteen thousand law enforcement complaints turned over but never acted on,

and violations of Indian Gaming and Violence against Women Act, among other irregularities.[38]

• 2004–present—Greed, graft, politics, and jealousy permeate Red Lake's association with the nearby casino industry. See "Tribal Members Suffer from Congressional Greed."[39]

No: Indigenous People and students of Indigenous realities should not allow this nation's leaders, its media, or its right-wing groups to use Red Lake as a platform for touting family values, God, the Christian Bible, lies about federal support, or hatred and violence of any kind. Rather, all people should heed the words of Navajo Nation President Joe Shirley Jr. after he offered his condolences to the victims of the school shooting at Red Lake:

We are all terribly saddened by the news about our relatives on their land in Red Lake in Minnesota. Unfortunately, the sad truth is, I believe these kinds of incidents are evidence of Natives losing their cultural and traditional ways that have sustained us as a people for centuries.[40]

What is lost, however, can be found. The authors in this book believe that if enough people awaken to the truths they offer, perhaps not only Natives but all of us can return to a time before deception. We can be motivated to challenge the hegemony that has continued to attack Indigenous worldviews in an effort to keep them from rising to their true destiny, a destiny that can benefit all the world. Time is of the essence. Perhaps this is what the eagles were trying to say as they flew over the Minnesota capitol, when both the red and white people gathered to mourn the Red Lake tragedy together.[41]

NOTES

1. Perhaps not coincidentally, I just took a break from writing and went to the university lounge, where I looked through a January 2005 issue of *Computer Games*, a glossy magazine left on a table. An ad for "The Punisher" shows a skull with large, red-blood letters stating, "Guns Don't Kill People. Three-Quarter Inch Holes in the Head Kill People," along with an illustration of torture and shooting. Apparently there are many children "showing interest in violence" besides "the Red Lake shooter."

2. The problem of what to call "Native Americans" or "American Indians" is complex. As the editor of this volume, I personally prefer the term "Indigenous" or "Indigenous Aboriginal" since "Indians" is really a term coined by the conquerors of the Indigenous Aboriginals who have lived in what is now known as the

Americas for thousands of years. I also try to capitalize the terms to emphasize the distinction, as one would emphasize a national category like "African." However, as divided as "Indian" people are themselves on this issue, I have allowed various descriptors to be used throughout the book. Depending on the context, each author may use one or more of the terms to convey some personal or professional nuance. "Indian" identity crises are one result of the language of conquest. For the purposes of this book, however, although honoring individual lineage is vital, I offer that "being Indian" is less about blood and more about worldview. The Kiowa author M. Scott Momaday sums my position up: "An Indian is someone who thinks of themselves as an Indian. But that's not so easy to do and one has to earn the entitlement somehow. You have to have a certain experience of the world in order to formulate this idea" (quoted in Peter Nabokov, *Native American Testimony* [New York: Penguin, 1992], 439). As someone whose mother did her best to turn me away from my own Creek/Cherokee heritage, as someone more Anglo in blood than Indigenous Aboriginal, I turn to my Sun Dance experience, my life with the Oglala and the Raramuri, and my lifelong research into understanding the Indigenous worldview within limitations I fully recognize, among other things, as my own grounds for the entitlement to which Momaday refers. At any rate, the issue of identity is crucial as it relates to the young teenage "shooter" responsible for the Red Lake tragedy.

3. Ceci Connolly, "Native Americans Criticize Bush's Silence: Response to School Shooting Is Contrasted with President's Intervention in Schiavo Case," *Washington Post*, March 25, 2005, A06.

4. "Bush Calls Red Lake Tribal Leader," UPI, 2005, http://washingtontimes.com/upi-breaking/20050325-030125-6463r.htm. Accessed March 25, 2005.

5. He illustrated this connection in his award-winning documentary, *Bowling for Columbine*.

6. References to demons and devils were also prevalent in media reports on the Red Lake incident. For example, the title of the *Time* magazine article was "The Devil in Red Lake" (*Time*, April 4, 2005).

7. Survey Reports, Pew Research Center for the People and the Press, January 19, 2000, http://people-press.org/reports/pring.php3?PageID=251. Accessed March 27, 2005.

8. Don Trent Jacobs (Four Arrows) and Jessica Jacobs-Spencer, *Teaching Virtues: Building Character across the Curriculum.* (Boston: Scarecrow Press, 2001), 161.

9. Christopher Kirchhoff, "Congress Bludgeons First Amendment," Council for Secular Humanism, Fall 1999, http://www.secularhumanism.org/library/fi/frontlines_19_4.htm.

10. Bill Moyers, "On Receiving Harvard Medical School's Global Environmental Citizen Award," Common Dreams News Center, December 6, 2004, http://www.commondreams.org/views04/1206-10htm. Accessed March 27, 2005.

11. D. Neiwert, "The Succubus," March 23, 2005, http://dneiwert.blogspot .com/2005/03/succubus.html.

12. National Socialist forum posting by Todesengel (he also posted as "NativeNazi") on March 19, 2004, at 1:15 a.m.

13. National Socialist forum, http://www.nazi.org.

14. National Socialist Frequently Asked Questions, http://www.nazi.org/ library/faq/#eco. The Red Lake boy who shot and killed his classmates and him-self stated on May 26, 2004, "I was wondering if there was a way to become a more active member, besides posting on this board. I can't really think of anything else to do."

15. In a posting to the National Socialist forum, http://www.nazi.org, he identified himself as follows on March 19, 2004, at 12:09 a.m. "Hello al. My name is Jeff Weise, a Native American from the Red Lake 'Indian' reservation in Minnesota."

16. Ibid., posting by "NativeNazi" on July 19, 2004, at 11:33 a.m.

17. Amy Forliti, "Funerals to Be Held for Shooting Victims," ABC News, March 26, 2005, http://abcnews.go.com/US/wireStory?id=615536. Accessed March 28, 2005.

18. See, for example, Mathew Barkhausen, "Tragedy at Red Lake: A History of Self-Hate among Indian Youths," March 24, 2005, www.alternet.org/ story/21594/.

19. National Socialist forum, http://www.nazi.org.

20. Ibid.

21. Lisa Falkenberg, as published in the San Antonio *Express-News*, December 13, 2004; University of Connecticut Health Center, http://www.uch.edu/ ocomm/features/stories/stories04/feature_religiosity.html.

22. Chris Bowers, "America Leads the World in Mental Illness," MyDD, http://www.mydd.com/story/2005/3/14/15253/7082.

23. Notably, President Bush plans to promote a proposal that would screen the entire population for mental illness and extend screening and psychiatric medication to kids and adults all over the United States, following a pilot scheme of recommended medication practice developed in Texas and already exported to several other states. The following report appeared in the June 2004 *British Medical Journal*: "A sweeping mental health initiative will be unveiled by President George W. Bush in July. The plan promises to integrate mentally ill patients fully into the community by providing 'services in the community, rather than institutions,' according to a March 2004 progress report entitled New Freedom Initiative." While some praise the plan's goals, others say it protects the profits of drug companies at the expense of the public; www.whitehouse.gov/infocus/ newfreedom/toc-2004.html.

24. Suppression of Indigenous cultural values was even part of the late Pope John Paul II's legacy. Representing the kinds of contradictions that are inherent

in orthodoxy, on the one hand he was a great spokesperson for Indigenous People, even apologizing for the historical oppression perpetrated by the church. On the other, he sanctioned (at least officially) the continuing evangelization of Indigenous People and forbade them to incorporate their cultural forms of worship in the churches or traditional use of churches for "non-orthodox" religious events. He also continued promoting a male-dominated system of religiosity.

25. "Lislakh" refers to the interrelated and historically connected peoples who share societal, cultural, language, and/or patrilineal roots within the context of Western civilization, including Germanic people and the heirs of the Roman Empire.

26. Wub-e-ke-niew (Francis Blake), *We Have the Right to Exist* (New York: Black Thistle Press, 1995), 144.

27. Larry Bivins, "BIA gets $108M Cut in Bush Budget," in *Argus Leader Washington Bureau*, March 8, 2005, http://www.argusleader.com.

28. "A Quiet Crisis: Federal Funding and Unmet Needs in Indian Country," U.S. Commission on Civil Rights, July 2003, www.usccr.gov.

29. Jane Costello, Scott Compton, Gordon Keeler, and Adrian Angold, "Relationships between Poverty and Psychopathology: A Natural Experiment," *Journal of the American Medical Association* 290.15 (October 2003): 2023–2029.

30. Amy Forliti (AP), "Tribal Chairman: Son Innocent in Shooting," *Grand Forks Herald*, March 29, 2005.

31. Historically, Indigenous People have been known for their affection for and treatment of children. Of course, drug addiction or alcoholism, reacting with historical trauma, poverty, and utter confusion, can lead to domestic violence.

32. Paul Tosto, "Red Lake Is Blue," *St. Paul Pioneer Press*, March 25, 2005, http://www.grandforks.com/mld/grandforks/11224976.html.

33. This list was extracted from the "Chronological History of Red Lake," by Erwin F. Mittelholtz, Beltrami County Historical Society, http://uts.cc.utexas.edu/Ðwoss/redlake2/chrono1.html.

34. Wub-e-ke-niew, *We Have a Right to Exist*.

35. Native American Press Ojibwe News, July 12, 2002, http://www.press-on.net/editorials/7-12controls.html.

36. Paul Wellstone may have been the last U.S. senator who was a true friend of the Red Lake Band. He fought for their rights, visited often, helped legislate funding for facilities, and donated annually from his own pocket to a shelter he helped build. His wife, Sheila, took part in the Equay Wiigamig's Indian Women's Coalition roundtable and Fall Feast. Former chairman of the tribe Bobby Whitefeather considered him to be a part of the People. See Amy Becker, "Notebook: From Blue Collar to Power Suits, They Came for Wellstone," *St. Paul Pioneer Press*, October 30, 2002. David Wellstone, during a memorial service for his father, told a story about the senator's recent trip to the Red Lake Reservation; the senator had seen an eagle fly over and commented that it was

a good sign. See Philip Pina, "He Was a Wonderful Father," *St. Paul Pioneer Press*, October 30, 2002, http://www.twincities.com/mld/twincities/4400215.html.

Paul McCabe, special agent from the Minneapolis Division of the FBI and FBI spokesman at Red Lake, was in charge of the investigation into the death of Senator Paul Wellstone. I speak about his unusual handling of the Wellstone case in Four Arrows, *American Assassination: The Strange Death of Senator Paul Wellstone* (New York: Vox Pop, 2004).

37. Jeff Armstrong, "Cover-up Claimed in Duluth Police Shooting of Native," NAIIP News Path, April 3, 2003, http://www.yvwiiusdinvnohii.net/News2003/0304/Armstrong030404DuluthShooting.html.

38. "Reservation Report: A Monthly Media Letter regarding American Indian Policies," *New Century Communications* 3.9 (June 2004): 2–8.

39. In addition to concerns about who receives profits, etc., the spending of tribal money for political action committees has been problematic. Millions of dollars in soft money has been donated to the parties by tribes. It's not easy to track the funds, and because tribal entities donate under various names, it is difficult to even account for how much is being spent. For example, in 1998, listings for Mille Lacs campaign contributions were found under the names "Mille Lacs Band of Chippewas," "Mille Lacs Band of Ojibwe/Grand Casino," "Mille Lacs Band of Ojibwe Indians," or "Chippewa, Mille Lacs." See Elizabeth S. Morris, "Tribal Members Suffer from Congressional Greed," a summary from Center for Responsible Politics, July 2003, http://www.ronan.net/~morris/page20.html.

40. Independent Staff, "Navajo Leader Gives Condolences over Red Lake School Shootings," March 25, 2005, http://www.gallupindependent.com/2005/mar/032505shootings.html.

41. It was reported that when members of the Red Lake Band, as well as many non-Indians, gathered on the steps of the state capitol to pray for healing in the wake of the Red Lake shootings, they looked up and saw eagles soaring overhead. See the Associated Press article, "Prayers for Healing Offered on State Capitol," http://www.rlnn.com/ArtMar05/PrayersHealOfferStepsCap.html.

INTRODUCTION

Four Arrows

The language of conquest is ultimately a language of deceit. It echoes in the corridors of every American institution, building illusion upon illusion while robbing all of us of our collective Indigenous wisdom. This book is an effort to expose and replace this deception. Although it speaks specifically to the colonization and oppression of America's First Nations and their potential contributions, which have been suppressed by the lies of our dominant culture, no single race of people can lay claim to "Indigenous wisdom." It lives deep within the heart of every living creature. Anyone who remains deeply aware of the rhythms of the natural world can remember it.

Unfortunately, it seems that most of us have lost or are losing this "primal awareness,"[1] largely because of the language of conquest. Of those who have not lost it, perhaps none have struggled as hard or have experienced such overwhelming efforts to force them to forget it as have the wisdom keepers of the various American Indian tribes. My friend Rick Two Dogs, an esteemed Oglala holy man and spiritual leader of the Medicine Horse Sun Dance, told me recently that those who remember and live the old ways are like weeds that continue to break through "the concrete streets" of the oppressors. This is why, he said, we must remember the old Lakota ways. "Ehanni Lakol wichohanki Tunkasila kiksuye." Grandfather remembers the old Lakota ways, and so must we.

In any book that praises or attempts to protect Indigenous wisdom, there is always the risk of either playing into or being accused of participating in the so-called Noble Savage Myth. Our authors are fully aware of the idea and the historical context and political motivations associated with this. However, they know also that many writers have intentionally thrown the proverbial baby out with the bathwater under the guise of legitimately deconstructing this myth. In this case, the "bathwater" symbolizes the false and largely artificial image of Indigenous People as being totally innocent, physically perfect, always fearless, highly instinctive and without cognitive skills, always wise and peaceful, without emotions, free of social restraints, relegated to the unlivable past, and so on. The "baby" represents authentic worldviews that may indeed offer us vital alternatives to the devastating effects of free-market globalization, greed, war, and ecological ignorance. To save the "baby," our contributing authors will describe aspects of Indigenous worldviews that can have meaning for contemporary lives of all people, while offering formidable rebuttals to the logic of those "researchers" who have concluded that "acknowledging anything positive in the native past is an entirely wrongheaded proposition because no genuine Indian accomplishments have ever really been substantiated."[2]

When people come upon a description here or there of authentic aspects of ancestral Indigenous thinking, many people recognize or remember the truths represented or revealed without the dehumanizing or political agendas associated with the aforementioned myth. See if this is true for you as you read the following assumptions about life that many of the varied and various Indigenous Peoples generally share:

- The natural world is ultimately more about cooperation than it is about competition.
- The concept of reciprocity can guide living systems toward balance.
- Human decisions are best made from the heart as well as the mind.
- Humans are entwined in and with Nature and the idea of "conquering" or "being in charge" of it rather than honoring the relationship is considered an aberration.
- Children are sacred and possess inherent value.
- A Great Mysterious Spirit is within all its creations.
- Material possessions are less important than generosity and generosity is the highest expression of courage.
- Diversity gives strength and balance to the world.
- Resolution of conflict should be about restoring harmony rather than enacting vengeance or punishment.
- Cognitive dissonance is a human frailty that is best met with humor and understanding followed by corrective resolution, not by rationalization or denial.
- Women are naturally wise and powerful and are thus vital for social harmony.
- Prayer and ceremony can help one connect to an invisible world and have value in maintaining health and harmony.
- Fear is a catalyst for practicing a great virtue such as generosity, patience, courage, honesty, or fortitude.[3]

- Ultimately, the only true authority comes from personal reflection on experience in light of a spiritual awareness that all things are related.
- Words are powerful entities and should never be misused or used deceptively.

This book is not about such assumptions per se. Rather, it intends to reveal why it is so difficult in these times to understand and embrace them. More specifically, it offers a long overdue scholarly challenge to the educational and ideological hegemony[4] that constitutes what might be thought of as a "fourth wave of killing the Indigenous." The story of this "fourth wave" is similar for Indigenous People around the world, but in America it goes something like this:

European invaders, government soldiers, and civilian opportunists launched the first assault with violence and disease. A genocidal effort to eradicate the people of America's First Nations was based in greed and rationalized by Christian fundamentalism. Politicians, courts, lawyers, the military, and corporations have been behind an ongoing second wave intended to control Indigenous land, water, language, culture, identity, and sovereignty. Academics have led the third wave of the attack with "scholarly" publications that erroneously attack the philosophies, worldviews, and histories of Indigenous People.

The fourth wave is the insidious accumulation of the first three, bringing anti-Indianism into the realm of a dangerous hegemony. It tends to support the first three waves with continuing anti-Indian legal interpretations, classroom instruction and textbooks, literature, films, and social commentary. It represents a new and growing level of erroneous "common sense" that prevents people from realizing the truth, not just about Indigenous People, but about life itself.

The contributions in this text address all four overlapping "waves," but especially focus on the third wave, which relates to more formal aspects of education and information dissemination. It seems that public education itself has become an enemy of truth seeking. For example, it is common for third-year university teacher candidates, even those from First Nations, to be surprised when they learn for the first time that the Christopher Columbus legacy is anything but positive. In the same way that the conservative radio personality Rush Limbaugh confuses millions of people about environmental issues like global warming (sufficient, for instance, to result in as much as a 50 percent reduction in contributions to environmental groups like the Union of Concerned Scientists[5]), the Ivory Tower rhetoric and "research" of authors like those mentioned below feed a growing mistrust of "Indian" values throughout society.

Robert Whelan's 1999 book, *Wild in the Woods: The Myth of the Peaceful Eco-Savage*, is but one example. Whelan, director of a think tank that specializes in pro free-market analysis of environmental issues, is one of a slew of authors whose "scholarly" publications dismiss any positive contributions of the Indigenous way of thinking and revise history in order to support their conclusions. For example, Whelan, after criticizing anti-Columbus rhetoric, concludes, "Indigenous peoples of the earth today have little to teach us about caring for the environment."[6] He says there is "a great deal of wishful thinking behind statements that claim that pre-Columbian native people lived as natural elements of the ecosphere. In fact, they could scarcely be more inaccurate."[7] And: "In fact we now know that the American Indians were forest-burners par excellence. As a result, it was not the forests which impressed the early settlers but the absence of them. To the Indians, trees had no value."[8] Referring to Indigenous Peoples of South America, he further states that it was the "decimation of the Indian population which resulted in the re-appearance of the rainforest!"[9]

Whelan writes well, provides many references, and travels around the world giving speeches that assert that "the green movement has been rightly perceived by many libertarians as a serious threat to both liberty and the market,"[10] a comment he made when he presented before The Stockholm Network, a European pro-market think tank. Whelan is the associate director for the Institute of Economic Affairs and is also Britain's leading anti-abortion activist. He recently proposed legislation to "sell Africa" to a multinational organization. His speeches and his writings are nonetheless convincing to many, as when he says in his book, "The American Indians were deadly serious about hunting. There was no sense of British fair play, or giving the quarry a sporting chance. The aim was to kill as much as possible as quickly as possible with the minimum risk to the hunter. There was no concern for conserving future stocks nor for taking only as much as was necessary to meet present needs."[11] Or when he unfavorably compares tribes like the Iroquois with modern paper mill owners: "Conservation would not have occurred to the Indian, lacking the necessary understanding of the physical world."[12]

In a subsection called "Dances with Garbage," he says North American Indigenous People were quick to exploit the peculiar legal status of their reserves, and uses gambling as an example of how Indian people are far from being free from corrupting consumerism. (Of course he ignores that such corruption stems from the shadow of dominant culture and oversimplifies the complexity of the casino phenomenon.) Similarly, he refers to a contract by the Campo Indians of Southern California who "charge millions of dollars for the dumping of waste under conditions which are far less stringent than those which waste processing companies would be obliged to meet anywhere else in the USA" as another example that there is nothing particularly of worth in Indigenous value systems. (And again, this ignores the deeper truths and implications of this absence of environmental regulations on Indian reservations!)

Whelan is but one of a growing number of authors publishing academic and popular books or articles that argue, like C. E. Kay does in "Aboriginal Overkill," a piece published in *Human Nature*, that Indigenous People historically never had a conservation ethic but rather acted in ways that were the absolute opposite of a conservation strategy.[13] Other authors offer "evidence" alleging that the Indigenous worldview and practices were responsible for such horrors as

- unrestrained cannibalism among the Hopi and Zuni as described by Dr. Christy Turner in the University of Utah Press release *Man Corn: Cannibalism and Violence in the Prehistoric American Southwest* (1999).
- constant violence, cannibalism, and warfare among the Anasazi and other Puebloans as presented in the University of Utah Press release *Prehistoric Warfare in the American Southwest*, by Steven A. Leblanc, whose newest book, *Constant Battles: The Myth of the Peaceful, Noble Savage*, published by St. Martin's Press (2003), concludes that technology and science have put mankind on the right trajectory for world peace in comparison to the barbaric behaviors of aboriginal people.
- civilian massacres that prove that the "humanity" of humans is a product of civilization and centralized governments that overcame the horrors of primitive life, as "documented" by Lawrence H. Keeley in *War Before Civilization* (Oxford University Press, 1997).
- child abuse and other social maladies that were far more pervasive in primitive societies than in ours and prove the superiority of Western culture, put forth by UCLA anthropologist Robert Edgerton in *Sick Societies: Challenging the Myth of Primitive Harmony* (Free Press, 1992).
- the demise of the buffalo, which according to Shepard Krech in his book, *The Ecological Indian: Myth and History*, was the fault of the Indians themselves (Norton, 2000).
- savagery reflected in difficult-to-pronounce Indian names like Ota Kte, "which translated as Plenty Kill and evoked a savage past," as stated in Michael L. Cooper's elementary school text, *Indian School: Teaching the White Man's Way* (Clarion, 1999).

- killing and mutilating women and children for the sake of honor, according to Albert Martin in his book *Sitting Bull and His World* (Dutton, 2000), a text for grades 5–8 that says, "White people did not bring war to the Great Plains" (39).

Such publications have done and are doing to American Indians what a number of "academic" authors have done in Australia to dismiss the value of the Australian aboriginal worldview. Interestingly, the vice president of the Australian Council of Professional Historians, Kathy Clement, recently edited a collection of articles from academic professors entitled *Whitewash: On Keith Windschuttle's Fabrication of Aboriginal History;* her book sets out to counter the influence of books like Keith Windschuttle's, which is "part of a range of writing that seeks to counter left-wing influence on people's thinking about the history of Indigenous Australians."[14]

These are examples of one side of the dual-edged sword academics have used against Indigenous People. The other side relates to how they typically ignore them. Several decades ago Francis R. McKenna categorized this policy of dismissal as follows:

> Academics generally have little interest in Indians. Scholars generally can be divided into three categories: (a) Those who are overtly racist. An example is John Greenway, a folklorist at the University of Colorado. Greenway posed the question, "Did the United States destroy the American Indian?" and answered, "No but it should have." (b) Those who exclude Indians from academic life. To illustrate, witness the rejection of the application of the American Indian Historical Society for participation in the International Congress of Historical Sciences; and (c) those who neglect to include the Indian in scholarly presentations. For example, the revisionist historian, Colin Greer, in an otherwise excellent collection of works of ethnicity in America, makes no mention of American Indians.[15]

These examples are, of course, more or less obvious and intentional, but such work filters down into the system to support a more subtle hegemony, one that the authors expose in this book. This "filtered" material is woven into the fabric of everyday communication from those who themselves have become "brainwashed" (in a sense) from years of learning that began in elementary school and pervades most media in the United States. Consider a recent special issue of *U.S. News and World Report* entitled "Defining America: Why the U.S. is Unique." Taking up the economic expansion of "the most innovative and wealthy society the world has ever seen," the author of an article entitled "A Nation on the Make" states, "A final element—place—provided both the resources to jump-start the transformation and the room for it to grow. The largely empty continent offered industrious new Americans land, timber, water and food."[16]

Empty continent? Scholars have estimated that the number of people living in North America before sustained contact with Europeans was 20 to 60 million. Demographics historian Henry F. Dobyns estimates that 120 million people occupied the lands.[17] The magazine's reference to a "largely empty continent" reflects how the writer was both influenced by and influences the kind of hegemony this book reveals.

Thus, the "fourth wave of killing the Indigenous" builds on the first three waves, pulling in decades of anti-"Indian" literature, films, and social commentary. Sometimes appearing as a smothering maelstrom, other times as an invisible poison, it ultimately emerges as a "common-sense" view of the world that automatically disregards truth. It represents the kind of hegemony that prevents people from realizing that social and environmental injustice are not a natural by-product of human nature; that the current form of global capitalism is not the only economic system available to humanity; or that living Indigenous cultures possess a measure of wisdom that may be vital for all of our futures.

This fourth wave is in reality an insidious form of cultural genocide against Indigenous People that tends to support

- ongoing ignoring of Indigenous People's legal rights and the legitimate relationship between the various First Nations and the federal government.
- legislation that attempts to abrogate Indian treaties or to deny federal support.
- efforts of white citizens to launch anti-Indian campaigns in connection with acquiring coal, timber, gas, fishing, and other land-use rights.
- suppression of Indigenous People's religious freedoms, as when museums display ancestral bones or religious objects, or when sacred medicine bundles are confiscated or destroyed by U.S. Customs officials or peyote ceremonies are disallowed. (I myself recently had my Sun Dance rope taken away from me at the Phoenix airport for fear I might "tie someone up with it.")
- the ignoring of cultural relevance in education as exemplified in implementation of laws like the No Child Left Behind Act.
- expropriation and exploitation of reservation lands, which ultimately pollutes, poisons, or extracts vital resources while robbing Indigenous

People of fair compensation or opportunities to litigate for environmental restoration.

These items represent just the tip of the iceberg. Volumes would be required to itemize attacks on American Indians and the deceptive language of conquest that supports these attacks. Moreover, new items emerge almost daily, from new discoveries of corruption against tribes to the deleterious effects of federal education laws on Indian children. Consider for example the use of Indian lands for military experiments. Gregory Hooks, chair of Washington State University's Department of Sociology, and Chad L. Smith, a professor at Texas State University at San Marcos, recently concluded in "The Treadmill of Destruction: National Sacrifice Areas and Native Americans" that dangerous military sites are disproportionately situated on American Indian lands, systematically exposing American Indians to extremely toxic and dangerous weapons and chemicals. So in addition to being pushed off millions of acres of their homelands to make way for weapons testing sites, American Indians remain at risk from unexploded bombs, land mines, nerve gases, and toxic materials, including nuclear waste.[18]

In noting and remembering such injustices against Indigenous People, the reader should also realize that the loss of Indigenous perspective is a loss to all people. As noted earlier, Indigenous worldviews, as varied as they are, have common associations that are significantly different from those operating in the dominant cultures of the so-called Western world. For example, assumptions about children, authority, community, language, deception, art, music, justice, competition, animals, religion, land, and money are often polar opposites from those that guide the typical American citizen's life and typical U.S. government policies. Although these assumptions are not exclusive to American Indian cultural paradigms and can be found in alternative philosophies in all societies, this book asserts that the wisdom of traditional American "Indians" is an essential ingredient for those wishing to mitigate the dominant American influence on domestic and world systems. Moreover, many First Nations citizens still maintain these values today and can help the process of transforming American culture.

Our goal is thus a lofty one. We hope to replace anti-Indigenous hegemony with understanding that is both truthful and constructive. We do not mean to say that Indigenous worldviews are always better ways for knowing reality than those that pervade Western culture. No worldview is epistemologically privileged in the sense that it is the only absolute truth and all others are false. The process of understanding nature, human nature, and the relationship between the two is an evolving one in many ways. Yet, as J. Baird Callicott says in his validation of traditional and Indigenous intellectual achievements,

> The Indigenous worldviews around the globe can contribute a fund of symbols, images, metaphors, similes, analogies, stories and myths to advance the process of articulating the new postmodern scientific worldview. Thus the contemporary custodians of traditional and indigenous non-Western systems of ideas can be co-creators of a new master narrative for the rainbow race of the global village. They have a vital role to play ... indigenous environmental ethics may complement a post-modern evolutionary-ecological/environmental ethic as well as vice versa. We may anticipate a global intellectual dialogue, synthesis, and amalgamation to emerge, *rather than an era of Western philosophical hegemony, or—just as bad—an era of intellectual balkanization, bickering, intolerance and ethnic cleansing.* (Emphasis mine)[19]

Popular authors from Arthur Schlesinger Jr. to Diane Ravitch continue to tell us that American society and schools should forget about soothing the pain of dispossessed groups of Indigenous People, that attempting to do so threatens the solidarity of our nation. We assert the opposite is true. It may be that ignoring the Indigenous wisdom upon which the United States Constitution was largely founded is what has led our great country into ever-increasing violence, chaos, inequity, and ecological devastation. The problem, although complex, has much to do with a calculated commitment to a very singular notion of a Eurocentric worldview, a worldview supported by manipulated hegemony that serves, not a democracy, but a plutocracy.

Charles Alexander Eastman (Ohiyesa) concluded his book, *The Soul of the Indian*, originally published in 1911, with these words:

> Such are the beliefs in which I was reared—the secret ideals which have nourished in the American Indian a unique character among the peoples of the earth. Its simplicity, its reverence, its bravery and uprightness must be left to make their own appeal to the American of today, who is the inheritor of our homes, our names, and our traditions. Since there is nothing left us but remembrance, at least let that remembrance be just![20]

Although more optimistic about the future of First Nations' people perhaps than was Ohiyesa in 1911, our authors nonetheless speak for this just remembrance while at the same time making the appeal for the way of seeing and being in the world about which he speaks, challenging the hegemony of those who misrepresent it along the way. Many of the noted contributing authors in this volume are of First Nations blood or are enrolled tribal members. Others have long focused their research on an authentic understanding of Indigenous history, philosophy, and contemporary realities facing Indigenous People, or at least have studied those aspects of colonialization that continue to oppress Indigenous consciousness in all of its forms.

NOTES

1. Don Trent Jacobs, *Primal Awareness: A True Story of Survival, Transformation and Awakening with the Raramuri Shamans of Mexico* (Rochester, Vt.: Inner Traditions International, 1998).

2. James A. Clifton, *The Invented Indian: Cultural Fictions and Government Policies* (New Brunswick, N.J.: Transaction Books, 1990), 36.

3. Don Trent Jacobs and Jessica Jacobs-Spencer, *Teaching Virtues: Building Character across the Curriculum* (Lanham, Md.: Scarecrow Press, 2001).

4. The word "hegemony" will be used often throughout our text and can be considered a more formal way of referring to the "language of conquest." The *Fontana Dictionary of Modern Thought* defines hegemony as "not only the political and economic control exercised by a dominant class but its success in projecting its own way of seeing the world, human and social relationships, so that this is accepted as 'common sense' and part of the natural order by those who are, in fact, subordinated to it." (Alan Bullock, *Fontana Dictionary of Modern Thought* [London: Collins, 1988]), 388. The term thus signifies the ability of the dominant social leaders to cultivate, through largely noncoercive means, a popular worldview that naturalizes their positions in a way that manipulates subordinate classes of people to consent to their own subordination and oppression, thinking that it ultimately serves their best interests. (This process was explored initially by Antonio Gramsci when he was being held as a political prisoner under Mussolini.) The important point here is that the language of conquest, i.e., cultural hegemony, is achieved relatively imperceptibly, as if the populace has been hypnotized into the realities it accepts, no matter how destructive they may be.

5. Don Trent Jacobs, *The Bum's Rush: The Selling of Environmental Backlash* (Boise, Idaho: Legendary, 1994). (See website at www.teachingvirtues.net.)

6. Robert Whelan, *Wild in Woods: The Myth of the Peaceful Eco-Savage* (London: The Environment Unit of the Institute of Economic Affairs, 1999), 23.

7. Whelan, *Wild in Woods*, 21.

8. Ibid.

9. Ibid., 23–24.

10. Robert Whelan, "Life on a Modern Planet," book review in *Free Life* 23 (August 1995). http://freespace.virgin.net/old.whig/fl23plan.htm. Accessed December 16, 2004.

11. Whelan, *Wild in the Woods*, 25.

12. Ibid., 28.

13. C. E. Kay, "Aboriginal Overkill," *Human Nature* 5.4 (1994): 379.

14. Kathy Clement, http://sonner.antville.org/stories/267764/, March 21, 2003. The relationship between anti-Indianism and right-wing efforts to discredit the logic of Indigenous wisdom considered "left wing" is apparent when one looks at the makeup of organizations that attack American Indians. An example is the obviously anti-Indian organization "One Nation." Situated in Oklahoma, its founding members include the Oklahoma Independent Petroleum Association, the Oklahoma Petroleum Marketers Association, and others who paid $10,000 membership fees to lobby against tribal sovereignty and power, which they claim are distorting the free-market American economy.

15. Francis R. McKenna, "The Myth of Multiculturalism and the Reality of the American Indian in Contemporary America," *Journal of American Indian Education* 21.1 (October 1981). http://jaie.asu.edu/v21/V2151myt.html. Accessed December 16, 2004.

16. Christopher Schmitt, "A Nation on the Make," *U.S. News and World Report* (June 28–July 5, 2004): 64.

17. Cited in Bruce E. Johansen, *The Native Peoples of North America: A History* (Westport, Conn.: Praeger, 2005), 4.

18. Gregory Hooks and Chad L. Smith, "The Treadmill of Destruction: National Sacrifice Areas and Native Americans," *American Sociological Review* 69.4 (August 2004): 558–575.

19. Baird J. Callicott, *Earth's Insights: A Multicultural Survey of Ecological Ethics from the Mediterranean Basin to the Australian Outback* (Berkeley: University of California Press, 1994), 9.

20. Charles Alexander Eastman (Ohiyesa), *The Soul of the Indian* (1911; Mineola, N.Y.: Dover, 2003), 45.

Immediately after hearing Frank Bracho's keynote speech on the subject of happiness and Indigenous wisdom, given to representatives from fourteen Indigenous cultures at the Sixth Annual Gathering of the Indigenous Peoples of the Americas Conference in 2004,[1] I asked him if he would write the opening chapter for this book. His eloquent and passionate words establish a mood of hopefulness and simplicity that offer the reader an anchor in preparation for the stormy and more disturbing insights that the subsequent chapters present. Without romanticizing Indigenous People or their histories, he nonetheless presents a convincing case that the concept of happiness has more to do with "being" than with "having" and that the Indigenous proclivity to live in accordance with natural laws is the saner path to follow. His logic shows why it is important for all people to become aware of anti-"Indian" education and hegemony.

Frank Bracho is a Venezuelan of partly Arawak heritage, which he proudly vindicates, although he prefers to present himself simply as "a human being in pursuit of his highest realization." A noted militant in native causes, he is the author of numerous books on health, the environment, and economics, and has served as the Venezuelan ambassador to India. During his eighteen years of distinguished public service in this capacity, he advised several presidents, served on several international bodies, was an active member of various national and international civic society organizations, and promoted socially responsible business practices.

***

A HUMAN PURSUIT

The attainment of happiness has always been a fundamental human aspiration. This is why all traditions of wisdom have made reference in one way or another to how it can be obtained, frequently conceiving happiness as the *sumum* or pinnacle of human achievement. Happiness as a goal has even been enshrined as a fundamental value for nations or governments. The United States' Declaration of Independence, for example, specifies "the pursuit of happiness" as one of the new nation's fundamental aspirations, and the fathers of this manifesto, such as Thomas Jefferson and Benjamin Franklin, made happiness a central good in their body of political ideas. Simon Bolívar, who led several South American republics to independence, did the same when he affirmed that the most perfect system of government is that which produces the greatest possible amount of happiness. In those eighteenth-century times, happiness was usually linked to feelings of safety and to personal and social stability. In spite of all the foregoing, such an ideal might seem too general or utopian to some skeptic-pragmatists of today, and some might even say, sarcastically, that if in those days the Gross National Product—the measurement that today's economists have enshrined as the supreme value of any national well-being—had existed, the founding fathers would have preferred it.

But the goal of happiness keeps returning to the agendas of leaders and nations, as a vital unsatisfied aspiration; nations as diverse as Bhutan, whose government recently declared, on the basis of ancestral Buddhist teachings, that "the National Happiness Product is more important than the Gross National Product,"[2] and England, where the government has decided to highlight the pursuit of well-being and social happiness in its public policies. At the international level, the desire for happiness is maintained as central. At the United Nations' Millennium Summit, held in 2000 in New York, Secretary General Kofi Annan presented a Gallup International poll, the biggest public opinion poll ever taken, covering about sixty nations, to the heads of state. The poll concluded that people value good health and a happy family as being more important than anything else.

On the subject of the pursuit of happiness, one of the more illuminating and renowned wisdom traditions has been that of the Indigenous Peoples. And among these, the wisdom of the Indigenous Peoples of the Americas greatly influenced the thinking of prominent revolutionary leaders in the eighteenth and nineteenth centuries in Europe and the Americas in their struggle against monarchic-feudal authoritarianism and in favor of more human, freer societies. Among them were leaders such as Franklin, Jefferson, and Bolívar.

Jefferson was convinced that Indigenous People who lived without the European forms of government generally enjoyed infinitely greater degrees of happiness. He honored them for not submitting to any laws or to any coercive power lurking in the shadows of government. He noted that the only control they needed in their societies came from their moral sense of right and wrong or, when the rare offense occurred, from exclusion of the offender from society.[3]

Bolívar also remarked about the peaceable character of a People who seemed only to want repose and solitude; who did not seek nor expect to lead by authority or to dominate others. Bolívar referred to the "Indian" as "everyone's friend" and as someone content with his peace, his land, and his family.[4]

In his first chronicles, even Christopher Columbus had commented the following, in relation to his encounter with the Indigenous culture of the "new continent": "They are the best people in the world, and the sanest. They love their neighbors as themselves. They are faithful and do not covet what others have . . . their speech is always sweet and gentle, accompanied by a smile."[5]

But before we go on with such great exaltation of the Indigenous People, whose lifestyles and perspectives were short-lived after European invasion into the Americas, let us stop here and try to determine precisely what happiness means. And, starting from this determination, let us make more objective judgments of the degree to which the ancestral Indigenous wisdom achieved it.

Information coming to Europe about the happiness and sanity of Indigenous self-government on the basis of the Natural Order truly influenced a series of revolutionary thinkers throughout several centuries from Thomas Moore to John Locke, Rousseau, and Marx. Although none of these got it quite right, their ideas, in turn, would return to the American continent to influence it in interesting ways. Despite their different ideologies (Moore's illustrated anarchy,[6] Locke's and Rousseau's emphasis on natural rights, Marx's communist society, etc.) and the diverse forms of ideology that stemmed from them, they all shared a core of belief that speaks of a profound influence from the Indigenous People's path to happiness and social harmony as reported by those who had observed it firsthand, such as Jefferson and Bolívar.

WHAT IS HAPPINESS?

Happiness can be understood as a state of satisfaction or contentment and well-being, based on our natural identity. Insofar as our natural identity is concerned, it is generally accepted that we human beings are matter and spirit, body and soul, depending on what we want to call our two characteristic identity components: the dense and the subtle.

The dimension of well-being in the concept of happiness refers to the more physical, dense, and external aspects of our being, while the dimension of satisfaction/contentment refers to the more spiritual, more subtle, and internal aspects of our identity.

We could also link the well-being dimension with health, as defined in the wide-ranging sense given by the World Health Organization (WHO). For WHO, health is "a state of complete physical, mental and social well-being, and not merely the absence of disease or infirmity."[7] This broad concept highlights the importance of affirmative and preventive health aspects (beyond the repair-cure thrust in which modern medicine has remained); it emphasizes health as a lifestyle in which, besides attention to health as such, there is attention to nutrition, housing, clothing, education, environmental quality, and the affection and protection afforded by community-based life.

However, it is evident that health cuts across, and has a continuity relationship with, the other, subtler, dimension. Both the term used by WHO, "infirmity" (disease), which comes from the Latin "infirmus," meaning lacking firmness or equilibrium, and the mental scope of health as cited in the WHO definition remind us of health's more subtle aspects. It has also been said that matter, in the final analysis, is but concentrated energy.

In reference to the *satisfaction/contentment dimension*, a prerequisite for happiness is wisdom, since it will give us the correct leads for differentiating that which makes us happy from that which does not. Being able to relate with our self and other beings from a perspective of love, compassion, and respect for all life, as well as feeling useful, are other fundamental requirements for a happy life. Relatedly, the eminent Chilean biologist Humberto Maturana noted that our biological essence is based on love and cooperation. In other words, we tend to become ill for a lack of love, but never for a lack of violence or aggressiveness.[8]

In spite of those links between well-being/health and satisfaction/contentment, it is evident that this last, linked to the more spiritual aspects, is the most crucial. As the Christian theologian Pierre Teilhard de Chardin believed, we are not human beings on a spiritual quest, but we are spiritual beings in a human experience.

Thus, in order to achieve happiness as defined above, the following basic needs emerge:

- with relation to the *well-being/health dimension:* health as such, nutrition, housing, clothing, physical exercise, environmental quality, education, and community-based affection and protection.

- with relation to the *satisfaction/contentment dimension:* wisdom, love, compassion, respect for all life, and feeling useful. (Bearing in mind that, if we are to be faithful to the higher hierarchical standing of the spiritual, the latter set of requirements should really come first.)

INDIGENOUS WISDOM AND HAPPINESS:
COMPARISON WITH MODERN SOCIETIES

How can we qualify ancestral Indigenous wisdom in relation to these benchmarks for happiness? And on the other hand, what can we say of modern civilization's performance in this regard? Let us proceed now to some considerations on these questions.

Insofar as the first, the Indigenous should not be idealized or romanticized, nor should we deny that they have also been subjected to their own degenerative process, in a cycle that seems to have been inescapable for all humanity. The forefathers and thinkers of the eighteenth century indulged, in point of truth, in a certain idealization of Indigenous wisdom, the idealization of he who tends to see in another that which he is deeply lacking, or simply the idealization of the simplifier or the one of limited knowledge. Not all Indigenous cultures encountered by the Europeans when they arrived in the Americas were at their highest stage of wisdom; some, such as the Aztecs, Mayas, and Incas, were in decline from their "golden years." Nevertheless, it is true that with reference to what was and is originally and ancestrally Indigenous, the expressions of admiration of Europeans and Americans who witnessed pre-contact Indigenous Peoples were not far from the truth. (When we speak of the originally or ancestrally Indigenous, it should be clear that, for us, being "Indigenous" is about more than skin color or race. It is a state of consciousness that embodies an intimate and respectful communion with Mother Nature and its laws; a respect for place and a way of seeing the world.)

Although it could seem that the term "happiness" did not always appear explicitly in Indigenous languages, their lifestyles and attending values did express the concept. For example, in the language of the Waraos, the ancestral aborigines of the Orinoco Delta in Venezuela, the word did exist as such, in the expression *"oriwaka." Oriwaka,* for the Waraos, has the following meanings: "wait together," "have a party," "joy of sharing with others," and "paradise where the dead are happy," meanings that highlight the importance of sharing, of joy, and of the transcendent as the key to happiness. In the Piaroa language (a Venezuelan Amazonian ethnic group), "happiness" is called *"eseusa"* and means principally "the joy of sharing with others," in value quite similar to the Warao concept. To the ancient *achaguas arawak*, who also inhabited Venezuela, their word "*chunikai*" meant both "happiness" and health" (which takes us back to the equation we earlier highlighted).

Insofar as the Mayas are concerned, it is interesting to note the importance given to happiness in the behavior prescribed by their moral code, known as The Pixab: "A thing is good as long as it harms no one. A thing is right as long as it contributes to *happiness* and life."

In the Maya language Q'eqchi, happiness is called *sahil ch'oolejil* and means literally "having a glad heart." Confirming the great centrality that the value of happiness had in daily Q'eqchi Maya life, the main social greeting is *masa' laa ch'ool*, which means: "How is your heart?"

The contrast with the European lifestyle served to raise conscious awareness among Indigenous Peoples about the merits of their ancestral lifestyle, relative to happiness. In this regard, the following reflection, made around 1676, by Chief Micmac in North America is eloquent:

> Which of these is the wisest and happiest—he who labors without ceasing and only obtains, with great trouble, enough to live on, or he who rests in comfort and finds all he needs in the pleasure of hunting and fishing? ... There is no Indian who does not consider himself infinitely more happy and powerful than the French.[9]

Or consider the following comparison by Chief Maquinna, of the Nootka nation, also in North America, after he learned the banking practices brought by white civilization:

> We Indians have no such bank; but when we have plenty of money and blankets, we give them away to other chiefs and people, and by and by they return them, with interest, and our hearts feel good. Our way of giving is our bank.[10]

Compare this with the greed and individualism that, despite the best wishes of such founding fathers as Franklin, Jefferson, and Bolívar, persisted in the bosom of the colonizing European culture. Such inclinations would lead, in the end, to the dismal practices of subordination and slavery to which the colonists would subject Indigenous Peoples, and the subsequent traffic of African blacks, as well as the growing mercantilist and corporate materialism which would later take hold. In this last regard, as far as the United States is concerned, analysts such as the historian Richard Beard have highlighted the narrow economic interests that truncated much of the high idealism of that nation's Declaration of

Independence, written in 1776, when it was translated eleven years later in 1787, into the nation's Constitution, which explains, among other things, why black slavery was not abolished in the latter (so that blacks were excluded from the rights proclaimed by the Declaration of Independence as universal to the human condition). In the end this omission cost the new nation dearly, since the question had to be settled some eighty years later by a dreadful civil war. On the other hand, starting from that war, corporations and wealth acquired decisive power in that nation, causing President Lincoln to voice the following concerns, prophetic in their portrayal of the subsequent developments of the United States:

> I see in the near future a crisis approaching that un-nerves me and causes me to tremble for the safety of my country. As a result of the War, corporations have been enthroned . . . An era of corruption in high places will follow and the money power of the country will endeavor to prolong its reign by working upon the prejudices of the people.[11]

Those narrow economic ambitions, of course, also played their part "south of the Rio Grande," truncating the dreams of solidarity and social happiness cherished by the founding fathers of the new republics in that region. The new landowner and commercial elites sought unscrupulous political and economic divisions for their own ends.

Perhaps we can find a root of all those inexorable forces of economic greed in the Industrial Revolution. This greed, alongside the great political and independence-seeking revolutions of the eighteenth and early nineteenth centuries, guided the course of the Industrial Revolution in spite of its rhetoric about ideals regarding social happiness. The great historian Arnold Toynbee has left the following judgment on the subject:

> There were paradoxical and *unhappy* human consequences of an increase in the production of material wealth. The cause of this social miscarriage was the motive of the entrepreneurs by whom the Industrial Revolution was launched. Their stimulus was *greed*, and greed was now released from the traditional restraints of law, custom, and conscience.[12]

Since then, greed has become so ubiquitous that it is today a central subset of debate, particularly in the light of events such as the great wave of corporate scandals which have shaken the world of late in generalized form, with cases as emblematic as Enron in the United States and Parmalat in Europe.

WELL-BEING/HEALTH DIMENSION

Coming back to the Indigenous contribution, the following statement by the North American indigenous leader Tenskwatawa, of the Shawnee, in 1805, has broad implications because it refers to the root and basic aspects of the happy Indigenous lifestyle, and its comparison to European culture:

> Our Creator put us on this wide, rich land, and told us we were free to go where the game was, where the soil was good for planting. That was our state of true *happiness* . . . Thus were we created. Thus we lived for a long time, proud and happy. We had never eaten pig meat, nor tasted the poison called whiskey, nor worn wool from sheep, nor struck fire or dug earth with steel, nor cooked in iron, nor hunted and fought with loud guns, nor ever had diseases which soured our blood or rotted our organs. We were pure, so we were strong and happy.[13]

Tenskwatawa's acute reflections are particularly relevant to illustrating Indigenous concepts concerning the physical well-being and health dimension with respect to the happiness concept, as well as its comparison with the invading civilization that attempted to impose itself over the Indigenous Peoples.

Smithsonian Institution studies by historians such as Francisco Herrera Luque and Manuel Cartay, the chronicles of the naturalist scientist Humboldt, and even the reports of many of the conquistadors, bear witness to the biological and health superiority of the Indigenous People over the European. Let us quote just one of these latter, as an example— the words of the conquistador Pedro Alvárez Cabral, who, in the face of the aboriginal world of what is today Brazil, expressed with admiration in 1500:

> They do not plow nor raise [animals]. There are no oxen or cows, nor goats, nor sheep nor chickens. Nor any animal used to living with men, nor do they eat except of that iñame (manioc), of which there is much here, and of those seeds and fruits of the land, and the trees which grow by themselves, and with this they walk as hardy and plump as we are ourselves not as much.[14]

Even in terms of curative practices for treating illnesses, the natives were generally superior. Smithsonian Institution researchers have pointed out in the case of Mesoamerica that the conquistadors had a general lack of confidence in their own medical skills, and frequently sought out Aztec practitioners for health complaints in preference to their fellow countrymen.[15]

Well-being as health, in the broader sense of the WHO definition, was in truth a *lifestyle* for the traditional native, where in respect and integration with the Five Elements of the Natural Order, that is to say, "earth," "water," "fire," "air," and "ether," the Indigenous Native obtained all he needed for his subsistence, including, besides health as such, the concomitant requirements of good nourishment, housing, clothing, education, physical exercise, environmental quality, and community-based affection and protection. Chief Seattle's famous manifesto for the most part is a hymn to the virtues of the Five Elements of the Natural Order as vital requisites for human welfare and life.

When health was lost, the Indigenous Person would turn to purification in order to recover it. As pointed out in the Maya Pixab, when disease, problems, pain, and desperation invade our days, it is necessary to perform a purification so that harmony will return, so that peace and *happiness* will return.[16] Purification involved diverse methods and depth, according to need: fasting, de-intoxication with multiple remedies, penitence, service to others, spiritual retreats, and so forth.

On the other hand, all the strength of the Indigenous culture, and all its wisdom in terms of well-being, could not withstand the overpowering European conquering onslaught, which in the end inflicted on the aboriginal peoples one of the greatest genocides that the history of humanity has ever known. At the end of the conquest and colonial rule, about 90 percent of the American Indian population had succumbed. This fatality rate was due less to the action of the musket (harquebus) than to imported diseases that decimated Indigenous Peoples. And these, less than direct contact with the Europeans, as is usually said, came fundamentally from the collapse of their physical and spiritual aboriginal lifestyle, in the face of the European colonialist assault and enslavement. This meant the collapse of their immunological systems, leaving them prey to all types of disease. This is the same fate which, indeed, awaits present-day humanity, which in the deepening of an anti-nature life and the destruction or contamination of the natural environment has gone so far that it now faces a similar collapse—as evidenced by the present proliferation of diseases of the most diverse types.

The exploitation of Indigenous Peoples continued in postindependence times under the domination of the "criollo" (mestizo, or mixed-race) culture in the new republics—in some ways, with even greater ferocity and contempt. This has been true up to contemporary times, when after five hundred years of servitude and resistance, a cultural and political Indigenous resurrection movement seems finally to have begun in the Americas. This movement has benefited from international and domestic legal conquests that have recognized the "rights of Indigenous Peoples" to their own ancestral cultures and habitats. This laudable achievement, nevertheless, must be tempered with the warning that in the ancestral Indigenous wisdom the concept of "rights"—if it ever existed as such— was subordinated to the more important concept of *duty fulfillment*. If one reads Chief Seattle's emblematic manifesto carefully, one can see that this is a charter of duties: duties to care for Nature, to respect other living beings, and so on; Seattle speaks little of rights. In this regard, the famous expression attributed to him: "The land does not belong to men, men belong to the land," typical of universal Indigenous wisdom, summarizes everything. The new kind of Indigenous sovereignty, empha-sizing only rights—a distortion brought by modern culture—has lent itself to abuses in some aboriginal territories, through the implemen-tation of projects that deprecate natural resources or projects opposed to the integrity of aboriginal culture. Such activities are promoted by Indigenous Persons who are alienated from their traditional culture, in tandem with unscrupulous foreign partners, sometimes acting outside the limits of more protective national laws.

SATISFACTION/CONTENTMENT DIMENSION

Let us turn now our principal attention to the satisfaction/contentment dimension of the concept of happiness. It has to do, as we have said before, with the more subtle, but also more crucial, dimension of happiness. Even with physical health, and in possession of many material assets and social relations, we can end up being unhappy, possibly because in having too much of all these things, we can end up as "possessed possessors" (having too much, like having nothing, is an extreme that conspires against hap-piness). When greed enters into play in this process, the matter becomes more serious. As we have said before, greed is anathema to happiness in a major degree, since those human beings who are consumed with greed are never satisfied. As Gandhi said so well: "The world has enough to satisfy everyone's needs, but not enough to satisfy a single one's greed." Greed makes us want to accumulate assets or money in an insatiable man-ner, frequently at the expense of the needs of others and of the Natural Order, against the precepts of love, compassion, and not harming life. "Goods" accumulated in this manner end up turning into "bads."

Jefferson originally excluded property from the category of "natural right" in the Declaration of Independence of the United States; this proclamation was reserved only for life, liberty, and the pursuit of happiness. Jefferson considered that property should have social limits, and therefore was more a "civil right"—subject to regulation. Private property and its "unhappy" usage through greed or avarice was seen by Indigenous cultures in the same manner, as shown by the following statement by Santee Sioux Ohiyesa (Charles Alexander Eastman):

> The tribe claimed the ground, the rivers and the game; only personal property was owned by the individual, and even that, it was considered a shame to greatly increase. For they held that greed grew into crime, and much property made men forget the poor. . . . Without a thought of same or mendicancy, the young, helpless and aged all were cared for by the nation that, in the days of their strength, they were taught and eager to serve. And how did it work out? Thus: Avarice, said to be the root of all evil, and the dominant characteristic of the European races, was unknown among Indians, indeed it was made impossible by the system they had developed.[17]

The most potent explanation for why having or enjoying things does not guarantee happiness is the ephemeral nature of possessions, and even relationships. Those who are attached are inexorably destined to suffer when possessions disappear—as inevitably they must—from our lives. This is why Indigenous People shun such attachments to objects, including, in a sense, the body, which can be the greatest attachment of all in spite of the certainty that it will also perish. From this emerges, then, the importance of focusing more on the "permanent," and this is only achieved in God's territory and in the territory of the soul, or to say it in more Indigenous terms, to the Great Spirit or Creator, and the spirit of each one of us.

Thus happiness ultimately comes from the works of the Creator, the Natural Cosmos, as evidenced in the sacred Thanksgiving Prayer of the North American Oneidas:

> Our mother earth takes care of all lives. Let's put our minds together. So be it in our minds. . . . To the one who made all things that we are thankful here on earth. Let's put our minds together. So be it in our minds.[18]

Separation from the Natural Order, thus, was and is for the traditionally minded Indigenous Person a separation from wisdom. The Oglala Sioux

Chief Luther Standing Bear spoke of such wisdom. He knew that man's heart, away from nature, becomes hard; he knew that lack of respect for growing, living things soon leads to lack of respect for humans too. So he kept his children close to nature's softening influence.[19]

Thus it is necessary to reflect on the degree to which the most ancient Indigenous gatherer cultures (those that had not entered the agricultural or industrial stages) were as primitive as present-day conventional wisdom would have us believe. The latter tells us that the evolutionary progression of man has ascended from gathering as the "most backward stage" to the industrial as "the most advanced." However, the gatherer cultures, on account of their depending on the intimate knowledge and mastery of the Natural Order, in order to be able to survive sustainably on the basis of its wild fruits, were, indeed, closer to a greater wisdom—from the Indigenous point of view, which emphasizes a full understanding of the Natural Order.

On the other hand, conventional wisdom would also have us believe that aboriginal cultures such as the Caribs, who populated Brazil, Venezuela, and the Caribbean, were more backward than the Aztecs and the Incas simply because they lacked the monumentality of the latter—as reflected in the great cities, temples, pyramids, and cultural achievements of the latter groups. But, could we not say, rather, that the Caribs were freer, happier, and wiser precisely because they avoided the striving associated with monumentality? Instead, they were happy to live within a low-intensity use of their natural environment through a decentralized gatherer-hunter-agricultural culture, in good measure itinerant, without the ties of monumentality and social stratification characteristic of the great American indigenous empires. Historical evidence seems to indicate that, in fact, the Caribs, known for their great devotion to freedom, remained in it deliberately, and, in truth, for the European conquistadors, were more difficult to subjugate.

WISDOM, NATURAL ORDER LAWS, AND HAPPINESS

For the Indigenous Peoples, therefore, the wisdom essential for happiness lies in being attuned to Nature and its laws. Among these the "The Law of the Oneness of Life" stands out: "All is one and all is alive"—the great Shaman maxim. If we humans are only "a thread in the weave of life"—as Chief Seattle said—then in consequence, as he said too: "Anything we do to the weave, we will be doing to ourselves."

We can thereby deduce the corollary that we must avoid doing harm to all life (the ama guaña commandment of the Incas, analogous to the ahimsa of Buddhists and Hindus) and, on the contrary, must profess love for all Creation. Creation itself, in truth, is an act of love; even our own lives as human beings come, generally, of the loving fusion between two beings. All Creation arises from love, is nourished by love, lives for love, and ends by dissolving itself into love. No wonder the First Commandment in the Christian tradition, coinciding with all the other major religions, refers to Love—in the "golden rule" that we find present in all religions and encompassing all the other commandments.

Another cardinal law of the Natural Order is "The Law of Impermanence," which says that "the only constant is that nothing is constant." In Indigenous cultures, death is not seen as something to fear, because it is understood to be a great teacher of this law. It reminds us that today we have to live to the fullest. In the Indigenous tradition, every "spiritual warrior" prepares for each battle as if it were the last, and by doing so achieves excellence. Impermanence teaches us to treasure the transcendent and the immortal as the most important elements for happiness. From the purported teachings of the legendary Yaqui sage Don Juan, the saying "always having death as companion and teacher" stands out as key to wisdom.

A third fundamental law is "The Law of Cause and Effect," which says to us that "every action produces a consequence or reaction." Thus, in every traditional Indigenous culture, the native is careful of all his steps; he is in a permanent state of alert to foresee the consequences of what he does, and he relates to the natural environment from a perspective of great respect so as not to cause consequences that would inevitably affect him negatively. For the same reason, in Indigenous wisdom, the notion of trying to repair any damages immediately is common, as is the notion of trying always for positive actions so as to obtain favorable effects. With regard to all of these aspects of Indigenous wisdom, the following teaching of Chief Joseph of the Nez Percé nation in North America is illustrative: "We were taught to believe that the Great Spirit sees and hears everything, and that he never forgets, that thereafter he will give every man a spirit-home according to his deserts. If he has been a good man, he will have a good home; if he has been a bad man, he will have a bad home."

In Venezuela, with relation to Indigenous cultures such as the Waraos and the Pemones, seeing how the law of cause and effect is venerated in their meticulous ancestral cultural behavior codes, full of taboos and "contras" (to repair damages or counterbalance their effects) and recommendations so as to better get along with the environment and other living beings, is admirable.

Other laws, such as "The Law of the Cyclical-Spiraled Movement of Life and Its Processes" (easily discerned by Indigenous People in their close communion with the seasonal cycles of gathering, planting, water, etc.), "The Law of Analogy" (stating that the microcosms reflect the macrocosms and vice versa), and "The Law of Complementary Poles" (which holds that what are apparently opposites actually are complementary), were also part of the vital cultural heritage of Indigenous wisdom.

HAPPINESS: A MATTER OF BEING MORE THAN OF HAVING

The foregoing discussion of happiness and Indigenous wisdom suggests that to reach happiness, we need to recognize that "being," which is linked to the transcendent and more lasting, is more important than "having," which is linked to the less transcendent and more transitory. In the case of ancestral Indigenous wisdom, "Being," in the most satisfying manner, in the form most conducive to happiness, was linked to the greatest possible integration with Creation, with the Natural Order and its laws. The Hopi Indians, so revered for their ancestral wisdom, summarized their creed of peace and happiness in the exclamation: "Techqua Ikachi," which means, "Blending with the land and celebrating life." This notion of life as a celebration reminds us of the teachings in the Quechua tradition of the Intij Inti, The Creator, who said at the genesis of the Indigenous People: "Go to the world to enjoy, because by enjoying you will learn, and by learning you will grow and by growing you will fulfill the sacred purpose of evolution." Does this not explain the general zeal of the traditional Indigenous Peoples for revering and respecting the Natural Order? Does it not explain why so many Indigenous People were contented to let things remain as the Great Spirit Chief made them? The statements of many American Indian leaders express a puzzlement over the white man's desire to change the rivers and mountains if they did not suit them.[20]

HAPPINESS: A VITAL LIFE MISSION

All of which brings us back to a fundamental aspect of the definition of happiness: its conformity with natural identity, with what we are in accordance with the Creator's designs, with our natural mission of existential life. In that light, perhaps there is some truth in the "noble savage" myth that speaks of the lost wisdom: "Men were happy only in a natural state."

Or, to say it in the reverse sense, if we achieve our natural identity we will automatically be happy, since happiness is our natural condition.

To be happy, however, each of us has to add our individual life mission to the common existential mission in the life we have as humans and living conscious beings. The following explanation of the Nawal concept of the Mayas summarizes this idea very well:

> Happiness and complete fulfillment in life are achieved by carrying through the work or function given to us at the moment of conception and birth ... No one comes to the world because he wants to come, say the Elders, who wisely assure us that we all have a mission to fulfill in life; a role to play to benefit humanity. Every human being has a Nawal that defines a particular personality and makes him different from other persons ... the life-mission will depend, then, on his qualities, aptitudes, virtues and defects as ruled by his Nawal, which is not more than a divinity that guides and helps the individual. It is his gift, his donation, his responsibility, and if he should resign the mission, he would fall sick, or worst of all, would die.[21]

We are happy, then, if we fulfill the mission to which we are destined as human beings, both in the cosmic sense as well as individually. We are happy if we are simply what we are meant to be. And this constitutes a path more than a destiny, in the here and now. Making an analogy with the simpler animal world: "The bird does not sing because it's happy, it's happy because it sings." Similarly, the bird does not fear the moment when the branch he is on will begin to creak, because it has wings to fly away. Like the wings to which we may appeal when physical death arrives, because, as Chief Seattle said, in the final analysis: "There is no such thing as death, but a change of worlds."

Some of the contributions to this book will likely challenge the reader's sensibilities. Some of the authors will be angry. Some may express a frustration with everything from the dominant culture that has corrupted the true way to happiness. As important as it may be to at last realize the falsities that surround us, it is even more important to remember that all of the work is ultimately about regaining our rights and responsibilities to find true happiness, and that consideration of the worldviews of Indigenous Peoples may indeed lead to a better way to achieve it.

NOTES

1. This conference, held at the University of Puerto Rico, April 25–31, 2004, was organized by Ramon Nenadich of the Centro de Estudios Indígenas

de las Americas in an effort to foster a collaborative effort between North and South American Indigenous Peoples to work and pray for world peace through recognition of Indigenous wisdom.

2. Frank Bracho, "Happiness as the Greatest Wealth," paper presented at the International Seminar on Operationalization of the National Happiness Product, Thimpu, Bhutan, February 18–20, 2004.

3. Bruce Johansen, *Forgotten Founders: Benjamin Franklin, The Iroquois and the Rationale for the American Revolution* (Ipswich, Mass.: Gambit Incorporated Publishers, 1982).

4. *Del Materialismo al Bienestar Integral: El Imperativo de una Nueva Civilización* (Caracas: Editorial Texto/Ediciones Vivir Mejor, 1995).

5. Peña Adrián Setién, *Realidad Indígena Venezolana* (Caracas: Centro Gumilla, 1999).

6. Thomas Moore, *Utopia*, trans. Paul Turner (London: Penguin Books, 1986).

7. See http://www.who.int/about/definition/en/.

8. Cited in Carlos Ponce Sanguines, *Tiwanaku, Espacio, Tiempo y Cultura* (La Paz, Bolivia: Editorial Los Amigos del Libro, 1981).

9. Kent Nerburn and Louise Mengelkoch, eds., *Native American Wisdom* (Novato, Calif.: New World Library, 1991).

10. Ibid.

11. Harvey Wasserman, *America Born and Reborn* (New York: Macmillan, 1984), 46.

12. Arnold Toynbee, *Mankind and Mother Earth* (London: Granada Publishing, 1978), 82.

13. Barefoot Windwalker, *"The Uncivilized" Native American*, http://www.barefootsworld.net/lovepeople.html. Accessed March 4, 2004.

14. Frank Bracho, *Claves del Futuro: Autodeterminación Humana y Leyes del Orden Natural* (Caracas: Editorial Texto/Ediciones Vivir Mejor, 2001).

15. John Verano and Douglas Ubulaker, *Seeds of Change: Readers on Cultural Exchange after 1492* (Boston: Addison-Wesley, 1993).

16. Ajpup Oxlajuj, *Fuentes y Fundamentos del Derecho de la Nación Maya-Quiche* (Guatemala: Editorial Serviprensa, 2001).

17. Charles Alexander Eastman (Ohiyesa), *The Soul of the Indian* (Mineola, N.Y.: Dover, 2003), 67.

18. H. W. Brands, "Founders Chic," *The Atlantic Monthly* (September, 2003), http://www.theatlantic.com/doc/prem/200309/brands. Accessed March 3, 2004.

19. Nerburn and Mengelkoch, *Native American Wisdom*.

20. Ibid.

21. Oxlajuj, *Fuentes y Fundamentos*.

ADVENTURES IN DENIAL:
IDEOLOGICAL RESISTANCE TO THE
IDEA THAT THE IROQUOIS HELPED   *Chapter 2*
SHAPE AMERICAN DEMOCRACY
Bruce E. Johansen

The Indigenous ideas and manifestations relating to the "pursuit of happiness" were incorporated into and helped shape the founding principles of the United States. In this chapter, the world's foremost authority on how the Iroquois Confederacy served as a model for American democracy exposes the agenda of well-known neoconservative guardians of culture and academy who seem threatened by multicultural perspectives in general and more specifically with any affiliation with Indigenous worldviews that might somehow challenge their "us versus them" version of reality. Perhaps there is a fear that acknowledging the legitimacy of Indigenous contributions to democratic ideals might expand to larger questions about free-market globalization and the corporate/religious authority behind it. Whatever the source of resistance to the truth about America's founding, Johansen's personal story of his decades-old battle with those who deny the truth is testimony to how the language of conquest continues to prevail.

Bruce E. Johansen is the Kayser Research Professor in Communication and Native American Studies at the University of Nebraska at Omaha Department of Communication. He is author of The Native Peoples of North America: A History *(2005),* Exemplar of Liberty *(1991, with Donald A. Grinde Jr.), and* Debating Democracy *(1998), as well as several other books and numerous articles and commentaries.*

***

This strange white man—consider him, his gifts are manifold. His tireless brain, his busy hand do wonders for his race. Those things which we despise he holds as treasures; yet he is so great and so flourishing that there must be some virtue and truth in his philosophy.

—SPOTTED TAIL (BRULE' LAKOTA), 1866

INTRODUCTION

I have long been enamored of Noam Chomsky's idea that some concepts are defined as being beyond the scope of permissible debate, even in a society that defines itself as devoted to democracy and open discussion. Part of my fascination stems from my involvement during the last three decades with the idea that the Haudenosaunee (Iroquois) Confederacy helped shape the political beliefs and institutions of the United States (and through it, democracy worldwide). Having explored this theme in several books,[1] I also have held a ringside seat as the rhetoric on this issue has evolved. Part of the evolution has been outright denial by a number of academics and popular commentators who believed, without much examination of the evidence, that the idea was a silly invention. It has been a wild rhetorical ride.

A pointed debate has developed along the way, especially during the last fifteen years, as controversy regarding this issue has been folded into broader controversies vis à vis multicultural education. I have compiled an annotated bibliography of ways in which the idea has been treated which by April 2004 included more than fourteen hundred items. Two volumes of these annotations are available in print as library reference books.[2]

During the 1980s, Mohawk artist, teacher, and culture bearer John Kahionhes Fadden gave such critics of the Iroquois influence on American government the nickname "Trolls" after European mythological characters said to charge tolls for passage over bridges (the nickname came from the idea that certain people seek to control access to the realm of established knowledge). The perils of academic gatekeeping have been well known among various Iroquois for many years.

This chapter examines the reactions of various academics, as well as several conservatives with household names and large audiences, who have sometimes linked the debate over the Iroquois and democracy with "Afrocentric" literature, especially Martin Bernal's *Black Athena*. These comments raise questions about the critics' assumptions, all of which point to a general conclusion: that conservative popular discourse on this subject is incredibly sloppy, a product of fear that European-centered perceptions of history and culture are losing their grip on the common values that we, as residents of Turtle Island (North America), are all expected to share. Without such a common core of knowledge (taught in the English language), the critics have argued, the United States may crumble into a jumble of scattered, self-interested bands. None of these commentators stop to ask the cost of ignorance of the large parts of our history that lack gender or racial qualifications for inclusion in the old-style European-derived "canon." Journey with me, please, as I pick my way through jungles of clichéd confusion.

Does multicultural education help us better understand each other through filters of race and culture? I think so. The idea that multicultural education contributes to a "Balkanization" of the United States is a myth, similar to the myth that national solidarity is supported by speaking English "only." Anyone who speaks a second or third language is richer, culturally, than the person who speaks only one language. Besides, if our vaunted freedoms mean everything, they also have meaning in languages other than English, and in cultures other than the mainstream.

DENIAL IN THE ACADEMY

Some of the more enduring critics of the Iroquois-influence idea continue to hammer away. One example is Laurence Hauptman, who, in a review of *Apocalypse of Chiokoyhikoy* (1997), does not spare invective. "According to its editors," Hauptman begins his review, "this minor, enigmatic document further supports those would-be academics who believe that the Iroquois Indians had an influence on the thought of . . . the institutions created by the Founding Fathers." Hauptman writes that he's "incensed" by the publication of this book. As usual, the ad hominem attacks of the "Trolls" do not brim over with decorum or respect for "would-be academics" whose opinions they consider to be in error. According to Hauptman, the annotations of the *Apocalypse* by editor Grinde have "as much depth as a comic strip."[3]

By 1998 Richard White, the celebrated New Western historian at Stanford University, was re-echoing earlier assertions of Elisabeth Tooker and William A. Starna, both of whom have now retired. In so doing, White invoked the invisible authority of uncited but presumably very authoritative historians. At the same time, White so wildly overstated the assertions of "influence" advocates as to make them sound ridiculous:

> The newer contributionist [sic] school has set its sights much higher. Native Americans, this new school says, gave us democracy and republican government and inspired our Constitution . . . Some of the literature has proved very popular with the tribes. The Six Nations, who were the central figures in the theory of American Indian democracy put forward by Bruce Johansen and Donald Grinde,[4] were quick to embrace their role in founding the Republic against whose birth many of their ancestors had, for good reason, fought bitterly. To oppose the American Indian origins of the Constitution was to oppose not just academics but sometimes quite vocal and articulate Native American people. Still, very few historians accepted the Grinde and Johansen thesis.

Both historians of Native American peoples and American historians in general have regarded it as a fabric of insinuation, invention, and misreading. The factual basis was weak and its own portrayal of Indian governance simplistic.[5]

As is common in "Troll" argumentation, White stopped only long enough to spew generalized invective, doing little to elaborate his blanket condemnations.

In *The Blank Slate*, Steven Pinker attacked the notion that an infant's mind is a more-or-less empty vessel (tabula rasa), arguing that the mind has an inherited universal structure based on demands made upon the species for survival, with some room for cultural and individual variation. Pinker, a chaired professor at the Massachusetts Institute of Technology, cites with approval arguments by J. O. McGinnis that the authors of the U.S. Constitution possessed a theory of human nature based on evolutionary psychology. McGinnis argues, according to Pinker, that the Constitution was designed to limit the drive for dominance and esteem so that it would not imperil government. On the same pages that cite McGinnis approvingly, Pinker disparages the idea that the Iroquois helped shape the Constitution as "a popular belief that . . . is just 1960s granola."[6] He stops there, settling for a half-dozen words of drive-by argumentation. It helps to have a sense of humor when one's decades of work are zapped in two deprecating words laced with absolute ignorance by a professor who, in other contexts, would like to be regarded as an intellectually capable commentator. For the record, I'll *never* refer to *The Blank Slate* as "Post-Freudian twaddle."

Donald S. Lutz, writing in *Publius: The Journal of Federalism*, offers a detailed examination of the Iroquois Confederacy, with special attention to its federalist attributes. The debate over Iroquois influence on the development of federalism is dismissed at the beginning of this article as an invention by "a few non-historians." "Historians," writes Lutz, "quickly concluded that such claims were ill-founded." Lutz cites Johansen's *Forgotten Founders*, calling its author "a journalist" (i.e., "a non-historian"). Along the way, Lutz struggles to squeeze the Iroquois League into a European framework: Is it "Aristotelian" or "Hobbesian"? Lutz, who is sure how to define "historian" and "journalist," and to declare that never the twain shall meet, cannot decide.[7] He seems to be making a case that only academics whom he regards as historians should have a crack at writing history. Lutz himself is a political scientist, not a historian.

DENIAL IN POPULAR MEDIA

Let us begin our tour of the popular media with a paragraph from Rush Limbaugh, who has been earning a multi-million-dollar annual income spewing stereotypical tripe to audiences of millions. He writes, in *The Way Things Ought to Be* (1992), "Multiculturalism is billed as a way to make Americans more sensitive to the diverse cultural backgrounds of people in this country."[8] Instead of seeing some value in the shared understanding that such education might bring, Limbaugh blasts it:

> It's time we blew the whistle on that. What is being taught under the guise of multiculturalism is worse than historical revisionism. It's more than a distortion of facts. It's the elimination of facts. In some schools, kids are being taught that the ideas of the Constitution were borrowed from the Iroquois Indians and that Africans discovered America.[9]

Limbaugh lavishes simplicity on his audience, ignoring all nuance of argument. The possibility of ideological amalgamation (say, that the Iroquois played a role in shaping a system that also has many European roots) escapes him. Similarly, Limbaugh discards the possibility that Africans may have migrated to the Americas by infinitely expanding the African contribution ("Africans discovered America") to make it sound absurd, a specialty of his rhetorical method.

The best general retort I have seen to Limbaugh appeared in *Native Americas*, a national American Indian news magazine; its editor, Jose Barreiro, writes:

> It may be wise to keep watch on the bigoted views of Rush Limbaugh. Because he serves as a barometer of the national climate, familiarity with the points of attack can be useful. But remember also this truth: Native Americans—Limbaugh's so-called savages—carried out a prescribed protocol of participatory democracy . . . This style of governance spawned confederacies and produced a palpable freedom, a shared experience that inspired colonial leaders, and that is more of America than Rush Limbaugh, from his glass-enclosed, push-button, overblown, self-aggrandizing world, will ever be.[10]

The next visit in our hall of rhetorical luminaries is with John Leo, longtime cultural commentator for the newsmagazine *U.S. News & World Report*. Leo reflected on Afrocentrism and Iroquois influence on democracy at least twice. In his November 12, 1990, column, Leo assails multiculturalism in school curricula, notably New York State's Curriculum of Inclusion. Leo hews to the "party line" of the curriculum's opponents, who assert that the influence of the Iroquois on American statecraft is being included in various school curricula only to appease the Iroquois, not because it is a factual part of history. In a February 1994 article, Leo writes, "In Upstate New York, a Native American lobby demonstrated how a curriculum can now be altered by adroit special pleading. After a visit by an Iroquois delegation to the state education department, the school curriculum was amended to say that the political system of the Iroquois Confederacy influenced the writing of the U.S. Constitution."[11]

The source of the debate here is New York State's Curriculum of Inclusion, an attempt to revise teaching about minorities which had several components, including one dealing with black studies and another, written by several Iroquois authors, entitled "Haudenosaunee: Past, Present, Future." This draft, which reached several hundred pages, contained suggestions of Iroquois influence on the development of democracy in the United States borrowed from work by my co-author Grinde and myself. These assertions quickly elicited blasts of venom from several trenchant opponents of multicultural education in general and Iroquois influence in particular.

The meeting with New York State Education Department officials at which Iroquois "lobbyists" were so often said to have pressured the department never occurred. Mohawk John Kahionhes Fadden, one of the authors of "Haudenosaunee: Past, Present, Future," wrote to me:

> For what it's worth on the debate issue . . . the idea for it was not the result of "lobbying" by the Iroquois as some of the detractors have written. The idea for the guide was brought up at a meeting at SED. The meeting resulted from a letter-writing campaign directed toward inaccuracies in a specific field-test draft, Social Studies 7 & 8: United States and New York State History. During that January 8, 1987 meeting the concept of a curriculum guide was suggested by Donald H. Bragaw, chief, Bureau of Social Studies Education, and was supported by Ed Lalor, director, Division of Program Planning. The idea did not emanate from the Haudenosaunee "lobbyists" who were there to address the draft mentioned above.[12]

Leo writes:

> The idea that the Founding Fathers borrowed from the Iroquois is a century-old myth. No good evidence exists to support it. But it is now official teaching in New York State. [It wasn't. It was part of a curriculum under development that was never implemented.] To the surprise

of very few, this decision shows that some school authorities, eager to avoid minority-group pressure and rage, are now willing to treat the curriculum as a prize in an ethnic spoils system.[13]

Leo's essay very concisely sums up the argument of many "influence thesis" opponents: The idea is "fiction" or "a myth," and is being imposed on innocent schoolchildren by a small group of somehow awesomely powerful, media-hungry Iroquois who want to muscle this falsehood into "mainstream" history. Leo gives no hint that a scholarly debate is going on here. To suggest that the idea is even debatable (and not pure fiction, "myth," or "the silliest idea I've ever heard") would undermine the assumptions of his arguments.

Leo returned to these themes in 1994. In a column titled "The Junking of History," Leo assailed the beliefs of people he calls "Afrocentrists" and those who deny the Jewish holocaust, calling their claims "pure assertion [with] a growing contempt for the facts." Leo included in his laundry list attempts to "transform facts into opinion" and "the supposedly strong influence of Iroquois thought on the U.S. Constitution, now taught in many schools."[14]

I was granted a rare privilege in the national mass media: two column-inches (as a letter to the editor) to refute Leo's two pages. My reply to Leo was published in *U.S. News & World Report*, April 18, 1994. "We have a genuine need to factor the accomplishments of non-white people into our history," I said. By comparing advocates of Native American influence on American ideas to the debunkers of the Jewish holocaust, Leo "has the debilitating problem for a social critic of not being able to tell historical wheat from chaff."[15]

Another example of the conservatives' "party line" was provided by Heather MacDonald in a collection of essays from the neoconservative journal *The New Criterion*.[16] MacDonald decries the Curriculum of Inclusion as a product of racial (mainly black) politics, resulting in the destruction of historical standards. She simplifies the thrust of multiculturalism to a banal slogan: "Hey, hey, ho, ho, western culture's gotta go!" Along the way, she argues that if multiculturalists amass enough power, they might demand not just Iroquois but Egyptian influence on the U.S. Constitution. This comment is an aside in a longer case against Martin Bernal's *Black Athena* which reduced everything multicultural to a contest of power-driven wills between racial groups battering down the walls of the European canon.

The syndicated columnist George Will drew from this ideological well several times. *Newsweek*, unlike *U.S. News & World Report*, never printed the replies I submitted. After his third misinformed swipe at multiculturalism, I wrote Will a tart personal letter and attached it to a stack of research. After that, his assault ended. In terms similar to those used in two previous syndicated columns (in 1989 and 1991), Will lambasted new explorations in African and Native American history under the title "Compassion on Campus" in 1993. "Religious fundamentalists try to compel 'equal time' in school curricula for creationism and evolution. But they are less of a threat than liberals trying to maintain 'fairness' for dotty ideas that make some 'victim groups' feel good—ideas such as that Greek Culture came from Black Africa [an allusion to Martin Bernal's *Black Athena*], or that Iroquois ideas were important to the making of the Constitution." [17]

Patrick Buchanan joined the fray about the same time as Will, using the same now-familiar fear appeals directed at multiculturalism during his 1992 presidential campaign. "The cultural war is already raging in our public schools," Buchanan writes in the Atlanta *Constitution*: [18]

> In history texts, Benedict Arnold's treason at West Point has been dropped. So has the story of Nathan Hale, the boy patriot who spied on the British and went to the gallows with the defiant cry, "I regret that I have but one life to give for my country." Elsewhere, they teach that our Constitution was plagiarized from the Iroquois, and that Western science was stolen from sub-Sahara Africa. [19]

"TRASH AND NONSENSE"

What is a professor to do when he finds the subject of his PhD dissertation and subsequent research (but not its substance) used as campaign fodder by a stump-preaching politician? Buchanan was quoted in another venue as saying: "When you see the idiocy that somehow the American Constitution was a direct descendant of the Iroquois Confederation documents—this is all trash and nonsense. The effort is to turn future Americans into people who despise their own history and background" [20] Really, Mr. Buchanan, trashing my European ancestors was not on my mind.

Some classical liberals, adopting the fear appeals of Will, Leo, et al., cranked up the volume on the issue of multiculturalism. The most notable was Arthur M. Schlesinger Jr., whose *Disuniting of America* (first published in 1992, revised in 1998) [21] made the now-familiar case that teaching "minority" history would undermine the common heritage of the European-centered "canon."

The 1998 edition of *Disuniting of America* was largely a replating of the 1992 edition, with added sources and a denunciation of "monoculturalists" on the right wing to balance Schlesinger's condemnation of "multiculuralists" on the left. Schlesinger displays no knowledge of what had become of the New York Curriculum of Inclusion (including its Native American component, "Haudenosaunee: Past, Present, Future") during the six years since his book's initial publication. The Haudenosaunee curriculum was not adopted by New York public schools. Instead, the state education department ceded ownership of it to the Haudenosaunee (Iroquois) Grand Council. The curriculum, having been smothered in the state education bureaucracy (at one point it was cut by more than half) remains unpublished to this day. Schlesinger, even in 1998, showed no awareness of the considerable debate over assertions that the Iroquois helped shape the character of democracy, despite the fact that he had given *Forgotten Founders* a very nice jacket blurb in 1982, calling it "a tour-de-force of ingenious and elegant scholarship, offering justice at last to the Indian contributions to the American Constitution."

By 1992, however, Schlesinger appeared to be ignorant of the published record, preferring buzzwords such as "feel-good" history, which he now said was a product of a "cult of multiculturalism," a brush with which he also amply painted Afrocentric curricula. Without engaging any of the facts of Afrocentric education or the case for Iroquois influence on political culture, these critics assume there is no factual case, and that feel-good fiction is replacing "the facts."

Mary Lefkowitz, a professor of classics at Wellesley College who wrote *Not Out of Africa*, a critique of Afrocentric education, also tried her hand at taking down the idea that the Iroquois helped shape democracy in a *Wall Street Journal* review of *The Menace of Multiculturalism*, by Alvin J. Schmidt, and *We Are All Multiculturalists Now*, by Nathan Glazer. The review began:

> Does the U.S. Constitution owe more to the 18th-century Iroquois than it does to the ancient Greeks? No, but many younger people may answer yes, because it is what they have learned in school. The history that children learn is not necessarily a record of what actually happened in the past; rather, it is often an account of what parents and teachers believe they ought to know.[22]

Later in the review, Lefkowitz acknowledges at least that the Iroquois had a government: "However impressive the governmental organization of the Iroquois nation, the inspiration behind the Constitution may once again be credited to the European Enlightenment, and the ancient Greeks."[23]

I replied to Lefkowitz in the letters column of the *Wall Street Journal*, asserting that giving credit to the Iroquois does not demean classical Greek or English precedents for basic United States law, but "simply add[s] an Iroquois role to the picture." I concluded: "We can have our Greeks, and our Iroquois, too."[24] We later exchanged e-mails, and she said that she had become acquainted with the Iroquois-and-democracy thesis in a commencement speech that Gloria Steinem had given at Wellesley.

Neoconservative lawyer Robert Bork weighed in with the observation that one of the many ways in which modern liberalism is destroying U.S. culture is "curriculum changes to accommodate multiculturalist pressures."[25] "It is everywhere," Bork moans.[26] Sounding so much like earlier assertions of this theme that he borders on plagiarism of Will, Leo, and others, Bork hauls out the notion that "in New York State it is official educational doctrine that the United States Constitution was heavily influenced by the political arrangements of the Iroquois Confederacy."[27] Bork strains to find a word that expresses the type of "political arrangement" maintained by the Iroquois. Bork also ignores the lively debate that had grown up over the issue, pontificating: "The official promulgation of this idea was not due to any research that disclosed its truth," but because "the Iroquois had an intensive lobbying campaign." Bork rests his case on assertions from John Leo's polemic, *Two Steps Ahead of the Thought Police* (1994), and Arthur Schlesinger Jr.'s *Disuniting of America*. There you have it in the book of Bork: *no* research exists on the subject, so why look for any? Why not trust a vaunted legal mind, a man who was once nominated to sit on the U.S. Supreme Court?

It is worth reminding ourselves at this point that most cultures are mixtures, and that no culture remakes itself in the image of another overnight. This may be easy to forget because the arguments over multiculturalism often seem to be presented without nuance, in stark shades of black and white: the Constitution derived from the Iroquois *or* from "our English heritage"; African thought swallowed the Greeks in one gulp *or* had no influence whatsoever. Nicholas Davidson provides an example of this absolutism in the *National Review* in an article entitled "Was Socrates a Plagiarist?" His piece is mainly a critique of Afrocentric education, but it begins: "Shakespeare and Locke are non-gratae at Stanford; New York schoolchildren learn that the Iroquois were the real source of the Constitution. Multiculturalism is on the march."[28] Noteworthy here, too, is the way in which Davidson elides the excision of "Shakespeare and Locke" (standing in for all of the European canon, both literary and political) from Stanford (presumably the Ivory Tower of liberalism), with the takeover by "the Iroquois" in New York (the public school system).

The debate over multiculturalism has popped up in several French newspapers, as well. In *Le Monde*, Henri Pierre describes debates over multicultural history in the United States, particularly Afrocentric ideas. He also briefly mentions the debate in the New York State Department of Education over the "Haudenosaunee: Past, Present, Future" guide asserting that Iroquois precedent helped shape the origins of democracy in the United States. Pierre thinks that the role of Native peoples in the founding of the United States should be recognized.[29]

The debate over multiculturalism in the United States has also been discussed occasionally in the British press. In his review of Schlesinger's *Disuniting of America*, Ambrose Evans-Pritchard, writing in the London *Daily Telegraph*, defended DWEMs—Dead, White, European Males— whom he said have suffered at the hands of "the American race-relations industry, [which is] amply subsidized by the public purse." "Education in America is becoming a form of therapy," he wrote. "Black school children in Portland, Oregon, are taught that Africans discovered America. In New York, the curriculum guide for 11th-grade history tells students that the Haudenosaunee political system of the Iroquois Indians was the inspiration for the American constitution."[30] As has been pointed out elsewhere, the proposed curriculum over which Schlesinger and this writer are gnashing their teeth was drafted by Iroquois writers, but not implemented by the state. Such nuances seem to have escaped nearly all conservative critics in their unrelenting pursuit of a political-correctness horror story. They accuse the Iroquois of fomenting historical fiction as they invent some history of their own. This is a wee bit Orwellian of them, if I may borrow from our English heritage.

THE OTHER SIDE OF THE RHETORICAL "TRACKS"

Having visited some of the more genial neighborhoods in our ideological Anglo-American "City on a Hill," let us cross the "tracks" into the rougher sections of town, where argument drowns in racist cant to which the genial folks Uptown would rather not lay claim. Richard Grenier's column in the Washington *Times* supplies an illustration. Grenier, a regular columnist for the *Times*, spars with notions of multicultural education, debunking "African-Americans' claim that Queen Nefertiti of ancient Egypt was black" and asserting that "Iroquois Indians have induced

New York State education officials to include in their 11th-grade syllabus the dogmatic assertion that the Iroquois Confederacy was a major influence on the U.S. Constitution."[31] He labels such ideas as "unfactual" and "racist." If the Iroquois can claim to have influenced the Constitution, then people of Mongolian descent have the right to insist that Genghis Khan also shaped it, he maintains.[32]

Into the China shop of debate, like a bull with an attitude problem, lumbered columnist Charley Reese of the Orlando *Sentinel*, who maintained that ideas such as Iroquois influence on democracy prey on gullible Americans who lack knowledge of their own history. Reese's version of history is simple: "*All* the institutions of American government are derived from our European culture. *None* comes from Africa or Asia or American Indians." Reese calls "ignorant" assertions that "our forefathers derived the idea of the U.S. Constitution from the Iroquois Confederation." Reese is just getting warmed up. "It's not even worthy of comment, except to point out that only a person 100 per cent ignorant of American and European history could make such a dumb statement." Before leaving the scene, our bull leaves a 24-carat lump of racist cant at the door: "The superbly educated authors of the American Revolution had *nothing* to learn from a primitive tribal alliance" (my emphasis).[33]

In the *National Review*, Jonathan Foreman bemoaned that "Baby Boomers" had infected Hollywood movies with liberal values based on their experience during the 1960s. Collectively, Foreman argues, these "Boomers" are shaping the media with their "delusions." He laments, by way of letting his conservative audience know just how stupid the Boomers can be, "We live in a society where some students are taught that the United States Constitution was inspired by the Iroquois, that the Greeks stole science from Africans, and that the Aztecs were sweeties who didn't really eat people like popcorn."[34]

Those who have crossed these ideological tracks in search of a *real* intellectual rumble should examine *The Menace of Multiculturalism*, authored by Alvin J. Schmidt. Schmidt, a professor of sociology at Illinois College, Jacksonville, is an opponent of multiculturalism who takes no prisoners. Schmidt's style of argumentation brings to mind the business end of a crowbar. At the beginning of a chapter titled "The Facts Be Damned," he lists a number of facts that he says multiculturalists have "invented." One of these is that "the Constitution of the United States was shaped by the Iroquois Indians."[35] He also denies the well-known fact that Crispus Attucks, the first casualty of the Boston Massacre (1770), was black (Attucks' father was Afro-American; his mother was Massachusset Indian).

Schmidt would rather history stress the cruel and violent aspects of Native American cultures, which he says squishy-soft multiculturalists downplay. He argues that American Indian cultures were environmentally destructive and that women in Native societies lived in virtual slavery. Calling the idea of "influence" a fabrication, he also asserts that multiculturalists exaggerate the role of Iroquois women. Elsewhere, borrowing from George Will, Schmidt calls the Iroquois influence idea "historical fiction." [36]

CONCLUSION

Eventually, in the rougher parts on this side of the intellectual tracks, the rhetoric gets really invidious. Dinesh D'Souza, a research fellow at the American Enterprise Institute, used a cover story in the business journal *Forbes* (under the title "Visigoths in Tweed") to target "a new barbarism—dogmatic, intolerant, and oppressive," that he says has "descended on America's institutions of higher learning . . . a neo-Marxist ideology promoted in the name of multiculturalism." He quotes William King, president of the Black Student Union at Stanford University, who cited a number of items of multicultural history before that school's Faculty Senate, including "that the Iroquois Indians in America had a representative democracy which served as a model for the American system." [37]

This reference to King would seem to represent the limit of D'Souza's investigation of the literature on the subject. And although D'Souza apparently does not know my name, or what I have published, this attack is personal—and all the more grievous for the invisibility of its target. For in fact D'Souza has just labeled me a "Visigoth in Tweed," a barbarian, an oppressor, a dogmatist, as well as a "neo-Marxist"—without even realizing that a debate is being engaged here. He has made himself an expert on the subject matter without giving evidence of having read any of the literature, an affliction he shares with many of the subjects of this essay.

I should not take any of this personally, of course. I have not yet decided much I would pay, for example, to see the looks on the faces of Limbaugh, D'Souza, et al., when they discover (if they ever do) that one of the main instigators behind "this Iroquois-Constitution nonsense" is a middle-aged Norwegian American from Omaha, Nebraska, who spends most of his average working day teaching undergraduates how to write newspaper and magazine articles. Given what I have heard them say, such a notion could jam their mental radar.

None of the authors cited above give any evidence of having read our books, nor those of Martin Bernal. It is a sad day in public discourse when one realizes by close association with an arguable issue that large audiences are being regularly informed on an intellectual level which approximates cocktail-party chitchat, doled out to audiences of millions in measured, authoritative-sounding tones which reinforce existing prejudices. This neoconservative chorus tells us that multicultural voices are "dumbing down" our collective historical memory. Actually, they are the ones doing the dumbing-down.

NOTES

The epigraph to this chapter is taken from Charles A. Eastman, *Indian Heroes and Great Chieftains* (Boston: Little, Brown, 1918; Mineola, N.Y.: Dover, 1997), 134.

1. Donald A. Grinde Jr. and Bruce E. Johansen, *Exemplar of Liberty: Native America and the Evolution of Democracy* (Los Angeles: UCLA American Indian Studies Center, 1991); Bruce E. Johansen, *Forgotten Founders: Benjamin Franklin, the Iroquois, and the Rationale for the American Revolution* (Ipswich, Mass.: Gambit Incorporated Publishers, 1982); Bruce E. Johansen, Donald A. Grinde Jr., and Barbara A. Mann, *Debating Democracy: Native American Legacy of Freedom* (Santa Fe: Clear Light Books, 1998).

2. Bruce E. Johansen, comp., *Native American Political Systems and the Evolution of Democracy: An Annotated Bibliography* (Westport, Conn.: Greenwood Press, 1996); Bruce E. Johansen, comp., *Native America and the Development of Democracy: A Supplemental Annotated Bibliography* (Westport, Conn.: Greenwood Press, 1999).

3. Laurence Hauptman, Review of *Apocalypse of Chiokoyhikoy*, by Robert Griffin and Donald A. Grinde Jr., *Journal of American History* 86.1 (1999): 220–221.

4. Donald A. Grinde Jr., *The Iroquois and the Founding of the American Nation* (San Francisco: Indian Historian Press, 1977).

5. Richard White, "Using the Past: History and Native American Studies," in *Studying Native America: Problems and Perspectives*, ed. Russell Thornton (Madison: University of Wisconsin Press, 1998), 232.

6. Steven Pinker, *The Blank Slate: The Modern Denial of Human Nature* (New York: Viking, 2002), 296–298.

7. Donald S. Lutz, "The Iroquois Confederation Constitution: An Analysis," *Publius: The Journal of Federalism* 28:2 (spring 1998), 99.

8. Rush Limbaugh, *The Way Things Ought to Be* (New York: Pocket Books, 1992), 204.

9. Ibid.

10. Jose Barreiro, "Bigotshtick: Rush Limbaugh on Indians," *Native Americas* (fall 1995): 43.

11. John Leo, "The Junking of History," *U.S. News & World Report* (February 28, 1994): 17.

12. John Kahionhes Fadden, personal communication, November 28, 1992.

13. John Leo, "A Fringe History of the World," *U.S. News & World Report* (November 12, 1990): 25–26.

14. Leo, "The Junking of History," 17.

15. Bruce E. Johansen, Letter to the Editor, *US News & World Report*, April 18, 1994.

16. Heather MacDonald, "The Sobol Report: Multiculturalism Triumphant," in Hilton Kramer and Roger Kimball, *Against the Grain: The New Criterion on Art and Intellect at the End of the Twentieth Century* (Chicago: Ivan R. Dee, 1995).

17. George Will, "'Compassion' on Campus," *Newsweek* (May 31, 1993): 66.

18. Patrick J. Buchanan, "America's Cultural War," *Constitution* (Atlanta), September 15, 1992, A-15. See also Patrick J. Buchanan, "Yes, a Cultural War Is Raging . . . ," *Post-Dispatch* (St. Louis), September 13, 1992, 3-B.

19. Buchanan, "*America's Cultural War*," A-15.

20. Peter Mitchell, "A Conversation with Buchanan," *Sentinel* (Orlando), February 27, 1992, A-5.

21. Arthur M. Schlesinger Jr., *The Disuniting of America: Reflections on a Multicultural Society*, Revised and enlarged edition (New York: W. W. Norton, 1998).

22. Mary Lefkowitz, "Out of Many, More Than One," *Wall Street Journal*, March 24, 1997, A-16.

23. Ibid.

24. Bruce E. Johansen, "The Iroquois: Present at the Birth," *Wall Street Journal*, Letter to the Editor, April 10, 1997, A-15.

25. Robert H. Bork, *Slouching toward Gomorrah: Modern Liberalism and American Decline* (San Francisco: ReganBooks/HarperCollins, 1996), 306.

26. Ibid.

27. Ibid.

28. Nicholas Davidson, "Was Socrates a Plagiarist?" *National Review* 43:3 (February 25, 1991): 45.

29. Henri Pierre, "L'offensive de la 'Afrocentrisme,'" *Le Monde* (Paris), March 7, 1991.

30. Ambrose Evans-Pritchard, "Down with DWEMs—America's New Apartheid," *The Daily Telegraph* (London), August 30, 1992, Books, 15.

31. Richard Grenier, "Historic Identity Crises," *Times* (Washington), March 27, 1990, F-3.

32. Ibid.

33. Charley Reese, "Americans: Knowledge of Past Is Key to Retaining Your Liberty," *Sentinel* (Orlando), February 1, 1994, A-8.

34. Jonathan Foreman, "Film I: Big Bad Brits (and Other Myths)," *National Review* (April 20, 1998).

35. Alvin J. Schmidt, *The Menace of Multiculturalism* (Westport, Conn.: Praeger, 1997), 43–44.

36. Ibid., 52–53.

37. Dinesh D'Souza, "The Visigoths in Tweed," *Forbes* (April 1, 1991): 81.

BIBLIOGRAPHY FOR FURTHER RESEARCH

Berman, Paul, ed. *Debating P.C.: The Controversy over Political Correctness.* New York: Laurel Books/Dell, 1992.

> Diane Ravitch contributes an essay to this book that opposes the "influence" idea. Reviewing the book in the *New York Times*, Frank Kermode comments: "Ms. Ravitch is wrong to deny the influence of the Iroquois (Haudenosaunee) in Upstate New York on the Constitution . . . with rancor substituting for argument."

Churchill, Ward. *Fantasies of the Master Race: Literature, Cinema, and the Colonization of American Indians.* Monroe, Maine: Common Courage Press, 1992.

> In the chapter titled "The New Racism: A Critique of James A. Clifton's *The Invented Indian*" (163–184), reprinted from *Wicazo Sa Review* 6:2 (spring 1991), Churchill takes up the "influence" debate through an analysis of Elisabeth Tooker's essay "The United States Constitution and the Iroquois League," first published in *Ethnohistory* (1988). He writes that Tooker attempts to "refute the 'myth' that the Six Nations Haudenosaunee Confederacy was a model of government which significantly influenced the thinking of the founding fathers in the process of conceiving the U.S. republic" (168). Tooker, writes Churchill, "has spent several years vociferously repeating her theme in every possible forum, and has actively attacked the credibility of scholars such as Donald Grinde and Bruce Johansen, the results of whose research have reached opposite conclusions." Churchill says that "when questioned closely on the matter at a recent academic conference, this 'expert' was forced to admit not only that she had ignored all Iroquois source material while forming her thesis, but that she was [also] quite unfamiliar with the relevant papers of John Adams, Thomas Jefferson, Benjamin Franklin, Tom Paine, and others among the U.S. founders." Churchill cites, among other sources, Grinde, *The Iroquois and the Founding of the American Nation* (1977); Johansen, *Forgotten Founders* (1982, 1987); Grinde and Johansen, *Exemplar of Liberty* (1991); and Barreiro, ed., *Roots of Democracy* (1988).

Clark, Joe. "Excerpts from Constitutional Minister Joe Clark's Address to Canada's First Peoples Conference." *Akwesasne Notes* 23:4 (fall 1992): 17–18.

In late February 1992, representatives of the three federalist parties in the Canadian House of Commons signed the report of the Special Joint Commission on the Renewal of Canada. The report contains a strong statement supporting Native American self-government. Minister Clark supports this case by arguing that Native Americans in North America had democratic self-government while most of Europe was still feudal. He describes the Iroquois Confederacy's emphasis on consensus. "That system was so impressive that it served as a model for Thomas Jefferson and Benjamin Franklin as they grappled with designing the American Constitution."

Deloria, Vine, Jr. "Comfortable Fictions and the Struggle for Turf: An Essay Review of [James Clifton's] *The Invented Indian: Cultural Fictions and Government Policies*" [New Brunswick, N.J.: Transaction Publishers, 1990]. *American Indian Quarterly* (summer 1992): 397–410.

This book of essays contains an abridged version of Tooker's 1988 *Ethnohistory* article on the U.S. Constitution and the Iroquois League. Deloria comments, on pp. 402–404: "Some years ago, Bruce Johansen published a little book entitled *Forgotten Founders* [1982, 1987] . . . A wave of nauseous panic spread through the old-boys' network of Iroquois studies since a commoner had dared to write in a field already dominated by self-appointed experts. Donald Grinde . . . published *The Iroquois and the Founding of the American Nation* [1977], elaborating on this 'heresy' which was becoming an open scandal.

"Damage control measures went into effect, and soon Grinde and Johansen found their NEH grant proposals turned down by readers who emphasized the orthodox interpretation of Iroquois studies. Conservative newspaper columnists, learning of the controversy, promptly marched into historical debates of which they had no knowledge whatsoever and chastised Johansen and Grinde and proposals by the two scholars to have an open debate over the topic were generally turned aside as if mere physical contact with the two would be a sign of incipient heresy.

"Into the fray rode Elisabeth Tooker . . . [who] demonstrated, to her satisfaction, the impossibility of the Six Nations having any relevance at all for American constitutional thinking. Tooker's argument is so wonderfully naive and anthro-centric that it makes the informed observer of the debate weep for her inability to free herself from the blinders which adherence to anthro doctrine has required she wear."

Deloria then recapitulates Tooker's argument (see Tooker, 1988, 1990) and says that "Johansen and Grinde have collaborated now to produce *Exemplar of Liberty* [1991] . . . which further extends the scope of materials that must be considered to make any sense out of this issue."

Hoeveler, J. David, Jr. "Original Intent and the Politics of Republicanism." *Marquette Law Review* 75 (summer 1992): 863.

Hoeveler, chair of the history department at the University of Wisconsin, Milwaukee, is discussing liberal and conservative interpretations of the doctrine of original intent. In this context, he discusses Arthur Schlesinger Jr.'s arguments in *Disuniting of America* (1992). In a footnote, Hoeveler mentions the New York State "Curriculum of Inclusion," asserting that "the curriculum guide for American history demanded that the 'Haudensaunee' [*sic*] (Iroquois) political system be acknowledged as influencing the development of the American Constitution."

Jacobs, Wilbur. "The American Indian Legacy of Freedom and Liberty." *American Indian Culture and Research Journal* 16:4 (1992): 185–193.

In this commentary regarding the debate over the "influence" issue, Jacobs, professor emeritus at the University of California, Santa Barbara, examines *Exemplar of Liberty* (Grinde and Johansen, 1991) in light of his readings in history while a research scholar at the Huntington Library. "Grinde and Johansen are doing pioneering work in Indian history, correcting the misdirected thinking of certain colonial historians and anthropologists. In so doing, they are spreading a new light of understanding and setting forth new themes for general American history and government." Jacobs examines the writings on the subject by Temple University anthropology professor Elisabeth Tooker and finds support for Johansen and Grinde's construction of history in the works of Lawrence H. Gipson, who observed that European colonists were exposed to Native American diplomacy and forms of governance on a repeated basis from the earliest years of settlement, setting a precedent for Benjamin Franklin's use of an Iroquois confederate model in his Albany Plan of Union and Articles of Confederation. Jacobs also calls on his readings of Carl L. Becker and William Brandon.

Landsman, Gail H. "The 'Other' as Political Symbol: Images of the Indians in the Woman Suffrage Movement." *Ethnohistory* 39:1 (summer 1992): 247–284.

Citing primary sources also used by Sally Roesch Wagner (1992 and earlier), Landsman describes the ways in which Native American (particularly Iroquois) examples helped shape the ideology of the women's movement from 1848 to 1920. Landsman then plugs the documentary record into an ethnohistorical framework, arguing that while the early suffragists utilized the Indian image extensively, they were activists who formed their opinions "not through the discovery of objective truth but in the context of validating and/or advancing the story of woman suffrage" (252). This article indicates the important role that mythmaking has played in the shaping of ideological movements throughout history. Landsman mentions the overall "influence" debate (citing Grinde, Johansen, and Tooker), but says only that such ideas "are . . . open to scholarly debate and ethnohistorical research" (p. 252). The files contain a letter from Landsman, dated February 25, 1993, asserting that her work is independent of Sally Wagner's, as well as differences between her arguments and those of Starna and other anthropologists.

Lewis, Martin W. *Green Delusions: An Environmentalist Critique of Radical Environmentalism*. Durham, N.C.: Duke University Press, 1992.

On p. 92 of *Green Delusions*, Lewis, an assistant professor of geography at George Washington University, argues that participatory democracy may not eliminate social repression. Instead, he believes it perpetuates "a tyranny of long-winded individuals [who are] immune to boredom." Lewis believes that the inefficiency of participatory democracy uses more of the earth's resources for decision making than do other forms of government. "Unable to hold up their own or their forebears' experimental efforts in communal living," writes Lewis, "they [eco-radicals] have turned instead to indigenous American social organization. One popular model of participatory democracy is the Iroquois Confederacy." Lewis finds the Iroquois to be "a particularly ill-considered exemplar. Admiring the Iroquois political system of that era for its democracy is akin to praising Nazi Germany for its enlightened forestry. The Five Nations not only engaged in a highly successful campaign of ethnocide against their competitors in the fur trade, the Hurons, but they also raised the torture of war captives (those whom they chose not to adopt, at any rate) to a high art."

Limbaugh, Rush. *The Way Things Ought to Be*. New York: Pocket Books, 1992.

Page 204: "Multiculturalism is billed as a way to make Americans more sensitive to the diverse cultural backgrounds of people in this country. It's time we blew the whistle on that. What is being taught under the guise of multiculturalism is worse than historical revisionism. It's more than a distortion of facts. It's the elimination of facts. In some schools, kids are being taught that the ideas of the Constitution were borrowed from the Iroquois Indians and that Africans discovered America."

Lyons, Oren, ed. *Exiled in the Land of the Free*. Santa Fe: Clear Light Books, 1992.

These impressive essays by eight Native American leaders and scholars present persuasive evidence that the American colonists and the U.S. founding fathers borrowed from the Iroquois Confederacy and other Indian political institutions in drafting the U.S. Constitution.

Maybury-Lewis, David. *Millennium: Tribal Wisdom and the Modern World*. New York: Viking, 1992.

This survey of aboriginal cultures around the world, prepared by Cultural Survival of Cambridge, Massachusetts, contains a well-developed description of the Iroquois League's origins and operations. It also mentions Cannassatego's advice to the colonies on unification in 1744, and Benjamin Franklin's use of the theme in the early 1750s. Both Franklin and Jefferson were impressed by Indian political systems, especially regarding egalitarianism. "There is an argument raging currently over whether or not the founding fathers of the United States of America consciously modelled their new nation on the Iroquois Confederacy. It seems to me, however, that the important thing is not whether they did or did not, but the fact that they *could* have. There were, after all, no models in Europe at that time for the kind of federal republic that the Americans established."

Schlesinger, Arthur M., Jr. *The Disuniting of America*. New York: W. W. Norton, 1992.

Schlesinger (on pp. 96–98) takes issue with "history for self-esteem," or "feel-good history," by which, he says, self-interested minority groups seek to express their points of view in school curricula. His target here is the New York State Curriculum of Inclusion, which features a Native American study guide entitled "Haudenosaunee: Past, Present, Future." This curriculum guide had been the object of a bureaucratic ideological battle within the state department of education for at least five years by 1992. Scholars on both sides of the issue worked as consultants on this guide under contract with the New York State Education Department. Until 1992, the guide contained references to the "influence thesis" which were reportedly excised after complaints by people to whom Vine Deloria Jr. referred in his essay (1992) as the "old-boys' network of anthropology."

Page 97: "In New York the curriculum for 11th-grade history tells students that there were three 'foundations' for the Constitution: the European Enlightenment, the 'Haudenosaunee political system,' and the antecedent colonial experience ... How many experts on the American Constitution would endorse this stirring tribute to the 'Haudenosaunee political system'? How many have heard of that system? Whatever influence the Iroquois confederacy had on the framers of the Constitution was marginal; on European intellectuals, it was marginal to the point of invisibility. No other state curriculum offers this analysis of the making of the Constitution. But then no other state has so effective an Iroquois lobby."

Schlesinger's book contains no footnotes or endnotes, so it is unknown what works he consulted before composing the above statements. He read *Forgotten Founders* in 1982 and endorsed it: "*Forgotten Founders* is a tour-de-force of ingenious and elegant scholarship offering justice at last to the Indian contributions to the American Constitution." (See letter, Schlesinger to Lovell Thompson, publisher, Gambit Incorporated Publishers, 1982.)

Wagner, Sally Roesch. "The Iroquois Influence on Women's Rights." *Akwe:kon Journal* (formerly *Northeast Indian Quarterly*) 9:1 (spring 1992): 4–15.

This is Sally Roesch Wagner's most detailed published description to date of how contact with Iroquois people helped shape the thoughts of Stanton, Gage,

Anthony, and other founders of modern feminism. See also Wagner (1988, 1989) and Grinde and Johansen, *Exemplar of Liberty*, chapter 11 ("Persistence of an Idea") (1991).

Warriner, Gray, director, producer. "More Than Bows and Arrows." Videotape. Camera One, 1995.

As described in the catalogue of Insight Media, New York: "This award-winning documentary illuminates the impact that Native Americans have had on the political, social, and cultural development of the U.S. Narrated by N. Scott Momaday, it examines how government, agriculture and food, transportation, architecture, science and technology, the arts, medicine, and language all have benefitted from Native American contributions."

Weintraub, David. "Iroquois Influence in the Founding of the American Nation." *Court Review* 29 (winter 1992): 17–32.

This very detailed summary of the Iroquois League and ways in which it helped to shape American concepts of democracy, written by a third-year law student at Touro College, Jacob D. Fuchsberg Law Center, won first prize in the American Judges Association/American Judges Foundation 1992 Law Student Essay Contest.

Wright, Ronald. *Stolen Continents: The Americas through Indian Eyes since 1492.* Boston: Houghton Mifflin, 1992.

Pages 115–116: The Iroquois Confederacy "still survive[s], still fighting for recognition of a nationhood that they believe they never surrendered to the parvenus who built the United States and Canada around them. They also feel ironic pride that European colonists took the Iroquois Confederacy as a model when contemplating a union of their own." Wright then recounts some of the events in this chain of events, such as the speech by Onondaga Sachem Cannassatego at Lancaster in 1744 calling on the colonists to emulate the confederacy. Wright places Benjamin Franklin at that meeting, a factual error. Franklin, still a printer by trade in 1744, published the proceedings of the Lancaster Treaty Conference, so he was undoubtedly familiar with Cannassatego's words. He did not attend treaty councils personally until the 1750s, however. Wright correctly points out that the bundle of arrows on the U.S. Great Seal is an Iroquois symbol, and that originally the bundle was to have contained five arrows (for the five original Iroquois nations) rather than thirteen, one for each original state. Wright describes the operation of the Iroquois League and historic comment on it through p. 120. He returns to the subject on pp. 320–342, ending with the 1990 confrontation at Oka, Quebec. Wright cites early books by Grinde and Johansen (1977, 1982, 1987), as well as Tooker's article and Johansen's reply in *Ethnohistory* (1988, 1990).

Chapter 3

BURNING DOWN THE HOUSE:
LAURA INGALLS WILDER AND
AMERICAN COLONIALISM

Waziyatawin Angela Cavender Wilson

In the previous chapter, Dr. Johansen referred to Rush Limbaugh's contribution to anti-Indian hegemony, placing him on par with a number of academics who work to dismiss the truth about the origins of U.S. democratic ideals. In many instances both radio personalities and academics use the same propaganda strategies to support a colonizing agenda.[1] This chapter adds popular literature to the list of "harmful and immoral ideologies" that must be "laid to rest, not from the reaches of historical inquiry or discussions of racism, oppression, genocide and colonization, but as values with which we indoctrinate our children."

Waziyatawin narrates both a scholarly study and a personal story that relates to the example of Wilder's famous book, Little House on the Prairie, *to show that, "Indeed, anti-Indian educational and ideological hegemony is so firmly established, most Americans cannot recognize it even when it appears before their eyes." The truth of her statement was reinforced just a few minutes ago when a good friend of mine who serves with me in a local Veterans for Peace chapter and who is usually a careful, critical thinker, sent me a recent* 60 Minutes *commentary of CBS correspondent Andy Rooney, referring to it as a "great comment" on U.S. policy. Rooney's piece, entitled, "Our Darkest Days Are Here," did speak eloquently of his sadness about the U.S. torture of prisoners in Iraq, but the anti-Indianism in his opening was not noticed by my activist friend until after I pointed it out: "If you were going to make a list of the great times in American history, you'd start with the day in 1492 when Columbus got here ... and perhaps beating Hitler and putting a man on the moon would be up near the top as well."[2]*

Waziyatawin Angela Cavender Wilson is a Wahpetunwan Dakota from the Upper Sioux Reservation in southwestern Minnesota. She received her BA in History and American Indian Studies from the University of Minnesota in 1992 and her PhD in American History from Cornell University in 2000. In 2002 Angela served as co-coordinator for the Dakota Commemorative March, a 150-mile-long, seven-day event to honor the Dakota people, primarily women and children, who were force marched November 7–13, 1862, from the Lower Sioux Agency to a concentration camp at Fort Snelling. She is currently an Assistant

Professor of American Indian History in the history department at Arizona State University and is author of Remember This! (De Kiksuyapo!) Dakota Decolonization and the Eli Taylor Narratives.

***

We have been lied to so many times that we will not believe any words that your agent sends to us.

—SHORT BULL (BRULE' SIOUX), 1890

How do a country and its citizens justify genocide and land theft? How do they transform obviously wrong or immoral actions into something righteous and worthy of celebration? To answer these questions one need only examine the beloved classic *Little House on the Prairie*[3] to observe how expertly Laura Ingalls Wilder crafted a narrative that transformed the horror of white supremacist genocidal thinking and the stealing of Indigenous lands into something noble, virtuous, and absolutely beneficial to humanity. Unfortunately, rather than recognize the perversion of morality inherent in Wilder's book, the American public celebrates the work as laudable children's literature and the author as an American icon.

This book and the entire *Little House* series have been best sellers and favorites among the American public since the first book, *Little House in the Big Woods*, was released in 1932. As First Lady Laura Bush kicked off her campaign to fight illiteracy at the beginning of her husband's presidency, she proudly characterized *Little House on the Prairie* as a childhood favorite.[4] Similarly, in 2004 the National Endowment for the Humanities and the American Library Association selected *Little House* as one of the fifteen books for their "We the People Bookshelf," chosen for exemplifying the theme of courage. Five hundred schools throughout the country were awarded the bookshelf of "classic" works. NEH Chairman Bruce Cole announced the program stating, "The *We the People Bookshelf* enables younger readers to examine the meaning of courage from many perspectives. These books inspire readers with stories of characters, real and fictional, who demonstrated personal courage when faced with difficult situations in uncertain times."[5] In their 2002 spring/summer issue, "Adventures across America," *Travel and Leisure Family* magazine promoted "A Little Drive on the Prairie," which encouraged readers to relive the fantasy of Wilder's pioneer days: "Pack your bonnet and steer your wagon to America's heartland, where pioneer houses and pageants bring the stories of Laura Ingalls Wilder to life."[6] From these examples it is clear that the *Little House* love affair runs through all levels of the American populace, from schoolchildren all the way to America's institutions, media, and even First Lady.

The destructiveness of this love affair hit me personally in October 1998 when my eight-year-old daughter, Autumn, returned from school in tears because she had heard "The only good Indian is a dead Indian" in Wilder's *Little House on the Prairie*, the book her third-grade teacher, Bev Tellefson, was reading aloud to her students. We were living on the Upper Sioux Reservation at the time, but like other reservation children my daughter attended Bert Raney Elementary in the Yellow Medicine East school district (YME), the public school in the town of Granite Falls, Minnesota, bordering our reservation. Very disturbed by the way this reading made her feel, Autumn asked me to speak to her class about "our side of the story." Autumn's teacher was a fervent Wilder fan and had already commented to us that she loved the books so much she made a point of attending the Laura Ingalls Wilder pageant held in Walnut Grove, Minnesota, every summer. Our close proximity to the Ingalls family homestead sites was certainly a factor in the contestation over the interpretation of this issue. I did speak to the class with the teacher's permission and then wrote a critique of the book. I then presented this to the YME school board at a special meeting called for the purpose of addressing this issue, along with a request that the book be removed from the school curriculum. This began a year-long controversy primarily over the issue of "book banning" that gained local, state, and national attention.

The first reaction to this controversy, particularly by non-Indigenous people, has generally been one of anger and confusion. While there has been frequent outrage that an Indigenous mother would challenge an American canon, there is also a great deal of bewilderment. How could anyone possibly challenge a much-loved classic? The general populace does not understand what could be objectionable, let alone racist or colonialist, about *Little House on the Prairie*, especially the generation that grew up with the white-washed television series of the same name starring Michael Landon and Melissa Gilbert. Even those who read the books frequently do not understand what might be offensive about them. Indeed, anti-Indian educational and ideological hegemony is so firmly established, most Americans cannot recognize it even when it appears on paper before their eyes.

When I presented my critique before the school board, several of the board members admitted that they loved the Wilder series, had read the books as children, and had read them as adults to their own children. They admitted frankly that they arrived at the meeting prepared to defend the use of the book in the classroom. These members were intimately familiar with the book, yet they were blind to the racism contained in its pages. However, after hearing my appeal and reading the four-page critique of the book I presented to them, all but one of the school board members were persuaded that the book was indeed racist and did not belong in the classroom. They voted to pull the book from the curriculum, at least temporarily, until a committee could be established to review the book more thoroughly. Elmo Volstad, the school board member who voted to keep the book in the classroom, did so on the grounds that he was against censorship. This prompted the article that appeared in the next issue of the Granite Falls newspaper, which reported that I "came before the school board asking for the book to be banned."[7] I had never used the term "ban," but this was enough to spark a debate over censorship throughout the state of Minnesota.

I argued that this was not a matter of book banning, but rather it was about making good decisions regarding curriculum in the schools. Clearly teachers, curriculum committees, and school boards make decisions all the time about what should be taught in the classroom and they don't call it censorship or book banning when they replace outdated material with more appropriate curricula. However, this is not the perspective of the American Civil Liberties Union, which views removing materials because of objectionable content as a violation of First Amendment rights. Thus after the teachers' union went to the Minnesota Civil Liberties Union (now the ACLU of Minnesota) about the *Little House* issue, they threatened to file suit against the YME school board unless they immediately rescinded their decision to pull the book temporarily until it could be further reviewed. According to them, "Under clear precedent set by the U.S. Supreme Court, public schools are permitted to take such action only where a work contains extraordinarily offensive material or for sound pedagogical reasons. *Little House on the Prairie* could not possibly meet these requirements."[8] As a consequence of the ACLU-Minnesota threat, on December 14, 1998, the school board voted unanimously to reinstate the book. The teacher had won and six books in the Little House series would continue to be taught in the Yellow Medicine East school district, two books per year in the third through fifth grades.

The ACLU, which prides itself on being a champion of rights for American Indians and other groups who have historically been denied those rights, is only committed to racial equality when it doesn't get in the way of First Amendment rights. Equal protection under the law does not seem to include children who face racism in the classroom or in the curriculum. Today the ACLU-Minnesota proudly declares the outcome of this controversy as its victory. However, from an Indigenous perspective, there was no sense of justice in this outcome.[9]

How is it that such dramatically opposed arguments could be made about a seemingly benign and favored book like *Little House on the Prairie*? This is the heart of the matter. Most Americans cannot even comprehend the problem because the problem helps them preserve their sense of superiority and entitlement to America's lands and resources. Those who have a vested interest in maintaining the status quo guarded every step in this process. Autumn's teacher at Bert Raney Elementary was white (as were the other elementary schoolteachers), the principal was white, the superintendent was white, the librarian was white, and all the school board members were white. Who at any of these levels would be able to recognize that there might be a problem? Which of them had specialized training in recognizing and addressing racism? How many of them grew up reading the Wilder books and watching the popular TV show? How many of them were capable of seeing racism in attitudes that had been normalized in their lives?

Some of the racism and anti-Indianism in the book is quite transparent. For example, we learn by the fourth chapter that Ma hates Indians and two other characters express the sentiment that "the only good Indian is a dead Indian." Even Jack, the family dog, hates Indians and growls whenever they approach. This hate and disregard for Indigenous life expressed in the book does not exist in a vacuum, separate from the actions of Americans during this era or subsequent eras. Rather it is reflective of the attitudes that attempt to justify America's treatment of its Indigenous inhabitants. This hate, coupled with tremendous greed, was often enough justification to incite the outright slaughtering of Indigenous People as well as the perpetration of gross human rights abuses in the nineteenth century. Just in the period of the 1860s (the decade of the Ingalls foray into Indian Territory), Indigenous People were brutally slaughtered at places like Sand Creek and Washita Creek, and nations such as the Dine, Apache, and Dakota faced forced removal and concentration camp imprisonment. The ideologies of this era supported these actions and resulted in horrific consequences for Indigenous People, and they are well represented in the Wilder text. In fact, this overt racism was the only racism my daughter could clearly identify in her eight-year-old mind, and she stated repeatedly that she felt like everybody must hate her because she is Indian. While she knew she felt violated and personally attacked because of attitudes expressed throughout the book, other than the blatant comments above, she could not pinpoint why.

When the book is given a critical reading, it becomes quite clear why an Indigenous child would walk away with feelings of shame, hurt, and embarrassment. There are literally dozens of derogatory, dehumanizing, and damaging messages—somewhat more subtle than suggesting the outright extermination of an entire race of people, but no less destructive in their outcome. The adjectives used to describe the Indigenous people in the book are revealing. There are at least eighteen references to Indians as "wild," a handful of references to Indians as "savages," numerous references to the Indians "throbbing drums" and "wild yipping," and Pa refers to them as "screeching dev—." In many other instances Indigenous People are compared with animals or characterized as animals: "Their eyes were black and still and glittering, like snake's eyes." "The wild, fast yipping yells were worse than wolves." In another telling passage we learn: "Laura thought [Pa] would show her a papoose some day, just as he had shown her fawns, and little bears, and wolves." In these examples, Wilder effectively dehumanizes Indigenous People by establishing their inferiority to white human beings and by suggesting they share more similarities with animals. On the second page of Wilder's story we are told that Pa wanted to leave their Wisconsin home and move further west because that is where the "wild" animals lived. "There were no settlers. Only Indians lived there." Even though Indigenous People had long lived and farmed in Kansas, we are taught to distinguish between their settlement of the area and white settlement of the area. One of the most offensive passages is a statement made by Laura as the Osage are moving from their territory. As she is watching the procession she begs, "Pa, get me that little Indian baby . . . Oh I want it! I want it! . . . Please, Pa, please!" Laura Ingalls wanted a little Indian baby just as she would want a pet.

We learn at one point that Pa does not believe the only good Indian is a dead Indian; his idea of a good Indian is one who will fight his own people to prevent them from attacking the white settlers illegally squatting on Indigenous lands. In this story, the one "good Indian" is Osage leader Soldat du Chene, who is willing to fight his own people as well as other Indigenous nations if they threaten the white settlers. By most standards he would be considered a traitor to his people, but not by the standards in *Little House*. Instead, he is revered and the "bad Indians" in the book are, of course, those who resented white intrusion in their territory and who posed the most significant threat to the Ingalls family.

The issue of white invasion of Indigenous lands is at the center of the story, but Wilder repeatedly seeks to justify white actions throughout the narrative. While Indigenous People are demonized, the whites in the story are glorified. One of the most dangerous aspects of the book, therefore, is the extent to which the reader develops an affinity with and adoration of the white characters in the story. The humanity of the Ingalls family is so convincing that their righteousness is firmly established. The underlying message embedded in this work is one widely familiar to American audiences; the white settlers are the heroes and the Indians are the villains. In creating such a dichotomy between the goodness of the Ingalls family and the badness of the Indians by whom they feel threatened, children reading this book are left to believe that Indians must be really bad if these good, moral, and wonderfully likeable people hate them. Most readers will never question how very "good" white people can hate Indians and still be considered "good."

The myth of manifest destiny is the pervading underlying theme throughout the work; it is introduced to the reader on the very first page, where we learn that "they were going to Indian country." Pa, Ma, Mary, Laura, and Baby Carrie are headed west in their covered wagon to make a new life. Rather than depicting this as an incredible act of violence, as invasion always is, it is celebrated and justified. In fact, the reader is encouraged to believe that this is necessary, inevitable, and even righteous. As they settle on the Kansas and Indian Territory border, Wilder writes, "Ma said she didn't know whether this was Indian country or not. She didn't know where the Kansas line was. But whether or no, the Indians would not be here long." Similarly, Mrs. Scott says, "Treaties or no treaties, the land belongs to folks that'll farm it. That's only common sense and justice." The fact that Indigenous People continued to be in the way as whites were moving in is apparent in Ma's comments throughout the book. For instance, at one point Ma derisively says, "I declare, Indians are getting so thick around here that I can't look up without seeing one." She fears Indian influence on her children and works diligently to teach her children to absorb her notions of civility and savagery: "Dear me, Laura, must you yell like an Indian? I declare, if you girls aren't getting to look like Indians! Can I never teach you to keep your sunbonnets on?"

Despite the fact that Wilder has already described the family move into Indian Territory, the Ingalls family is frightened and angry when two Indigenous men go into their house. "Those Indians were dirty and scowling and mean. They acted as if the house belonged to them." In this example we see the perverted logic of colonialism at work. While the

Ingalls family is more than willing to invade Indigenous lands, showing no respect for Indigenous rights, they expect Indigenous People to accept their presence and theft without repercussion. In the world of colonialism created and supported in Wilder's fiction, Indigenous people become the aggressors and the thieves, "stealing" the hard-earned products reaped from land the Ingalls family (unjustly) occupies. At the end of the story, the Ingalls family packs up what they can to head back to Wisconsin because they are informed that the U.S. government is sending over soldiers to "take all us settlers out of Indian Territory." While they are sad to leave their beautiful home, Pa is not too disappointed because they have profited from their stay, "Anyway, we're taking more out of Indian Territory than we took in." They have exploited the land as best they could.

In an attempt to argue a more benevolent reading of *Little House*, some may try to distinguish Laura's fascination with Indians from the racism of other characters in the book. In this argument Wilder is not characterized as racist, but rather her accounts are considered to be accurate depictions of racist nineteenth-century attitudes. Her art is merely a reflection of the times. For example, toward the end of the novel, "Her eyes were full of tears and sobs kept jerking out of her throat," as Pa told her to look at the long line of Osages finally leaving the area. The fact that she was saddened to see the Indians go (just after her pleading for an Indian baby), some might say, is an indication that she is not racist. Laura is not the only one who is moved at the site of the Osages moving westward; even Ma says she "didn't feel like doing anything, she was so let down." From an Indigenous perspective, however, this bit of nostalgia is unconvincing evidence of a benevolent attitude. A twinge of remorse in the act of invading provides no grounds for celebration unless it prompts the invaders to leave. If there is no subsequent action, this bit of sadness means little, especially when other thoughts and actions reveal a far more consistent pattern. Thus we learn at the beginning of the next chapter, "After the Indians had gone, a great peace settled on the prairie." In the end of the volume, it is not Indian removal that caused the Ingalls family to finally leave the area, but rather the threat of U.S. soldiers.

Not only is Wilder's description of Indigenous People in the story consistently derogatory, even when Laura presents something superficially positive, it is also couched in negativity. For example, in one instance, Laura reveals, "She had a naughty wish to be a little Indian girl. Of course she did not really mean it. She only wanted to be bare naked in the wind and the sunshine, and riding one of those gay little ponies."

Thus even here the sense of white superiority is apparent and a desire for anything associated with Indians is considered shameful and "naughty."

In light of all the derogatory messages embedded within the *Little House* text, it would be difficult for any child to remain unaffected. Without critical intervention, Indigenous children would likely be hurt and ashamed, while non-Indigenous children would further internalize ideologies of white superiority and manifest destiny because of their reinforcement and validation within the story. In my daughter's classroom, even as the teacher interspersed such comments as "people do not talk that way today" to try to diffuse the racism expressed in the book, she was far from able to offer a critical intervention, since her own love of the stories came through more vividly than anything else. After reading six books in the *Little House* series by the end of fifth grade, children at Bert Raney Elementary are thoroughly indoctrinated with Wilder's racism, and the children most hurt in the process are the Dakota children from Upper Sioux. One of the other Dakota parents whose daughter was in the same third-grade classroom asked her daughter if she felt bad reading *Little House* and her daughter said "No." However, when her mother pressed her, asking, "Doesn't it bother you when they say bad things about Indians in the story?" her daughter answered, "No, I just pretend I'm not Indian." Realization of this disturbing choice for Indigenous youth, to either allow the feelings of hurt and shame to take hold or to shut off that hurt through dissociation, was one of the most disturbing realizations for all the Dakota and white parents who felt *Little House* had no place in the classroom.

When my daughter first told me about her experiences with the Wilder book, I could not even fathom a scenario in which a teacher or school official would want to continue using materials that were hurtful to a child. I thought surely the teacher would apologize, reassure me that she never intended to harm my child, and then make the necessary changes to rectify the situation. In fact, rather than demonstrating any sensitivity to the racism, the teacher dug in her heels on the issue, insisting on her need to continue using the materials for educational purposes. The teacher loved the entire series and no amount of evidence about the offensiveness of the writings were going to change her mind. In spite of the teacher's extreme position, in 1998 I still wanted to believe that education was the key to ending racism, that when individuals were exposed to an intellectual argument that demonstrated racism their minds would change, even if the change occurred person by person. In my first discussion with the school board, this seemed to hold true. With my careful critique, I changed the opinions of all but one school board member. When the dozens of examples of racism in the book were illuminated and they could begin to view the book through Indigenous eyes, they were surprised and a few were somewhat embarrassed that they hadn't seen it before. Warren Formo, the school board chairman, told a delegation from Upper Sioux that their "eyes had been opened" as a result of this controversy, welcome words in any discussion of racism.[10] The educational success experienced in this first meeting, however, was short-lived. I soon realized that wherever racism is prevalent, intellectual arguments frequently hold little sway.

As the local news spread to the state and national levels, I was dumb-founded by the racist assumptions which began to surround the issue. Writers in editorials criticized the "chip on my shoulder," insisting that Wilder offers an accurate portrayal of the past and therefore should continue to be taught.[11] This perspective always shocked me because Wilder's attitudes were racist in the 1860s, the setting of the *Little House* story, they were racist in the 1930s when the book was published, and they remain racist today. I agree that there is a difference between a critical discussion about racism in a nineteenth-century context and an uncritical discussion which serves instead to indoctrinate new generations of children in racist ideology. In my daughter's classroom, clearly it was a matter of the latter. Another letter to the editor directed the question to me: "Have you ever read another book besides 'Little House'?" Her argument was that if I had read other books I would realize *Little House* is not so bad and that it is in fact one of the "most wholesome books you can read."[12] As a doctoral candidate in American history at Cornell University in 1998, I found the assumption that I was an ignorant and poorly read Indigenous woman both ironic and offensive. A similar comment came from Paul Sellon, Mitchell superintendent of schools, who referred to the Wilder novels as "history." About the "American Indian mother" who raised the complaint, he stated it was unfortunate that anyone would want to "wipe out history."[13] In spite of my educational background, I was positioned on the opposite side of "educators" and "historians," a way to effectively delegitimize my intellectual position and capacity.

Another argument routinely articulated was that all books are offensive to someone, so if all offensive books were removed from the classrooms and libraries there would be nothing left. In fact, when a crew from Nickelodeon came to our reservation and school district to produce an episode on the *Little House* issue for their children's program *Nick News*, Linda Ellerbee publicly advanced this argument in the final production.[14]

This kind of argument disallows degrees of offensiveness and distracts from any acknowledgment of issues of power and control. When then Superintendent Bob Vaadeland repeatedly denied that power was part of the equation, I finally asked him why we didn't have erotica in the elementary school library or in the children's classrooms. He told me I was being ridiculous, that there were no similarities at all because erotica was clearly inappropriate for children. I argued that it was precisely the same thing. Erotica is not allowed in the schools because it violates the general public's sensibilities about what is appropriate for children. While I don't believe erotica should be in the classroom, the question demonstrates that those in power, usually in accordance with the values of the general populace, make determinations about what is appropriate for children. Similarly, though KKK literature is an obvious part of American history, why don't schools promote the incorporation of their writings directed at children such as *Kloran (ritual) Junior Order Ku Klux Klan* or the booklet for the branch of the Women's Klan established for teenage girls, *Ritual of Tri-K Club*? They don't because it would again violate the same sensibilities. At issue here, then, is whose sensibilities determine the point of violation and who has the power to enforce those sensibilities.

This reality was confirmed to me in 2001 during a diversity awareness training workshop when I presented the *Little House* controversy to a group of Phoenix-area teachers and staff. Upon completion of my presentation, a high school librarian came up to me and confided that she continuously exercises her power to decide what should stay and what should go in the school's library collection. She stated that the previous summer she and her staff were horrified to discover some very old books with extremely racist children's jump-rope verses on the shelf, many of which were created during the slavery days in the Old South. The staff quickly discarded the books, thankful that they caught them and disposed of them before someone else discovered them. They immediately recognized the overt racism in the books and as a small group made the decision that they were inappropriate for a school library today. Unfortunately, racism against Indigenous People is not readily recognizable to the various levels of gatekeepers in educational institutions.

If Indigenous People maintained control over the education of our children, literature which helped to justify our extermination and land dispossession would clearly violate our sensibilities. *Little House on the Prairie* would not need to be pulled today because it would never have made it into the curriculum or the libraries in the first place. However, in the context of colonialism, the people who have the power to make such decisions have directly benefited from Indigenous extermination and land dispossession (indeed, the YME schools sit on land stolen from the Dakota Nation). They have a vested interest in maintaining the status quo, in this case that which helps to justify their very presence in our homeland. In this tenuous moral position the monumental racism in a book like *Little House* must be minimized and placed on the same level as someone from the Christian right, for example, who might find the reference to the color purple in a piece of children's literature offensive because they feel it endorses homosexuality. There is no room for an acknowledgment that advocating genocide moves the issue beyond one of petty offensiveness.

Americans recognize this in other contexts. For example, if a teacher were to uncritically use a Nazi primer in the classroom for educational purposes (the kind typically used as part of Hitler Youth programs in Nazi Germany), there would be outrage from nearly all segments of society. In fact Europe went through a de-Nazification program after World War II, and any literature deemed anti-Semitic was removed. For example, *Ich Kampfe*, the 100-page handbook distributed in the early 1940s to each new person enrolled in the Nazi party, was systematically destroyed by the Allied De-Nazification Commission at the end of the war.[15] Along with the banning of the Nazi party and general reforms on German education and culture, textbooks written under the Nazis were withdrawn and were replaced with new ones. Obviously this notion of removing books because of objectionable content would fall under various American definitions of book banning and censorship, but the difference in the equation is *power*. The Allied forces had the power after World War II to dictate what the Germans should and should not be reading. In that context Americans clearly understood the link between promoting a specific ideology in written literature and the implementation of that ideology in atrocious governmental policies. Furthermore, they recognized the danger in allowing anti-Semitic and racist agendas in the classroom. We see a similar recognition in global politics today. The current Bush administration has supported the de-Baathification of Iraq to eliminate the ideologic residue of Saddam Hussein's political party, the Arab Baath Socialist Party. In the "Report on the Transition to Democracy in Iraq" created in fall 2002, plans for this de-Baathification include new textbooks as part of the educational reform.[16]

The real issue, then, is not that Americans are opposed to banning literature—or at least replacing problematic existing literature with more appropriate literature. Instead the question is, why does our society today still advocate the indoctrination of American youth in racist and genocidal ideologies regarding Indigenous People? It does so because the United States government is still in power, it still considers the Indigenous population an expendable one, and it is still in the business of exploiting Indigenous lands and resources with the eager help of the corporate world. Even in the late twentieth century, for example, government sterilization policies were aimed at Indigenous women and administered through the Indian Health Service (in direct violation of the United Nations Convention on the Prevention and Punishment of the Crime of Genocide). This aptly demonstrates U.S. disregard for Indigenous life even in recent times. The purposeful targeting of Indigenous communities for toxic and radioactive waste disposal by national and multinational corporations with full governmental sanctioning offers another example of contemporary beliefs in America regarding the expendability of Indigenous People.[17] The American government and its citizens cannot seem to recognize the destructive ideologies because they have become essential to the ongoing colonization of Indigenous People and land bases. To question those ideologies would jeopardize America's capacity to further exploit Indigenous People and lands. Yet this is precisely what needs to happen.

As an antidote to current anti-Indianism and colonialism in American educational institutions, Americans must engage in the decolonization of curriculum and literature available to our schoolchildren, similar to the de-Nazification or de-Baathification this country has supported in other contexts. While this is a project in which we must engage at all levels of society and in all contexts, the literature read by our children is an appropriate place to start. This decolonization project will require Indigenous People and our non-Indigenous allies to continue to challenge the hegemonic structures which have justified and advocated our ongoing oppression and colonization. Justice demands that these harmful and immoral ideologies be laid to rest, not from the reaches of historical inquiry or discussions of racism, oppression, genocide, and colonization, but as values with which we indoctrinate our children.

Six years after our experience with the *Little House* controversy, our family still feels its effects. While writing this article I asked my (now teenaged) daughter Autumn what she thinks about the issue today, and she simply stated that she tries not to think about it too much because when she does it still hurts. Indeed, the anger, frustration, and hurt resulting from our battles have not subsided. Fortunately, despite the school's efforts to instill in her a sense of inferiority, she remains fiercely proud of being Dakota, in part because of our critical intervention in 1998. In recent years I've watched my daughter courageously and consistently fight other issues of racism in her schools on a near daily basis and because of that I am filled with a profound sense of hope. While we lost the fight over *Little House on the Prairie* in a southern Minnesota school, Autumn reminds me that the spirit of resistance to anti-Indian hegemony is active and preparing for the future struggles. Perhaps next time Americans will not cling as tightly to their oppressive ideologies and there will be sufficient support for more lasting and comprehensive positive change.

NOTES

The epigraph to this chapter is taken from James P. Boyd, *Recent Indian Wars under the Lead of Sitting Bull and Other Chiefs* (Philadelphia: Publishers Union, 1892), 207.

1. Rush Limbaugh, *See I Told You So* (New York: Pocket Books, 1993), 68.

2. Andy Rooney, "Our Darkest Days Are Here," *60 Minutes,* CBS, May 23, 2004, http://www.cbsnews.com/stories/2004/05/20/60minutes/rooney/main618783.shtml. Accessed December 17, 2004.

3. The main title of this chapter is taken from an excellent editorial written amidst the *Little House* controversy which erupted in Minnesota in 1998. See W. Roger Buffalohead, "Burning Down the House: A Little 'Teaching Moment,'" *The Circle* 20.2 (February 1999).

4. For example, see Associated Press, "New 1st Lady Set to Fight Illiteracy," *The Arizona Republic,* January 20, 2001.

5. See the National Endowment for the Humanities website, www.neh.fed.us/, for further information. For this news story visit www.neh.fed.us/news/archive/20040316.html.

6. Sunshine Flint, "A Little Drive on the Prairie," *Travel and Leisure Family* (spring/summer 2002): 14–18.

7. Faith Kammerdiener, "*Little House* Pulled from YME Curriculum," *Advocate Tribune,* October 29, 1998.

8. Letter to Superintendent Bob Vaadeland from Lucy A. Daglish, Dorsey & Whitney LLP, December 11, 1998.

9. For their statement on this issue visit their website at www.aclu-mn.org and view "Little House on the Prairie (Direct-Won)" under their category for Censorship.

10. Cited in Tom Cherveny, "YME reinstates 'Little House,'" *West Central Tribune* (Willmar, Minnesota), December 15, 1998, front page.

11. V. G. Haaland, Letter to the Editor, with the headline "Let's Not Continue with Chip on Our Shoulders," *Advocate Tribune* (Granite Falls, Minnesota), November 12, 1998.

12. Lea Pederson, Letter to the Editor, "Today's Books, Entertainment More Offensive Than 'Little House,'" *West Central Tribune* (Willmar, Minnesota), December 8, 1998.

13. Associated Press State and Local Wire, Mitchell, South Dakota, "Historians, Educators Defend Accusations against 'Little House' Series," December 8, 1998.

14. *Nick News* #166, "Book Banning," Lucky Duck Productions, New York.

15. This work is now available in the United States with an English translation, Ray Cowdery, *Ich Kampfe (I Fight)* (Rapid City, S.D.: U.S.M., 1982).

16. Paul Berman, "Learning Not to Love Saddam," *New York Times*, March 31, 2003.

17. For numerous examples of this see Winona LaDuke, *All Our Relations: Native Struggles for Land and Life* (Cambridge, Mass.: South End Press, 1999), and Ward Churchill and Winona LaDuke, "Native North America: The Political Economy of Radioactive Colonialism," in *The State of Native America: Genocide, Colonization, and Resistance*, ed. M. Annette Jaimes (Boston: South End Press, 1992), 241–266.

(POST) COLONIAL PLAINSONGS:
TOWARD NATIVE LITERARY
WORLDINGS

Jodi A. Byrd

Chapter 4

In this chapter, Jodi Byrd extends the discussion of hegemonic literature like
Little House on the Prairie, *explaining the importance of "reworlding" literary assumptions and definitions so that they can finally speak to the true histories
of Indigenous peoples. She tells us that this "worlding of a world" is the work
of the settler whose "discursive colonization naturalizes the European order as
dominant in the land by imaginatively transforming the Native Other into an
empty referent." She reminds us that the problem with hegemony is that "one
never does have to think about it, and all too often, Native scholars and authors
are left with the task of confronting the unthinking hegemonies" that continue
to shape academic knowledge about Indigenous People in ways that support their
own dominant desires and assumptions.*

*In recent years, more and more authors are attempting to record history
truthfully. Documentary films like* The Invasion of Panama *or* Farenheit 911
and books like Big Lies: The Right-Wing Propaganda Machine and How It
Distorts the Truth, The Pinochet Files, The Best Democracy Money Can
Buy, *or my own,* American Assassination: On the Strange Death of Senator
Paul Wellstone, *are growing in number as a way to deconstruct relatively recent
deceptions about official U.S. policies and practices. Such books are beginning
to awaken millions of Americans to difficult truths about American leadership
and are serving to begin new conversations. Still, authentic conversations about
Indigenous People, their history, contributions, perspectives, and desires are desper-
ately lacking. Books like Chrisjohn and Young's* Shadows and Substance in the
Indian Residential School Experience in Canada *may reveal hard-to-imagine
atrocities against Indian people—but contributions from contemporary Indigenous
voices that could guide us into the future are largely unheeded. Jodi A. Byrd's is
one of these voices and her call for those in charge of literary offerings to allow them
to emerge will serve readers who are interested in understanding how the lived
experiences expressed by Indigenous writers must inform postcolonial theorizing.*

*Jodi Byrd is a citizen of the Chickasaw Nation of Oklahoma. She received her
PhD in English from the University of Iowa, focusing on ideological formations
of Indigenous People with current postcolonial discourses. She currently teaches*

courses on American Indians in film for the University of Iowa's American Indian Native Studies Program.

***

Elizabeth Cook-Lynn has recently identified anti-Indianism as "probably the foremost challenge to U.S. history and art."[1] A discursive and imaginative violence that continues to shape U.S. intellectual and artistic expressions, anti-Indianism functions as a deep-seated colonial hegemony that vilifies and dehumanizes Indigenous People as a means to justify genocide and support imperialism. In *Anti-Indianism in Modern America*, Cook-Lynn suggests that a critical analysis of anti-Indianism within the field of literary studies is long overdue and provides a substantial starting point for scholars to engage those colonialist discourses informing works by Native and non-Native writers alike. By marking the hegemonic influences and lineages of contemporary literature about American Indians, Cook-Lynn reveals the propagandistic nature of anti-Indianism in stark detail. Anti-Indianism is a process by which our cultures, histories, and knowledges are transformed into a U.S. national patrimony where our very presence speaks to some essential "American-ness" that each citizen regardless of ethnic or racial origins may claim. It is not a stretch then that Cook-Lynn argues in her book that the narratives of James Fennimore Cooper's and Louis L'Amour's vanishing Americans are the direct ancestors of more recent contributions to the genre that include Ian Frazier's laissez-faire and voyeuristic forays to Pine Ridge in his 2000 memoir *On the Rez*.

Frazier's book, which has been roundly critiqued by Sherman Alexie and other Native reviewers, remains popular because of its nonthreatening accessibility and its assured entitlement and access to "Sioux" culture and history. Writing of his own interest in Pine Ridge and providing his credentials for observing life on the reservation, he invites his readers to identify affinities they might have for particular tribes, as if Native cultures were a veritable buffet line of choices for the discriminating consumer. "Indeed," he writes,

> the Indians of America are so varied that I think you could find an appropriate tribe for almost anyone . . . As we get older, we learn our affinities—for certain foods or kinds of music or seats in an airplane or professions or physical types among the sex we happen to be attracted to. Just through an affinity for a particular part of the country, a person narrows down the number of tribes that would be right for him or her. In the same way that I have gotten used to my liking for hot sauce

and my aversion to crowds, I accept that my affections veer toward the Oglala Sioux.[2]

Cook-Lynn has criticized Frazier for turning a tourist's gaze toward the reservation and for reducing the diversity of "Sioux" cultures into a monolithic type that he represents as Oglala. In her book, Cook-Lynn further describes how Frazier's tourism manifests at a public reading of his work. When asked by an audience member to reflect upon the conflicts that arise when non-natives write about Indians, he replies with the observation, "Well, I know that Indian writers have said critical things but I just have never thought about it."[3] In response, Cook-Lynn counters with her own question and a challenge: "If writers themselves never think about it, who will?"[4]

The problem with hegemony is that one never does have to think about it, and all too often, Native scholars and authors are left with the task of confronting the unthinking hegemonies that continue to shape academic knowledges about Indigenous People. One of Cook-Lynn's primary concerns is to restructure Native studies to reflect the intellectual sovereignty of Native nations and to resist the fetishization of political independence by academic hobbyists, tourists, and writers of fiction and memoir. She argues that the past 150 years of Indian resistances should rather "be seen in the context of the Third World struggle of our time in which a very large field of learning must be explored."[5] That large field of learning to which she refers includes the work of Homi Bhabha, Edward Said, Gayatri Spivak, and other intellectuals whose scholarship provides frameworks for thinking about colonialisms and their resistances under the rubric of postcolonial theory.

Yet while Cook-Lynn advocates for Native scholars to engage questions of transnationalism, colonialism, and cosmopolitanism within American Indian contexts, she later charges postcolonial theory with anti-Indianism when she examines how "postcolonial scholarship defames the native voice."[6] This defamation, according to Cook-Lynn, occurs through a variety of literary and academic discourses, from the celebration of writers like Louis L'Amour, James Fennimore Cooper, and others who play "cowboys and Indians" in their writings, to attacks on the legitimacy and "authenticity" of Native voices who rise to challenge the anti-Indian hegemony still practiced in Western academic institutions. Given the tendency of many postcolonial scholars and writers to cast Indigenous People as relics or remnants of a distant, conquered past, especially as they reflect upon the US' own supposed postcolonial status, gained in its revolutionary break from England, Cook-Lynn's argument highlights, for Native scholars venturing into the quagmire of Western epistemologies, the contradictory agendas within postcolonial critiques of empire, globalization, and cosmopolitanism.[7] How then might one resolve Cook-Lynn's own ambivalence between disrupting such forms of anti-Indianism on the one hand and her continued call for "Third World" scholarship as a means to address emerging indigenous voices on the other? It seems to me that postcolonial theories are situated on a precipice between providing a forum to consider the colonization of Indigenous People on a global, international scale and becoming yet another means through which Western academia discredits and invisibilizes indigenous worldviews. How scholars and writers tip the scales depends upon their evocation of worldviews that have been constructed and perpetuated, or denied and abjected, through the act of colonization.

The passage from Ian Frazier's *On the Rez* quoted above demonstrates a fundamental desire to consume indigenous knowledges and peoples to such a degree that the Native other is defamed through a recasting as something wholly available to anyone with an affinity or liking. The rest of the book provides a travelogue of Frazier's experiences in and around Pine Ridge, the people he meets, and how he considers making "Indians" more accessible to mainstream America. Published a year after President Clinton's 1999 visit to Pine Ridge, Frazier's book ostensibly takes up Clinton's challenge to provide "a gift to the 21st century"[8] by documenting how conditions on the reservation are not bleak but rather vitally important for those wishing to "be Indian" and that the warrior tradition is alive and well in the game of basketball. Positioning himself as an outsider with insider sensibilities, he details his desire to "be an uncaught Indian like them," a textual performance of what Philip Deloria has defined as "playing Indian."[9]

The same year that Frazier's memoir received popular and critical attention, Blackfoot author Stephen Graham Jones published his first novel, *The Fast Red Road: A plainsong*, to little fanfare. His novel, which has yet to receive the consideration it deserves, tells the story of a young mixed-blood Indian named Pidgin who attempts to recover his father's stolen body as they travel dusty Western highways inhabited by a bizarre cast of cowboys, grocery store clerks, rodeo clowns, thieves, and body snatchers. *The Fast Red Road* is a fictional travelogue that looks at life off the reservation and on the borders between Native nations and the U.S. government. But unlike Frazier's account, *The Fast Red Road* is not interested in framing twenty-first-century Indian country within the language and narratives that dominate U.S. desire. Instead, Jones' book confronts popular myths and images of American Indians and the "wild west" at the same time that it provides sharp insights into the historical violences that have carved the US out of Indigenous Peoples and lands. Echoing Gerald Vizenor's trickster narratives as it fragments and then reassembles into a daunting and at times absurd novel, the narrative resists the idea that Indianness is something that one can contract through affinity, or as one of the characters phrases it, through a communicable disease.

The first chapter, "Black Tea: An Old Man Has a Narrative Experience with Prescription Laxatives," revels in the scatological within trickster stories and provides a counterpoint to Ian Frazier's consumer-oriented buffet line of Indian cultures. The old man referenced in the chapter title appears as a Shoshone who is forced by Litmus Jones into a shared macabre vision of an all-you-can-eat buffet that morphs as he stares from BBQ and mashed potatoes into steaming piles of human parts and entrails linked to Columbus' arrival in the new world. Throughout the opening chapter, Litmus, as his name suggests, emerges as the author-as-trickster whose tests call into being a carnival of images, sounds, and smells that force the characters to "see through" the buffet to the reality of what is being fed to paying customers, and demands that readers wake from the gloss of conspicuous consumption. From the $18.76 price for the meal that evokes the Battle of Little Big Horn of that year to the memories of the massacres that lie beneath the rhythm of the William Tell Overture and the Lone Ranger's mythic west, the scene which is little more than "a weak drive-in movie you're supposed to laugh at" becomes a detailed evocation of death and destruction.[10]

The opening plainsongs of *The Fast Red Road* provide compelling insights into this dialectic of postcolonial literary analysis and Native philosophical traditions, which have at times seemed incommensurable. The nascent connection between Native American literary studies and postcolonial theory that Cook-Lynn gestures toward demands that scholars concerned with colonial discourse analysis within literatures of empire consider how British and then deep settler colonialism inform discussions of citizenship, diaspora, and authority within the US. Yet, on either side of the terrain, those involved remain guarded, tenuous, and occasionally resistant, which may account to some degree for Cook-Lynn's own ambivalence about the theory. That postcolonial theories have largely ignored Indigenous Peoples in the Americas remains, as Eric Cheyfitz has recently noted, "surprising, if not a complete scandal."[11] American Indian scholars have often approached the question of postcolonialism with a thinly veiled skepticism in part because the theory appears depoliticized in its emphasis on the "post" and its declaration that "the era of formal colonialism is over."[12] As Thomas King writes in "Godzilla vs. Post Colonial," such theories have little to do with the historical knowledge and memories Indigenous People have of themselves and their relations with European colonial powers.[13] This sentiment is typical of other Indian scholars who have often argued that postcolonial theories are unable to speak to the experiences of Native peoples because our decolonial struggles are still ongoing.[14] As the buffet scene from Stephen Graham Jones' novel graphically demonstrates, there is nothing "post" about an ongoing U.S. federal Indian policy that systematically dismantles the sovereignty and treaty rights of Native nations, forcibly appropriates their lands, and degrades Native cultures and languages through forced assimilation, relocation, and allotment.[15]

It is in this climate that Native authors have translated tribal aesthetics into written traditions as they identify and engage colonial symbolic orders. These questions surrounding postcolonial theory's ability to represent and engage Native histories and lived experiences stem from concerns Native scholars have about how authority and representative experiences are established in the first place. But because postcolonial theory arose from anticolonial struggles and provides methodologies through which to articulate how colonialism propagates itself discursively, the promise of collaborations between postcolonial theory and Native literary studies remains enticing. Native literatures in the Americas are shaped by diaspora, resistance, and nationalism as well as implicated in similar questions of cosmopolitanism and complicit intellectualism. Such theoretical considerations would foreground concerns over nationalism rather than ethnographic performance, decolonial struggles over marginal inclusions. Further, postcolonial and transnational theories provide vocabulary and methods with which to investigate how Native literatures are canonized as well as for whom, and to what end, they are written.

At stake, then, are the possible theoretical formulations that challenge postcolonial theory to engage Indigenous Peoples in deep settler societies while retaining the necessary distinctions of intellectual sovereignty of Native cultures that mark the work of scholars such as Robert Allen Warrior, Craig Womack, and Elizabeth Cook-Lynn. The issue here is a matter of transforming the postcolonial to account for those processes through which the discursive colonialisms of Native peoples remain intact even within theories developed to challenge Western hegemony. Gayatri Spivak identifies this discursive practice of colonialism as the force which "oblig[es] the native to cathect the space of the Other on his home ground."[16] As the Native is forced to invest emotionally within that Otherness, Spivak tells us, there is a "worlding the world of the Native" that accompanies that process whereby the Native internalizes or comes to see her/himself as Other. This "worlding of a world" is the work of the settler, whose discursive colonization naturalizes the European order as dominant in the land by imaginatively transforming the Native Other into an empty referent. The Indigenous laws and languages are negated and denied as the settler finally declares the land uninhabited.

By denying that original peoples or histories exist, the colonizer obscures the processes through which the Native self has been transformed into a blank Otherness that can then be controlled and consumed. Spivak's reformulation here of Martin Heidegger's "The Origin of the Work of Art" parallels, with one crucial difference, what Choctaw novelist and scholar LeAnne Howe has defined as *haksuba*. The word arises from Choctaw cosmology and describes what happens in this world when the Upper Worlds and Lower Worlds collide:

> Haksuba or chaos occurs when Indians and non-Indians bang their heads together in search of cross-cultural understanding. The sound is often a dull thud, and the lesson leaves us all with a bad headache . . .[17]

Whereas Spivak's understanding of worlding implies an emptying out of meaning and presence that marks the arrival of the colonizer, Howe provides us with a definition of worlding in which Indigenous People retain discursive control through which to recast and engage the arrival of the European settler. *Haksuba* recenters indigenous agency, troubling the notion of Spivak's worlding by incorporating the European into Southeastern cultural and political contexts. Howe's evocation of *haksuba*, or chaos, between indigenous and European worldings resists positioning the arrival of the colonizer as an epitomizing moment for Indigenous Peoples; Europeans are worlded instead into indigenous histories that span centuries and remain centered in land and relationships.

The scene that begins Stephen Graham Jones' novel performs the chaos that ensues as indigenous worldings bang heads with the hegemonic structures of consumer culture. The Shoshone man in the buffet line becomes Old Man, the Blackfoot creator, who initiates a creation-in-reverse as he begins reading tabloid newspaper accounts of the narrative yet to come. Jones' novelistic plainsong, a wordplay both upon European liturgical traditions and Plains Indian songs, interweaves each character's stream of consciousness and becomes in these moments a collage of histories that draws upon Western and indigenous aesthetics and evokes medieval monophonic vocals as well as the polyvocal call and response of traditional Blackfoot songs. The resultant discord forces these traditions into a collision of cultures where meanings open out upon one another to create an interdependence of referents within Indigenous post-contact symbolic orders rather than a textual performance Homi Bhabha might identify as hybridity or mimicry. At the very least, Jones forces the English language into multivalent meanings that are *almost the same but not quite*[18] of Indigenous vocabularies which, as Chickasaw poet Linda Hogan describes, "refer to entire systems [where] one word will open out into a variety of meanings that take in and summon together an entire region of the world."[19] The multivalent force of Jones' text demands that the reader submit from the outset to the temporal refractions and spatial distortions that structure the plot in order to naturalize within the self the shift of historical perspective that Litmus facilitates. In Litmus' moment of awareness in the buffet line, indigenous historical presences pierce the tenuous façade of U.S. consumer culture to reveal the foundational colonialist and genocidal policies that created the United States.

The distilled awareness that emerges in the opening buffet scene asks readers to adopt interpretative strategies by which to "see through" the interreferentiality of Jones' text to access worldings that have been denied. As the novel progresses and new characters are introduced, these strategies help clarify Jones' use of imagination to transform lived experiences rather than capturing or conveying cultural capital. Stiya 6 is such a character and is introduced as one of seven cashiers with the same name in Squanto's, a chain of grocery stores in the Southwest named for the Northeastern Indian, who in U.S. national mythologies of Thanksgiving, taught the Puritans how to grow corn and survive in the new world. As the cultural mediator who initiated the settler into the ways of the land, the Squanto in national holiday remembrance supplies the first cross-cultural supermarket to feed starving Puritans. Inside Jones' parodic store of the twenty-first century, this remembrance is memorialized and mocked by cash registers that are "done up like a Mayan temple, vegetables corkscrewed around mini teepees trailing paper smoke . . . [and] . . . all the cashier girls wearing the exact same nametag [. . .] Stiyas all."[20] Like the macabre buffet that starts the novel, Squanto's is a pan-tribal pastiche, this time of crass Indian marketing tools and ironies. However, the scene, and more specifically, the character of Stiya 6 whom it introduces, raises the ante in the novel's explicit concerns with the colonialist violences that underpin the historical memories that began in the buffet line and continued into Squanto's.

Stiya 6's name originates in an 1891 publication sponsored by the U.S. War Department and written by Marianna Burgess, a white teacher and dormitory matron at Carlisle Indian School in Pennsylvania. Assuming the identity of an Indian graduate of Carlisle named Embe, Burgess' fictional memoir, *Stiya, or a Carlisle Indian Girl at Home*, presented the story of a young girl who returns home to her Pueblo family after years at boarding school. According to Leslie Marmon Silko, Burgess's character was an abjection of all her fears and racism toward Pueblo culture[21]; Stiya ventriloquized horror and disgust at the lewd practices and dirty lives of her family for the white Christian woman who created her. Rather than revert to savagery, Stiya instead resolves to transform her parents to the standards of the civilized living she had been given at Carlisle.

There are a number of important elements to unpack here as a white woman performs Indianness to chastise Pueblo graduates to remain true to their indoctrination in white culture. If the worlding the world that Spivak locates in the settler allows him to master and name the land within his own narratives and histories, then Marianna Burgess' textual playing Indian cathects the space of the Other from the outside in. Additionally, it provides a how-to narrative that is as much about the abject othering white women have undergone in dominant culture as it is about forcing young Pueblo women to naturalize themselves as the same. The book was sent to all female graduates after they had returned home in order, Silko tells us, to prevent them from regressing to their pre-Carlisle ways. The goal of General Pratt's boarding school was to "kill the savage to save the man"; the hope was that the young men and women stolen from their families would quickly assimilate and disappear within urban landscapes to solve once and for all the Indian problem facing the US at the end of the nineteenth century.

In the light of this policy, Stiya's story functions as a discursive stopgap to patch the worlding students had already received when it started to crack in their return to their communities. Within Jones' novel, Stiya 6 becomes a mass-produced referent who has no identity or meaning outside what other characters invest in her. She is, as Gerald Vizenor might argue, a post-Indian, "an occidental invention that became a bankable simulation"[22] whose purpose is to perform as a spectacle of Indianness for Squanto's customers. Jones, it could be argued, repatriates Burgess' Stiya only to reconstruct her again as an empty referent whose cultural capital and bankability reside in her ability to represent. Her passive participation highlights the hegemonic modes of assimilation that manifest as bankable identities, commodifying meaning and value in U.S. consumerism.

It might be tempting to categorize the fragmentation and disjointed ironies of *The Fast Red Road* as yet another example of a late-capitalist postmodernism where the rapid-fire collages signify a disruption within the absurdity of master-narratives of genre, identity, and indigeneity. However, Jones seems to hold onto and reassert the centrality of Blackfoot cosmologies that are fully activated within his text. Informed by what Craig Howe has defined as the spatial, social, spiritual, and experiential elements of indigenous histories and oral traditions,[23] Jones reminds us that worldings are always in process, never complete or wholly inaccessible. While Vizenor's idea of the post-Indian emphasizes an emptied signification, Jones identifies within his characters some quality of "Indianness" that remains nontransferable. Among the worldings of natives and arrivants and the bankable identities these collisions produce, Jones is less interested in examining how Indianness becomes an empty referent than he is in the ramifications of what that emptying out might mean for Native worldings.

The resistant aesthetic of Jones' novel lies in its ability to narrate the cognitive dissonances and multivalent awareness that inform contemporary Native knowledge and to defamiliarize the definitive notion of a solid "Indianness." The indeterminacy that haunts every level of self-identification in the novel emphasizes an attentiveness to social interactions in which the self can only be understood in relation to others and to the land. Though there are a number of moments within the text that deconstruct the worlding of Indigenous People within the US, Jones also challenges us to further complicate Spivak's delineation of "worlding the world" by demonstrating the *haksuba* that LeAnne Howe describes in the collision of worlds. Jones' characters struggle in between worldings as they cross back and forth between the indigenous traditional knowledges that inform the aesthetics of the text and the racial categorizations and assimilations that U.S. colonialism seeks to consolidate.

While Jones begins with Vizenor's idea of the bankable, he ends with the removal of these simulations from the symbolic in which they create meaning. Littered throughout the text are apocalyptic apocrypha that, like Stiya 6 and the buffet, hint to other histories that lurk beneath the surface of consolidated significations. Drawing in and disavowing Franz Kafka's "The Wish to Be a Red Indian,"[24] Jones presents readers with apocalyptic narratives of "vanishing Indians" that ultimately figure instead a death from the symbolic order. Simulations of Indianness cease to function in the novel as crossbloods and non-Native tricksters refuse categorization. But death in the novel is not permanent. Characters reincarnate as or appear in other characters, and Jones again projects forward beyond the novel possible Native worldings in which the self might be represented in counterpoint to U.S. colonial discourses.

Given the Native worldings and guilty knowledge of the U.S. consolidation of indigeneity that Jones' text engages and the play between going Indian and Indian going, the question we should ask of postcolonial theories is not whether they apply to Indigenous Peoples within deep settler societies but whether they can be sufficiently decolonized to speak to the lived experiences of Native peoples. But as I said earlier, there is another lingering problem: postcolonial theories present significant concerns for Native scholars because they deconstruct into yet another colonialist discourse when applied unexamined to Native contexts. The call in postcolonial theory for scholars to distinguish between the "pure" colonialism of British imperialism and the analogous "racial" stratifications of the US demonstrates within its own theoretical models a moment in which an already worlded Other, in this case the postcolonial scholar, continues to other the indigenous within the consolidated borders of the US.

As Jones' novel reveals in the opening buffet scene and the worlding of Stiya 6, the paramount goal in the assimilation of indigenous identity within colonialist narratives is to solidify borders and boundaries which were never solid in the first place and then to invisibilize that process entirely. The transformation of externally colonized nations of people into racially othered citizens of the state can then be disappeared within a melting pot of an internal colonization that is masked as racial disenfranchisement rather than the actual colonization that precipitated it. This totalizing narrative of the colonizer's worlding further disregards the intricate treaty histories and decisions in cases like the 1831 *Cherokee Nation v. Georgia* that transformed Native nations from foreign and sovereign principalities into "domestic dependent nations" that could be removed and relocated at will as U.S. Manifest Destiny made, exceeded, and remade borders. Theories that posit the US as postcolonial or resist such a categorization entirely, critically examine the US as an imperial superpower and assume a completed internal worlding of solid boundaries and national borders. What is missing from these theorizations, however, are those discursive processes through which Native peoples could have been viewed as citizens of the land. As Jones' novel suggests, by shifting slightly the focus of attention from the gloss of national and capitalistic concerns, it is possible to "see through" the consolidated borders and assimilated knowledges to the fractured boundaries and identities that continue to underpin the US.

In his challenge to the American literary canon, Craig Womack states that "tribal literatures are not some branch waiting to be grafted onto the main trunk. Tribal literatures are the *tree*, the oldest literatures in the Americas, the most American of American literatures. We *are* the canon."[25] I would extend this challenge to postcolonial theory and suggest that Native literatures and studies are not a branch waiting to be incorporated into theoretical discussions of colonialism and its resistances. Native peoples in the Americas have been resisting European and then U.S. colonialisms for over five hundred years. By reworlding postcolonial literary theories to speak to the lived histories of Indigenous Peoples and by engaging the literary worldings such as those deployed by LeAnne Howe and Stephen Graham Jones, Native American literary studies can provide new directions for postcolonial theories to engage more fully and then dismantle the discursive work of colonization.

NOTES

1. Elizabeth Cook-Lynn, *Anti-Indianism in Modern America* (Urbana University of Illinois, 2001), 3.

2. Ian Frazier, *On the Rez* (New York: Farrar, Straus, and Giroux, 2000), 91.

3. Cook-Lynn, *Anti-Indianism in Modern America*, 23.

4. Ibid.

5. Ibid.

6. Ibid., 19. Cook-Lynn's book includes a chapter with this title in which she discusses how the academy discredits Native voices, particularly in David Stoll's attacks on Rigoberta Menchú and the "accuracy" of her claims of ethnic cleansing that occurred in Guatemala.

7. For instance, when Ajaz Ahmad writes about ethnic minorities' struggles with racial stratification in the US , he notes, "Even if we discount the few remnants of the indigenous population which had been exterminated in the process of genocidal colonization—some other ethnic minorities had been assembled over a century or more." The oldest and most significant minority experience in the US according to this framework is African American (81) while Indigenous Peoples, it is assumed, have been eradicated through a complete and successful genocide. Often within postcolonial analyses of U.S. history, Native voices are dismissed as irrelevant, if not nonexistent, and at any rate, are now seen as part of the broad mosaic of ethnicities that comprise U.S. national identities. See Ajaz Ahmad, *In Theory* (London: Verso, 1992), 81–82.

8. Remarks by the president to the Pine Ridge Indian Reservation community, July 7, 1999. See http://www.nativeculture.com/lisamitten/clinton.html.

9. See Philip J. Deloria, *Playing Indian* (New Haven: Yale University Press, 1999).

10. Stephen Graham Jones, *The Fast Red Road: A Plainsong* (Tallahassee: FC2, 2000), 13–20.

11. Eric Cheyfitz, "The (Post)Colonial Predicament of Native American Studies," *Interventions* 4.3 (2002): 406.

12. Patrick Williams and Laura Chrisman, "Introduction," in *Colonial Discourse and Postcolonial Theory*, ed. Patrick Williams and Laura Chrisman (New York: Columbia University Press, 1994), 2.

13. Thomas King, "Godzilla vs. Post Colonial," *World Literatures Written in English* 30.2 (1990): 10–16.

14. In addition to Thomas King, a number of other Native scholars and authors have weighed in on the "postcolonial," including Jace Weaver, Craig Womack, Robert Allen Warrior, Joy Harjo, and Sherman Alexie. Additionally, a number of scholars working in the field of Native literary studies have discussed its uses and limits, including Arnold Krupat, Elvira Pulitano, and Julia V. Emberley.

15. As many Native scholars and activists argue, the "post-" attached to the colonial functions as yet another dismissal of indigenous issues just as they start to come to the fore within academic dialogues. However, the "post" within postcolonial theory has been a point of contention since the theory emerged in the 1980s. For the writers of *The Empire Writes Back*, postcolonialism begins at the moment Europeans first land; for others, like Stephen During and K. Anthony Appiah, the "post-" is more affiliated with that in "postmodern" and has less to do with demarking the passing of an era. Still, for me, the "post-" remains a problematic suffix to an otherwise useful body of theoretical work that focuses on colonial discourse analysis and I leave it intact in order to place myself within those discussions.

16. Gayatri Spivak, *A Critique of Postcolonial Reason* (Cambridge: Harvard University Press, 1999), 211.

17. LeAnne Howe, "The Chaos of Angels," *Callalloo* 17.1 (1994): 110.

18. See Homi Bhabha, *The Location of Culture* (London: Routledge, 1994).

19. "Some Change in the World—A Conversation with Linda Hogan." See http://www.usca.edu/posttimenotes/Faculty/hogan.pdf.

20. Jones, *The Fast Red Road*, 111.

21. "Leslie Marmon Silko's Introduction to Our First Catalogue of Native American Literature." See http://www.lopezbooks.com/articles/silko.html.

22. Gerald Vizenor, *Manifest Manners: Postindian Warriors of Survivance* (Hanover: University Press of New England, 1994), 11.

23. Craig Howe, "Keep Your Thoughts above the Trees: Ideas on Developing and Presenting Tribal Histories," in *Clearing a Path*, ed. Nancy Shoemaker, 161–179 (New York: Routledge, 2002).

24. Franz Kafka, *The Complete Stories* (New York: Schocken Books, 1971), 390.

25. Craig S. Womack, *Red on Red: Native American Literary Separatism* (Minneapolis: University of Minnesota Press, 1999), 6–7.

Chapter 5

CONQUEST MASQUERADING AS LAW

Vine Deloria Jr.

Jodi Byrd revealed how dominant "literacy" falsifies the truth about postcolonial realities and how it tends to ignore the great truths of authentic Indigenous perspectives. In this chapter, Vine Deloria Jr. explains how such delusion has corrupted the law of the land, which is supposed to be based on a foundation of truth, justice, and equality. In what I believe to be one of Dr. Deloria's most insightful excursions into contemporary reality, he explains how American jurisprudence, especially as it relates to its treatment of Indian people, has largely been based on the idea that "the non-Christian peoples who would be discovered, and dispossessed, had a moral flaw that justice should take into account, in ways that would rationalize injustice." He demonstrates that decisions in U.S. law concerning Indigenous People go beyond a mere violation of logic, revealing a consistent prejudice that is even today identifiable with a language of conquest. Finally, in another challenge to "the fourth wave," he points out that "the so-called savage Indigenous ideas and practices for addressing wrong-doing, if seriously examined, would be understood as superior to U.S. law."[1]

Vine Deloria Jr., a Hunkpapa Lakota enrolled as a member of the Standing Rock Sioux, is the author of more than twenty books, including Red Earth, White Lies, Custer Died for Your Sins, God Is Red, *and* Spirit and Reason. *Recipient of a number of awards, including the 2002 Wallace Stegner Award and designation as the 2003 American Indian Festival of Words Author, Vine is a professor of history at the University of Colorado. As an Indian activist and attorney (the only Indian attorney in the early Wounded Knee trials, who has helped many tribes besides the Lakota), he has earned international acclaim as a leading voice for American Indians.*

***

An ancient apocryphal anecdote relates that Justice Oliver Wendell Holmes, responding to a lawyer who had just presented his argument before the Supreme Court, chastised the lawyer for asking the Court to do justice, commenting that it was the task of the Court to determine the law, not to ensure justice. Law is a formal institution designed to make the arbitrary and whimsical behavior of the governing elite seem to have an aura of rationality and balance. As everyone knows, wealth directs the outcome of any judicial decision and as Voltaire noted, at its worst law allows both beggars and rich men to sleep beneath the bridges of Paris. But, as the judge suggests in the Clint Eastwood movie *Hang 'Em High*, people feel much better when a person is executed by an order of a court rather than being victim of a lynching.

A survey of the history of federal Indian law reveals that it is possible to be legally condemned and lynched at the same time. Although guaranteed justice in the federal courts, Indians have discovered that far too often legal doctrines purported to ensure their political and treaty rights are used to confiscate their property, deny their civil rights, and deprive them of the benefits that accrue with United States citizenship. So bizarre are the rulings of the federal courts when deciding an "Indian" case that the decisions appear to have come through the Looking Glass of Lewis Carroll.

During the 1940s Felix S. Cohen, the solicitor of the Department of the Interior, organized a scholarly task force to survey the laws and cases dealing with Indian rights and to create a "handbook" of Federal Indian Law. The purpose of this document was to provide an authoritative source of legal doctrines so that U.S. attorneys could bring the full measure of federal resources to bear against Indian plaintiffs who sought justice in the Court of Claims. Since its publication courts and lawyers alike have elevated the handbook from a mere source of information to the status of a treatise—an elevation it has never deserved. The perspective of the handbook suggests the inevitable end of Indian political existence and the merging of Indian rights into domestic American law. Thus treaties, the primary document establishing a relationship between indigenous nations and the United States, have been submerged by strange interpretations of case law so that illogical but comfortable fictions comprise its primary substance.

In traditional political intercourse between nations the treaty has been the primary formal expression of agreements that benefit contending parties in an international setting. In the archives of the ancient Middle Eastern nations—the Chaldeans, Babylonians, Assyrians, and Persians— we find instances of treaty-making that testify to this basic means of establishing political relationships among and between nations. In the Old Testament we find the idea of the covenant not only between God and His Chosen People but also between the Hebrews, later Jews, and nations with whom they had dealings. The United States itself has made treaties with almost all foreign nations and for most of its first century of political existence, over eight hundred treaties with the Indigenous People of North America.

While international treaty-making has followed a reasonable and logical course of development, the treaties with Native Americans have been negotiated, ratified, and concluded under a cloud of impotence so that clear promises have dissolved into rhetoric when put to the judicial test. Federal Indian law actually begins with a sleight-of-hand decision that proclaimed that the United States had special standing with respect to ownership of the land on which the Indigenous People lived. This nefarious concept was called the "Doctrine of Discovery." Originating early in the European invasion of the Western hemisphere, this doctrine, as articulated by the Pope in the famous Bull Inter Caetera, by which he gave to Spain all lands hitherto discovered or to be discovered in the world. It was, as it turned out, the greatest real estate transaction in history.

European politics quickly seized on the opportunity and when Portugal and Spain divided Central and South America, with the Pope's approval, in the Treaty of Tordesillas the doctrine was broadened so that any Christian nation could "discover" lands previously unknown to Europeans and was immediately vested with legal title regardless of the claims and rights of the existing inhabitants. This doctrine in truth is merely an agreement among thieves similar to the division of the United States by the Cosa Nostra wherein each family rules a certain area and is not to be bothered by other thieves in the normal course of events.

The problem with international law is that it secures only the rights of large nations that are able to defend themselves and invade their smaller neighbors at their pleasure. Any sense of the ethical or moral dimensions of life is completely absent, and therefore establishing enforceable legal rights of the smaller nations depends on the sense of honor possessed by the larger nation or the interest of another large nation in the continued existence of the smaller nation. The United States quickly took its place as one of the favored nations after two wars with Great Britain so that no other nation could or would challenge how the United States dealt with its Indigenous People. Only recently, when the United Nations committees began accepting complaints from nongovernmental groups representing the indigenous nations of North America, did the fate of the people become an international issue.

All efforts to revise, systematize, and comprehend the subsequent statutory and case laws dealing with the natives in the United States have been passed and decided under the shadow of this doctrine. The degeneration of the indigenous political status began with a minor case in which two non-Indians contested the title to lands in Illinois, one laying claim under a purchase conducted by English officials in 1773 when England was the dominant power on the continent, the other claiming title under American laws passed after the United States had succeeded Great Britain. Chief Justice John Marshall in his opinion recited a basic history of the Doctrine of Discovery that borders on slapstick comedy. "The potentates of the old world found no difficulty in convincing themselves, that they made ample compensation to the inhabitants of the new, by bestowing on them civilization and Christianity, in exchange for unlimited independence."[2] One wonders how long the potentates struggled to convince themselves to adopt theft as a fundamental principle of international law.

Originally the papal commission was to provide for the conversion of the natives to the Catholic faith. Thus it would seem that instead of seizing the newly discovered lands and enslaving their people, the Christian nations would have provided schools, priests and ministers, and a handful of teachers to demonstrate the benefits of Christianity by living exemplary lives. Quite obviously the track record of the Europeans was already besmirched by their actions before America became one of the elite nations. Marshall finessed the religious part of the doctrine quite easily and provided a justification the United States would thereafter use to disenfranchise the indigenous nations. So he wrote: "Although we do not mean to engage in the defense of those principles which Europeans have applied to Indian title, they may, we think, find some excuse, if not justification, in the character and habits of the people whose rights have been wrested from them."[3] So the justification of theft was that the Indigenous People lacked character and had bad habits and therefore had to be denied the basic rights of all peoples as identified in the Declaration of Independence and other American state documents.

Nothing was ever specified as to the perceived character and habits of the Indigenous People that would have justified depriving them of basic human rights. So the popular mood was to adopt the idea that the natives were inferior as a matter of fact. At their foundations, then, the legal doctrines most eagerly embraced by non-Indians were religious—Indians were not Christians and there was doubt they ever would be, since their habits were different from any of the European settlers. This condition, once articulated in law, reflected the popular view and became the philosophy of the settlers. The native peoples would always be something less than human—except on those occasions when it was necessary to pretend they were equals, such as treaty-making time, when they temporarily achieved full status.

This principle has been repeated in various guises in most case and statutory law. First, the clergy accused the natives of being in league with the devil, since they could do some marvelous things, including healings of illnesses that could not be done with European medicine. The literary world saw Indians primarily as bloodthirsty savages and Cooper's books suggested that they should all be driven westward from their eastern lands. Finally, the American educational institutions promoted the idea that intellectually Indians were the mental equivalent of the eight-year-old white person. Thus white schoolchildren were encouraged to read Henry Wadsworth Longfellow's poem *Hiawatha* so they could understand Indians. As invasions of Indian country escalated, epidemics depleted indigenous nations, and the natives were forced to move westward. What was happening on a continental scale was justified by arguing that history dictated that the natives were doomed to vanish from the world stage. The farmer, it was argued, always supplanted the hunter; the merchant and businessman then supplant him in term. Civilization is never defined as a recognizable state of being, and the gift of Christianity only grudgingly assisted the natives in coming to grips with the conditions imposed on them.

The Cherokee crisis in the 1830s provided the final rhetorical slogan used to eliminate the rights of the natives. The state of Georgia passed laws extending state jurisdiction over the Cherokee lands, effectively negating the laws and rights of the Cherokees. The first of two cases decided whether the Cherokees had sufficient political standing to file a case in the United States Supreme Court as an original court, given that they were a foreign nation. After a review of many rhetorical concepts, the court described the Cherokees as a dependent, domestic nation, an entirely new concept in law in that many small European nations lived under the protection of a larger nation without being considered domestic to its boundaries. The Doctrine of Discovery implied that such status might apply to the Indigenous nations because they were adopting European ways. The Cherokees had an organized government modeled somewhat after the federal government. They had their own alphabet and even published a newspaper in their own language. Surely they were making great and visible advances toward the European model of society.

The Doctrine of Discovery, however, was used to negate the obvious similarity of the Cherokees to the people around them. There was a glimmer of hope. Among the concurring opinions was that of Justice Johnson, who, although concurring with the majority, suggested that the Cherokees were on the verge of becoming a nation with rights in the international arena. According to him they resembled the wandering Israelites in the desert—they did not own lands in the ultimate sense required by the Europeans but did have political status as a nation. They were what one might call an incipient or an expectant state, waiting only for recognition by the larger nations. The Cherokees believed they had reached the civilized state; John Marshall believed they had not.

Marshall instead compared the relationship of the United States with the Cherokee nation as that of a "ward to a guardian." But this description supported the idea that they would eventually achieve the status of fully independent nation. Presumably at some later date the Cherokees could join the community of nations since wards reach maturity and eventually handle their own affairs. But wardship also implies that for the present the ward is in a learning state, a pupil or, in theological terms, a person receiving the Holy Word and nearing conversion. And that is exactly how the Supreme Court would choose to see Indigenous nations. They were believed to exist in perpetual wardship, and thereafter any decisions they might make, outside of ceding lands, would be suspect. Unfortunately race, not intellect or culture, determined the nature of the American trust perspective.

Not everyone supported or understood the Supreme Court's position, and it is ironic that people visiting Indian tribes could see immediately that the natives already had all the necessary characteristics of a nation. In 1832, about the time that John Marshall was writing his opinion, Henry Marie Brackenridge, a well-known explorer and fur trader, visited Arikara villages near present-day Bismarck, North Dakota. After becoming familiar with these villages he commented:

> We here see an independent nation with all the interests and anxieties of the largest; how little would its history differ from that of one of the Grecian states! A war, a treaty, deputations sent and received, warlike excursions, national mourning or rejoicing and a thousand other particulars, which constitute the chronicle of the most celebrated people.[4]

In spite of the opinion of the Supreme Court, then, the indigenous nations continued to display the very characteristics that small European nations exhibited which gave them protection in international law. If the uneducated frontiersman could see the national characteristics of the Indigenous People, why could not others see it also?

In fairness, there was a good argument on the other side that looked with some degree of realism on the dilemma in which the United States found itself. It had made treaties with many small indigenous nations, none of whom could be compared favorably with the larger European nations that commanded the respect of the United States. Was the government to allow each and every small nation to file a case in its Supreme Court? The result would have been complete chaos and would have reduced the Supreme Court to a court of original jurisdiction for Indian claims. But here as in so many instances in history, people forget the obvious. There would have been no case whatsoever had the United States fulfilled its treaty obligations to the Cherokees and prevented Georgia from discriminating against them. In the second case, *Worcester v. Georgia*,[5] the Court did rule in favor of enforcing the federal laws passed to fulfill the treaty responsibilities, but it did not clarify the status of the Cherokees.

At this point the weakness of the separation of powers as practiced by the United States revealed itself. President Andrew Jackson refused to comply with the Supreme Court decision and protect the Cherokees. Nor did the Court dare command him to do so with a court order. While the justices simmered in resentment and cries in Congress raised the issue of national honor, there was no way to secure the rights of the Cherokees absent a major crisis about the nature of the federal government and its relationship to the states. That crisis was to come in 1861 with the election of Lincoln and the start of the Civil War. Jackson's political nullification of the powers of the Supreme Court permanently cowed the Court, and thereafter Indian cases were avoided whenever possible. When the Court had to decide them, justices usually threw logic and precedent to the winds and wrote opinions that were often personal and lacking rationality. Almost every Supreme Court decision since then has leaned toward an accommodation among the branches of the federal government and supported the powers of the states except where the evidence is overwhelmingly in favor of the Indians. The fictions—discovery, dependent domestic nation, and wardship—have become the mythical pillars on which federal Indian law has been built. It is, consequently, a twilight zone where wholly illogical and arbitrary beliefs are generated.

As is the tradition in American law, as cases were decided the decisions were accepted as the natural interpretation of basic legal principles even though their reasoning was absurd. When examining evidence in the courts, judges and justices who lacked any firsthand knowledge of the Indigenous People simply accepted as valid old stereotypes generated by the clergy, novelists, and social scientists. Thus the people who stood to gain the most by the reduction of Indian rights became influential policy makers in Indian affairs. Their fantasies about Indians became gospel as the courts agreed with them, and the courts agreed with them because they posed as experts.

The suspicion that the Indigenous People's "character and habits" were not up to par was enhanced with the advent of the theory of evolution. Indians were then seen as representing the first steps taken by primitive man in marching up the gradual incline of cultural evolution, finally to arrive at the state enjoyed by the white citizens of the United States. The natives were believed to be subject to the "survival of the fittest" evolutionary doctrine, which supplanted God's Will as the doctrine explaining planetary history. Convinced that the Indians would vanish according to the dictates of this natural law, sympathetic scholars rushed to visit the Indigenous People and record what they could of the culture of Indian nations. This effort at preservation only reinforced the image of the native peoples as wholly other, since the data recorded dealt mostly with the customs and practices of the people before contact with whites. Little attention was paid to the conditions under which the people were living. Unfortunately this condition continues to prevail among non-Indians today; credibility is always given to non-Indian scholars and their opinions on an indigenous group, while members of these nations are viewed with suspicion and mistrust. Although the testimony of academic scholars has assisted the natives in some instances, such as the fishing rights cases in the Pacific Northwest, the use of badly gathered data has also hindered the protection of legal rights, as seen in the testimony offered in the Indian Claims Commission hearings and in the recent Kennewick Man case.

It is important to note that while the courts almost always follow public opinion or reflect the pressures of the president or Congress, social science seems to follow the trend of the courts, although its data is supposed to be neutral, derived according to scientific principles. The mixture of law and social science began in earnest in the 1880s and can be seen most clearly in the Crow Dog case. In 1881 Crow Dog killed Spotted Tail, one of the Sioux chiefs most favored by the United States in developing its reservation and educational programs. The relatives of Crow Dog made peace with Spotted Tail's relatives and compensated them for the loss of their kinsman according to Sioux custom. The Sioux believed they had preserved civil and criminal jurisdiction over crimes committed by one tribal member against another in the 1868 treaty.

The government had other ideas. Crow Dog was arrested, indicted for murder, tried, and sentenced to death in a territorial court. Released to visit his relatives, Crow Dog walked through a blizzard to surrender himself for execution on the appointed day and his feat was written up in highly emotional articles in the newspapers. He appealed to the Supreme Court, and since the 1868 treaty was involved, the case became a major event in measuring exactly how much control the government had over the domestic activities of reservation Indians, particularly those who had preserved their laws and customs. The Court found that the Sioux had indeed preserved their rights to enforce their own criminal law. A statute passed after the treaty was made, purported to give the federal government jurisdiction over Indians, had a disclaimer clause that exempted Indian nations that had specifically preserved their rights by treaty. The Sioux were in this category.

The opinion, if we can believe the logic involved, represents a strange mixture of popular stereotypes and social science beliefs and is worthy of discussion. In upholding the statute and treaty provision, the opinion, by Justice Matthews for a unanimous court, offers its justification for the decision. Describing the unfairness in subjecting the Indians to the laws of the United States and enforced in the manner the government wanted, Matthews writes:

> It [the law] tries them not by their peers, nor by the custom of their people, nor the law of their land, but by superiors of a different race, according to the law of a social state of which they have an imperfect conception, and which is opposed to the traditions of their history, to the habits of their lives, to *the strongest prejudices of their savage nature; one which measures the red man's revenge by the maxims of the white man's morality.*[6] (Emphasis added)

Few scholars have examined the stereotypical understanding of Indians and the clash of cultures represented in this statement. Sioux traditional jurisprudence in a case of an Indian killing another tribal member required the families of the people involved to make every effort to compensate the injured party so that the killing would not disrupt the tribe by later acts of vengeance. This legal theory is called compensation and is found in many so-called savage nations as the guiding principle. It seeks at all costs to alleviate the damage done by a careless or evil act and reduce the injury suffered by the group as quickly as possible.

The vaunted "white man's morality," held up for all to see and exemplified in the decision to execute Crow Dog, follows the theory of retribution, in which society imposes the death penalty following the "eye for an eye" practice of the Old Testament and some Middle Eastern peoples who have an extremely heartless jurisprudence. It is still the primary legal theory behind the popularity of the death penalty, and today we have refined it to include a ceremonial cursing at the defendant by relatives of the deceased, who will not be satisfied or find "closure" until they see the wrongdoer executed. That this practice does not cultivate acts of revenge very often is testimony to the complexity of our society, not its moral superiority. In the Old West such vengeance was commonplace.

In the eyes of many contemporary philosophers of law, the Sioux practice would represent a much higher state of civilized behavior than the crude vengeance-inspired act of execution. Yet the popular and social science beliefs of the 1880s understood the indigenous people as living in a state of savagery without any comprehension of the various theories underlying criminal codes. The logic displayed here is based on popular stereotypes, not on the actual practices of the people.

As a result of the decision in *Ex Parte Crow Dog*, the civilized peoples demanded that the laws be changed so that no more killers could be freed on a technicality. In 1884 Congress passed the Seven Major Crimes Act, which gave the federal government complete jurisdiction over seven crimes, headlined by murder, should they occur on an Indian reservation and the wrongdoer and victim be members of the tribe. The constitutionality of the act came under judicial scrutiny almost immediately when two Indians killed another Indian on the Hoopa reservation in California. The wrongdoers were indicted and tried in the federal district court.

The opinion of the Supreme Court, again a unanimous decision, was perhaps the most puzzling of the nineteenth century. The traditional interpretation, and the consensus of experts today, is that the United States is authorized to deal with Indians by the treaty-making and commerce clauses of the Constitution. Yet the court soundly rejected the received law and argued as follows:

> We think it would be a very strained construction of this clause [commerce], that a system of criminal laws for Indians living peaceably in their reservations, which left out the entire code of trade and inter-course laws justly enacted under that provision, and established punishments for the common-law crimes of murder, manslaughter, arson, burglary, and the like, without any reference to their relation to any kind of commerce, was authorized by the grant of power to regulate commerce with the Indian tribes.[7]

The Court then suggested that the power to deal with Indians might derive from ownership of the land, perhaps the most radical interpretation of the Doctrine of Discovery ever articulated. "The right to govern may be the inevitable consequence of the right to acquire territory,"[8] said the Court. In effect the Court found the Seven Major Crimes Act to be constitutional on extra-constitutional grounds. Property ownership has never conveyed special political rights. Exactly how this line of reasoning convinced the other justices and the press remains a secret. It does suggest that laws dealing with Indian matters are sometimes interpreted as a display of personal ignorance and pique. There is certainly no sense of fidelity to previous decisions or logic here. Rather, it seems like the justice took a fictional road never traveled. Yet law professors today are pledged to pretend that this fiction represents some kind of mystical validation of legal creativity.

In 1903 the Supreme Court had occasion to take a case involving treaty provisions. In 1867 the Kiowas and Comanches made a treaty with the United States that required the signature of three-fourths of the adult males henceforth in order legally to cede lands to the federal government. The Jerome Commission met with the tribes in 1892. The government demanded that the tribes agree to sell some of their lands and secured the approval of 456 adult males, well over the number of signatures required. However, the tribes disputed the count and alleged that the interpreters had misrepresented the terms of the agreement, and therefore the number of signatures was short of the requirement. There were actually 725 adults eligible to consent. The government then and now was known to manipulate figures until they had the necessary number.

In 1900 Congress passed an entirely different bill in place of the original agreement. The Kiowas sued to void the bill. In the Supreme Court opinion, every excuse but the kitchen sink was cited to justify finding the amended agreement to be constitutional. The logic is so convoluted that scholars have not yet decided exactly what it meant. "To uphold the [Indian] claim," the Court said, "would be to adjudge that the indirect operation of the treaty was to materially limit and qualify the controlling authority of Congress in respect to the care and protection of the Indians, and to deprive Congress, in a possible emergency, when the necessity might be urgent for a partition and disposal of the tribal lands, of all power to act, if the assent of the Indians could not be obtained."[9] Could reasoning be more spurious?

Under the Doctrine of Discovery, the natives are to have undisturbed occupancy, and under previous cases the Court promulgated the idea that occupancy was as "sacred as fee simple,"[10] so presumably the United States was charged with defending native titles from all predators—except perhaps itself. The Court even cited some cases in its opinion suggesting that occupancy was indeed sacred and to be heeded by the courts. But it took refuge in the idea that since the United States owned the legal title, it could act as it wanted with regard to Indian property. With regard to the power of Congress, there was no question of its emergency powers. But what was the emergency?

Purchasing Indian land cannot possibly come within the scope of a national emergency and, in fact, the only possible reason for purchasing the land and reducing the tribal landholdings would be if the United States had lost a war to another large nation and was required to surrender a part of its territory within which the Kiowa and Comanche lands were located. To suggest that the existence of emergency congressional powers justifies attaching a rider to an appropriation bill to force an agreement on these two smaller nations is quite a jump in logic. The Court, however, had not finished its analysis. "It is to be presumed," the opinion went on, "that in this matter the United States would be governed by such considerations of justice as would control a Christian people in their treatment of an ignorant and dependent race."[11] Judging from the results of this Christian charity, little had changed since the Papal Bulls gave away other people's lands.

The Court neatly sidestepped the fact that in the treaty negotiations it was the United States that had insisted on including the three-quarters requirement as a means of showing the Indians that its word was good. In a wholly ironic argument the Court continued: "When, therefore, treaties were entered into between the United States and a tribe of Indians it was never doubted that the power to abrogate existed in Congress, and that in a contingency such power might be availed of from considerations of governmental policy, particularly if consistent with perfect good faith towards the Indians."[12] But where was the good faith? Certainly it was not in forcing the Indians to accept an agreement that Congress had substituted for the one they negotiated.

The worst was yet to come. In a sudden incomprehensible twist the Court said: "In effect the action of Congress now complained of was but an exercise of such [administrative] power, a mere change in the form of investment of Indian tribal property, the property of those who, as we have held, were in substantial effect the wards of the government."[13] While there was a small payment of cash per capita as a result of the land sale, the idea that at any time, without the consent of the Indians, Congress could simply confiscate Indian lands and issue a small dividend certainly did no justice to the Doctrine of Discovery, upon which rested all of the American claims to valid land title.

The historic strands of racial prejudice seemed to come together in a dissenting opinion filed by Chief Justice Rehnquist in the Sioux Nation Black Hills case in 1979. He was content with the historical findings of the lower courts—the Court of Claims and the Indian Claims Commission—that the United States had acted honorably toward the Sioux. The logic in his opinion strayed considerably from the norm: "There were undoubtedly greed, cupidity, and other less-than-admirable tactics employed by the Government during the Black Hills episode in the settlement of the West, but the Indians did not lack their share of villainy either." The reasoning is apparently that while the federal government did act with the vilest motives in the transaction, we know that the Indians sometimes beat their wives; therefore the score is even and the Indians should not recover.

Then he launched into a diatribe regarding "revisionist" historians who had changed the case by inserting unreliable conclusions into the evidence offered the lower court. "It seems to me quite unfair to judge by the light of 'revisionist' historians or the mores of another era actions that were taken under pressure of time more than a century ago. Different historians, not writing for the purpose of having their conclusions or observations inserted in the reports of congressional committees, have taken different positions than those expressed in some of the materials referred to in the Court's opinion." [14]

Rehnquist's opinion was so outrageously outside the boundary of polite jurisprudence and good taste that Justice Blackman chastised him in a footnote. Reviewing Rehnquist's first accusation, Blackman pointed out that he had failed to identify any materials that fit Rehnquist's description. He then noted: "The dissenting opinion does not identify a single author, nonrevisionist, neorevisionist, or otherwise, who takes the view of the history of the cession of the Black Hills that the dissent prefers to adopt, largely, one assumes, as an article of faith." [15] Yet it is not difficult to identify Rehnquist's source of discontent. In his mind the character and habit of the Sioux had been painted so darkly that the prejudicial images cultivated for more than a century were to him an accurate summary of the case. The Doctrine of Discovery implied that the non-Christian peoples who would be discovered, and dispossessed, had a moral flaw that justice should take into account (in ways that would rationalize injustice).

Law is often a means of expressing and enforcing the prejudices of the majority. In the Indian case, law quite often does not deal with facts but with beliefs accepted as facts. The belief that God appointed the Pope to rule over planet earth until the Second Coming of Jesus produced for many of the world's people a kind of legal limbo where justice could not be served, nor was it ever intended to be served.

NOTES

1. As quoted in an anonymous peer review for this text.
2. *Johnson v. McIntosh*, 8 Wheat 543, 572 (1823).
3. Ibid., 589.
4. Henry Marie Brackenridge, "The Arikara Villages," cited in Lloyd McFarling, *Exploring the Northern Plains 1804–1876* (Caldwell, Idaho: Caxton, 1955), 31.
5. *Worcester v. Georgia*, 6 Pet. 515 (1832).
6. *Ex Parte Crow Dog*, 109 U.S. 556, 568–569 (1883).
7. *U.S. v. Kagama*, 118 U.S. 375, 378–379 (1885).
8. Ibid., 380.
9. *Lone Wolf v. Hitchcock*, 187 U.S. 553, 564 (1903).
10. There are many cases that explain this phrase; see, for example, *U.S. v. Sands*, 94 F2d. 156 (1938), County of Oneida, *New York v. Oneida Indian Nation*, 470 U.S. 226 (1985), *U.S. v. Adair*, 723 F2d, 1394 (1981).
11. 187 U.S. 553, 565.
12. Ibid., 566.
13. Ibid., 568.
14. 448 U.S. 371, 435 (1979).
15. Ibid., 421–422.

TRADITIONAL NATIVE JUSTICE: RESTORATION AND BALANCE, NOT "PUNISHMENT"

Chapter 6

Rudy Al James (ThlauGooYailthThlee-
The First and Oldest Raven)

In the previous chapter, Vine Deloria Jr., not only pointed out some disturbing elements in the American justice system, he also suggested that Indigenous approaches to conflict resolution and social control have much to teach American jurisprudence. In this chapter, Rudy Al James, using an example of Kuiu Kwáan Traditional Tribal Court justice and a specific, rather famous case, shows why Indigenous justice represents "a higher state of civilized behavior." Rudy offers a glimpse into how traditional Native justice systems have served Indigenous People for thousands of years in restoring balance in communities.

Indigenous assumptions about justice contrast with Eurocentric ideas about vengeance and punishment, and have proven to be more successful in bringing harmony back into traditional as well as non-Indigenous communities. For example, the case described in this chapter parallels successful wilderness therapy programs for adjudicated youth, programs that have in effect borrowed from Indigenous wisdom. I am reminded of a story about a Lakota youth who killed another youth in a fight. The community met to decide the offender's fate and elected that the family of the slain child would adopt his killer to be their own son. The decision resulted in the adopted youth growing up to be a model citizen and great leader. The community was restored. What would have happened if U.S. law had prevailed?

Rudy Al James is a spokesman and historian of the Kuiu Kwáan tribe of Alaska and Secretary-General of the United Native Nations. He was raised in a remote Tlingit village in southeastern Alaska and is active in working for a continuation of the Tlingit people's cultural heritage and spiritual values. He also serves as the Lead Judge for the Kuy'di Tribal Court and the Combined Tribal Court of Tlingit Law. He is a member of the Board of Directors of the International Human Rights Association of American minorities and is author of Devilfish Bay: The Giant Devilfish Story *(1997).*

***

On July 12, 1994, Judge James Allendoerfer of the Snohomish County Superior Court of Washington state made a historic decision that in essence recognized the legal system of the Kuiu Thlingit Nation by deferring sentencing on two Thlingit youth from Alaska who had been charged with armed robbery in Everett, Washington, thus enabling the Tribal Court to utilize its own justice system. This was the first time that a court of the United States cooperated in such a manner with a Traditional Tribal Court on a felony court case which occurred off Tribal ground, concerning an assault by Natives against a non-Native. This recognition substantiated the capacity of the Traditional Tribal Court to exercise authority based on Traditional Tribal Law.

The Traditional Tribal Court, headed by myself as the Lead Judge, banished the youths to separate sites on remote uninhabited lands in Southeast Alaska. There was no way that the boys could communicate with each other. The barest of tools and necessities were supplied. The youths were essentially left to individually fend for themselves. Heat for comfort in their minimum shelters and for cooking and washing came from wood that they gathered, cut, and chopped. Water was packed in from nearby streams; there was no indoor plumbing or electricity. Physical work was required to meet all their various physical needs. Although there was a real danger for personal catastrophe or loss of life, it was both a rite of purification to cleanse the youth and allow time for inner reflection and a gentle form of punishment. The Elders believed that placing the boys out in an environment away from society, with no modern conveniences or amenities, would allow them to observe and participate unencumbered with the marvelous and wondrous working of Mother Nature.

The case generated excitement and increased interest in Tribal Sovereignty, Traditional Tribal Law, Traditional Tribal Courts, and culturally relevant solutions for problem solving that have served Indigenous Peoples for thousands of years. The sentence imposed by the Combined Thlingit Court made sense. For the first time in years, there was serious talk of taking responsibility for injury, restitution, and healing. This particular case telegraphed through law and justice circles the world over.

A fundamental difference exists between Traditional Tribal Law and its implementation as opposed to the Anglo-American legal-judicial system and its practices. Each of the two systems has vastly different procedures and results. The impetus for subjecting these Indigenous youth to the Traditional judicial system grew mainly out of a recognition of the horrendous recidivism ratio—nearly 90 percent—by the Anglo-American judicial process as opposed to the nearly zero recidivism rate for those placed with the Traditional Tribal Court.

The grandfather of one of the young men, Theodore Roberts, when asked why he "sent the feather" to ask for help from the tribal court and why he preferred banishment over prison for his grandson, replied, "In the White Man jail, they'll never have a chance." Now adults, one young man is counseling troubled youth, and the other is pursuing his education and actively involved in a project to continue restitution for the victim of the crime.

The concepts of Traditional Tribal Law wield considerable influence today, as evinced by worldwide attention focused on the Thlingit banishment case, *Washington vs. Roberts/Guthrie*. According to Dr. Y. N. Kly, the Executive Director of the International Human Rights Association of American Minorities, a United Nations nongovernmental organization with roster status, the 1994 case represents the cutting edge of changing attitudes toward crime, restitution, punishment, and cooperation between jurisdictions. In a press release titled *US Court Recognizes Tribal Court*, he stated,

> This is the first time the United States Court system has cooperated with a Traditional Tribal Court on a felony court case, which occurred off Tribal ground, concerning an assault by Natives against a non-Native. The successful handling of the case by the Kuye'di or Kuiu Kwáan Tribal Court of Southeastern Alaska could prove one of the most significant events in recent Indian history.[1]

Reporter Chi Chi Sileo of the newsmagazine *Insight on the News* observed:

> The *Roberts/Guthrie* case grabbed international attention because it was the first time that an American court had, in effect, turned jurisprudence over to a tribal one ... But tribal justice is not a new concept; in fact, the federal government long has recognized Indians' rights to establish and administer their own courts.[2]

Of course, this recognition has been anything but consistent; nonetheless, people in the larger society are now calling for the very things that Tribes have always relied on: reconciliation, victims' rights, community values, restitution, and rehabilitation. On June 4, 1996, U.S. Supreme Court Justice Sandra Day O'Connor delivered a speech at the Ninth Indian Sovereignty Symposium in Tulsa, Oklahoma, in which she said that we in the United States have three types of sovereign entities: the federal government, the states, and the Indian Tribes. Each of the three sovereigns has its own judicial system and each plays an important role in the administration of justice.[3]

Traditional tribal justice systems are important to the inherent sovereignty and self-determination of each Indigenous Nation. The Traditional Tribal Court has the ability to provide the most appropriate, culturally relevant, and just solutions to social conflicts. The United States Congress recognized the importance of Traditional Tribal Law through passage of the 1993 Indian Tribal Justice Act (25 USC), which states in part:

Sec. 2. Findings: The Congress Finds and Declares that:

1. There is a government-to-government relationship between the United States and each Indian tribe;
2. Congress, through statutes, treaties, and the exercise of administrative authorities, has recognized the self-determination, self-reliance, and inherent sovereignty of Indian tribes;
3. Indian tribes possess the inherent authority to establish their own form of government, including tribal justice systems;
4. Tribal justice systems are an essential part of tribal governments and serve as important forums for ensuring public health and safety and the political integrity of tribal governments;
5. Congress and the Federal Courts have repeatedly recognized tribal justice systems as the appropriate forums for the adjudication of disputes affecting personal and property rights;
6. Traditional tribal justice practices are essential to the maintenance of the culture and identity of Indian tribes and Indigenous People.[4]

PRINCIPLES OF TRADITIONAL TRIBAL LAW

Indigenous traditional legal systems have been handed down from generation to generation since time immemorial and are a relevant and essential part of modern tribal justice. Traditional Tribal Law is based upon the universal moral code as defined by a nation's traditional tribal Elders and its traditional tribal or village councils. It is a publicly defined legal process in which law and morality are interconnected and based upon ethics and spiritual beliefs that originated in the acts of will of sovereign Native American lawmakers. It is the fundamental part of tribal justice and serves to ensure public health and safety; it is the appropriate forum for the adjudication of disputes affecting personal and property rights and encompasses all levels and aspects of society, both domestic and international. It incorporates respect, restoration, restitution, justice, and balance. It serves to ensure public health and safety and provide appropriate avenues in the adjudication of disputes affecting personal and property rights, domestic and international issues.

Traditional Tribal Law is culturally relevant, commonsensical, and practical, with the goal of achieving justice and restoration of balance, all based upon respect. It incorporates healing and restitution, which are historically grounded in the lifestyles and culture of the tribes of the Americas. Traditional Tribal Law obligates tribal leaders, Elders, and tribal judges to act in concert with the leaders of the families to protect their tribal members, including children and grandchildren—those yet unborn and all living things. It requires leaders to protect their lands, waters, and resources for the seventh generation yet unborn.

Women express keen interest in Traditional Tribal Law because of the broad rights and powers enjoyed by the feminine gender under this ancient system, including the women's tribunal, in which women adjudicate certain crimes against the female membership. When reviewing United Nations General Assembly Covenants and Resolutions, one finds that "new" standards and norms of behavior toward women and children that are being promoted have much in common with Traditional Tribal Law. These concepts are not "new" at all, but have their roots in the ancient ways of our Indigenous Peoples.

Traditional Tribal Law works for the people, rather than the people working to serve tribal law. Therefore, under Traditional Tribal Law there is more flexibility and creativity than that which is found in most modern litigation processes. Conversely, the adversarial approach of Anglo-American law is largely based on statute, ordinance, rules, and regulations. Infractions of law in this system have a prescribed formula of punishment for the lawbreaker which often results in little or no restitution. Inherent in this system is the approximately 90 percent recidivism rate and a concomitantly dismal rehabilitation rate.

The primary goal of the Indigenous legal process is to bring about healing, restitution, and restoration, with very limited focus on punishment. There are few crimes that may warrant capital punishment: namely murder, sexual crimes against the feminine gender, and infidelity. The female Elders of the victim decide the fate of the perpetrator of crimes against women. Needless to say, in ancient times, very few men dared to commit acts that would place them in front of a woman's tribunal. Infidelity was dealt with directly by the offended husband, who was allowed to kill the male offender. The female offender was severely dealt with by her brothers or other male family members, which sometimes resulted in the forfeiture of her life.

From the earliest times of social awareness and comprehension, the Indigenous child was taught that no one stands alone. All family, clan, and tribal members were part of the whole. There was no "go it alone philosophy," no "I can take on the world by myself" thinking. Each member was obligated and responsible to the whole, and his or her personal actions reflected on the entire people; such individual action could bring shame or glory.

When an individual committed an infraction of law, his or her whole family, clan, and Tribal Nation were held equally guilty until proper restitution and all the attendant protocols were achieved to the satisfaction of the Elders of both sides of the issue. When people fully understand the consequences, there are very few lawbreakers.

Employing the fundamental protocols and facets of Traditional Tribal Law along with utilizing the Peacemaker (the Gowukáan, for the Thlingit-speaking peoples) greatly reduces the cost of conflict resolution. Litigants can save time and money, forgoing the expenses of the immigrant court and lawyers by utilizing the Traditional Tribal Court. Thus they have the opportunity, through their Elders, to be a part of creative problem solving. It is natural for parties to a case to want to have some control in deciding the future of those involved in litigation. The utilization of Traditional Tribal Law to resolve grievances or legal issues allows individuals, families, clans, and tribes to retain that control.

The principles of respect inherent in Traditional Tribal Law apply to any age and all generations. Balance is maintained when interactions between persons occur in an environment of mutual respect and cultural understanding. Rules of evidence are much broader than in the Anglo-American system of justice. Traditional Tribal Court judges desire nothing to be hidden from them. The evidentiary system operates exceedingly well within the current Traditional Tribal Court systems and has been a powerful tool in cross-jurisdictional interactions with non-Native courts. It is impossible to experience Manifest Injustice in the Traditional Tribal Law setting.

There are many commonalties that exist between the tribes with regard to Traditional Tribal Law. This aspect allows the Kuiu Kwáan Traditional Tribal Court to operate cross-jurisdictionally, especially where other tribes desire neutrality. Per requests of other Indigenous Peoples and Tribes, the Kuiu court has acted as a surrogate court, holding numerous court hearings in Alaska, Canada, South Dakota, Montana, and Washington state, rendering adjudication to a broad spectrum of Indigenous Peoples. The operations of the Kuiu Kwáan Traditional

Tribal Court have assisted many non-Thlingit-speaking Peoples. Indeed, the majority of the cases adjudicated have been for non-Thlingit members of other nations.

ETHICAL, NOT ADVERSARIAL, SYSTEM

There is no notion of "winners" or "losers" in the tribal court setting. There is no single Native American approach to law and culture, as there are more than one thousand tribes and villages in the Americas, each with its own way of dealing with law and justice. But there are fundamental similarities. Chief among these is an approach that emphasizes mediation and resolution rather than a contest between lawyers.

Among the Thlingit, the Peacemaker holds an office of the highest importance. His duty is to serve as an intermediary; he goes between the Elders of the victim(s) and those of the perpetrator(s). He is a highly respected Elder of impeccable credentials. The small and less important cases may be settled to the satisfaction of both parties by his skill and diplomacy. The more serious cases involve the Elders of both sides of the issue. The Traditional Tribal Court will be composed of anywhere from three to twelve Elders or more depending on the importance of the case.

The purpose of a tribal hearing is to establish the facts, determine the extent of the infraction of law, and negotiate the form of appropriate settlement or restitution and return of balance. The process involves the Elders of the lawbreaker(s) and the Elders of the victim(s). The Elders of the victim(s) meet in session separately to discuss an appropriate program for restitution and restoration, and may suggest certain other terms for the consideration by the Elders of the perpetrator(s). The Peacemaker serves as the "go-between" for both sets of Elders.

Law must not be confused with justice. Laws may be followed to the letter, but that does not mean justice has been done. Tribes are interested in a holistic, universal, larger sense of justice. Separation of church and state has little place in tribal settings; prayer asking for wisdom and guidance from the Creator prefaces tribal hearings. Sentences may include ways to make lawbreakers reflect upon their moral behavior or infraction of law. The close bond of a tribal community is a strong deterrent and a powerful motivator to monitor people's personal lives.

The goals of the tribal court are to protect heritage, tradition, culture, religion, and family tribal members, as well as those who may be visiting or who are passing through tribal territories. Tribes do not condone criminal acts by anyone, regardless of status as a tribal member. In some respects, tribal court judges have more judicial independence than that of their counterparts in the international, state, or federal court system.

Indigenous Nations are homogenous communities, and often the sentences are pragmatic and unique when compared to those typical of other peoples and cultures. There was the case of an Indian who broke another man's arm during a bar brawl. The offender's punishment was to spend the winter chopping wood for the man's family. One morning the wife of the victim saw the offender chopping wood and invited him in for coffee; a week later, she asked him in for dinner, and within months the family's friendship had been reaffirmed. Compare this to what might have happened in a non-Native court. The offender might have done some jail time, and he and the victim would have remained resentful and angry at each other. There would most likely be no reconciliation, no reintegration back into the community. In the meantime, the fellow with the broken arm wouldn't have any firewood for his family.

One of the goals of the Traditional Tribal Court is to set an environment for healing and restoration. When all the terms of the two sets of the Elders have been met, the Gowukáan of Thlingit society will call for a public gathering much like a Potlatch. He leads a review of all aspects of the issue. After a proper introduction and welcome of all the leaders and prestigious Elders present, he states the order of business and then makes a call of inquiry to the Elders of the victim(s) and asks them if they are satisfied that all their conditions and terms have been satisfactorily met. If the answer is affirmative, he makes a call to the Elders of the lawbreaker(s) to publicly inform them of the answer. The Gowukáan asks the Elders of the lawbreaker(s) if they have any reservations concerning the requirements of the restitution and restoration process. If the answer is that they have no reservations, then the Gowukáan dons splendid dancing regalia taken from the deer, the symbol of peace. He then puts on a remarkable headdress covered with soft white feathered down. A low quiet beating of a drum commences and the Peacemaker starts a slow, deliberate, and dignified dance, chanting as he moves. From time to time the movement of his head loosens some of the white down, which falls softly to the floor, signifying that peace is now returning to the peoples and the land. It is the Traditional "Dance of Peace." At the conclusion of the dance and chanting, the Gowukáan makes the solemn announcement, "Peace has now returned to the land and peoples and this matter of the infraction of law will never be spoken of again! This portion of tribal history will be forever sealed! It has ever been thus!"

In reality, the lawbreaker(s) will be given a second chance because all the conditions, terms, requirements, restitution, restoration, and rehabilitation have been satisfactorily met. There will be no stain on their personal record. This episode in their life will be completely blotted out, as if the infraction had never happened. Traditional Tribal Law strictly forbids anyone to ever talk about or mention this incident again. Their record will be clean. It will be as if they had been born again. This unique Indigenous process allows the lawbreaker(s) to choose go on and lead a respectable life, and if in the future he or she is called upon, he or she will be able to hold high office.

Under the Anglo-American judicial system, by contrast, those who break the law will carry the stain of their infraction the rest of their lives. It will largely determine their quality of life, hindering them in whatever activity or initiative they attempt to pursue. Such things as bank loans, home mortgage loans, or holding public office will be denied them. Most of the time they will be relegated to a marginal lifestyle. Nearly all personal initiatives will be negatively affected by their record of infringement of law. It matters not whether their negative action was committed when they were young; the passing of years does not obliterate the record even if they have satisfactorily completed a jail or penitentiary sentence and made restitution. The lawbreaker is generally not allowed to hold significant positions of responsibility. The convicted lawbreaker in the Anglo-American judicial system will lead a greatly compromised life.

UNEQUAL LAW ENFORCEMENT
AND DISPROPORTIONATE INCARCERATION

Indian tribes generally mistrust American courts, and the history of American jurisprudence and Indians involves incidences of prejudice, interference, and even cruelty. The Superior Court in Rapid City, South Dakota, has a dark history of persecution of Lakota, Dakota, Nakota peoples: Indians are often barred from wearing regalia, feathers, or beads in the courtroom, while non-Natives appear tattooed in low-slung pants, stomachs bared with rings in their navels.

Indigenous Alaskans and other Indians know from experience that it is not uncommon for them to be treated harshly by law enforcement agencies and the courts. They know that hostility toward Indians may run high and that sympathy for Indian values is lacking. Persons who violate the law should suffer the penalties, but the issue in Indian Country is the inequality of the punishment.

During the 1970s, the United States Commission on Civil Rights conducted an in-depth investigation concerning the administration of justice involving urban American Indians and stated, "In Arizona and New Mexico, Indians suffer from severe handicaps when it comes to the administration of justice."[5] All too often Indian people have experienced bias, brutality, and unfairness in their contacts with the state systems of justice. As tribal Elder Byron Skinna of Klawock, Alaska, stated in 1992, "I think in the non-Native courts 'justice' means 'just us.'"

At a time when America fights a "war against terrorism" on foreign shores, there is terrorism being perpetrated against the First Peoples of the Americas. The name Adelia Godfrey has become synonymous with human rights violations and the ugly, systemic abuse of children in the United States. Godfrey is now (at this writing) serving time in the women's prison in Pierre, South Dakota. Investigations have revealed that this young Indian girl's only crime was to be one of five Indian girls violated at a juvenile institution in North Dakota. Godfrey was subjected to cruel and inhumane treatment while in the "care and custody" of the state of South Dakota, transported across state lines, placed in a windowless cell, stripped and four-pointed on the floor, and molested. (One young girl subsequently committed suicide, and the molestation case remains unresolved.) During a contact visit at the Sisseton County jail prior to her transfer to Pierre, Godfrey admitted to resisting a law enforcement officer who had inappropriately handled her body. While waiting to see Godfrey, the Kuiu Family and Child Welfare Specialist and I witnessed a diminutive, nine-year-old Sisseton-Wahpeton girl chained like a dog to a railing in the waiting room of the jail. When the Child Welfare Specialist asked her name and why she was there on a Saturday morning, the child didn't know. Jail documents show no record of the child having ever been in custody or heavily chained to prevent escape from a secure, lockdown facility.

These are not the first reported instances of abuse of minor Indian children in South Dakota. Data received at an international gathering of Spiritual Leaders, Chiefs, Honored Elders, Traditional Headsmen, and Warrior Societies held by the Tsisistas (Northern Cheyenne) Nation in Lame Deer, Montana, December 5–9, 2002, detailed the findings of the Lakota, Dakota, Nakota Human Rights Commission concerning illegal actions and human rights violations perpetrated against Indigenous Peoples by agents and assigns of the state of South Dakota.

The commission found that state courts disregard the United States Constitution Supremacy Clause, provisions of the Indian Child Welfare

Act (25 USC 1901 *et seq.*), and provisions of United Nations covenants and accords to which the United States of America is signatory (especially provisions of the Covenant on Civil and Political Rights). Further, the commission found that the sovereign political status of Indigenous Peoples in South Dakota is in chaos, with no legal, coherent doctrinal base for decisions arbitrarily applied to Indians, resulting in dozens of diverse, inconsistent, and illegal opinions regarding Indians. Assaults on the Lakota, Dakota, Nakota Peoples at the hands of the agents and assigns of the United States of America and its illegal political subdivision, the state of South Dakota, are gross, systematic, and persistent. Gross: Elders, men, women, and children have been illegally arrested, jailed, transported away from ancestral homelands, and fined (violating certain international treaties and accords. Systematic: a consistent pattern of state policy, overt governmental actions, and institutionalized practices impose conditions of life detrimental to their ability to continue as a people. Persistent: These problems have occurred regularly and over a long period of time, violating their human rights, resulting in ethnocide, genocide, and forced assimilation. Injustices to the Lakota, Dakota, Nakota are sufficiently severe to warrant United Nations involvement.

For an example of the inequity, consider the case of an Indigenous man who had been found guilty of drunk driving on several occasions and then was found guilty of a subsequent violation of driving under the influence of alcohol. He was sentenced to five years in the Idaho State Penitentiary.[6] Another Indian man, who drove a car while under the influence of alcohol, caused an accident involving another auto, seriously injuring innocent people. He was sentenced to a lengthy term in the Idaho State Penitentiary.[7] Both sentences were legally within sentencing guidelines. However, about one hundred miles north, a non-Native wealthy businesswoman operating a motor vehicle under the influence of alcohol drove her automobile on the wrong side of a state highway, struck an oncoming car, and killed a young Indigenous father and his two young children. The victim's father had not been drinking alcohol nor was he under the influence of narcotics. The woman's blood alcohol level was .17 nearly four hours after the accident. This woman was charged with three counts of vehicular manslaughter.

The woman was not arrested at the scene of the accident nor fingerprinted until after sentencing. She finally received a sentence of twelve months in the county jail, to be served in the county of her residence, which was not the same county in which the accident occurred.

She was further allowed work-release time so that she could attend to her business during the week. A fine was imposed, with some probation.[8]

A tribal Elder stricken with advanced Parkinson's disease was arrested and fined in Klawock, Alaska, for "thinking about going fishing"; he was carrying a creel on his hip and a fishing pole in his hand. A non-Native visitor near Fairbanks, Alaska, shot a bear without a license and went unpunished.

These cases illustrate the problem of unequal treatment which is so ubiquitous in Indian Country, and help explain why many Indigenous people place so little faith in state and federal judicial systems. It is no wonder that Indigenous people prefer going to tribal court rather than through the Anglo-American court system, still so thoroughly permeated by a language of conquest!

NOTES

1. Y. N. Kly, "US Court Recognizes Tribal Court," Press Release of IHRAAM, May 25, 1998, http://canadiangenocide.nativeweb.org/ihraam1.html. Accessed July 15, 2004.

2. Chi Chi Sileo, "When Cultures Clash, Should Punishment Fit the Criminal?" *Insight on the News*, October 24, 1994, 7.

3. Ibid.

4. P.L. 106-559, chapter 38, Indian Tribal Justice Act, enacted December 1993.

5. The Southwest Indian Report, Report of the U.S. Commission on Civil Rights, 1973.

6. *State of Idaho v. Norton Black Eagle.*

7. *State of Idaho v. Dion Smith.*

8. *State of Idaho v. Janice K. Hess.*

Chapter 7

WHERE ARE YOUR WOMEN?:

MISSING IN ACTION

Barbara Alice Mann

Once the prejudices and purposes of anti-Indian hegemony are exposed from within revisionist history, corporate-controlled media, the academy, literature, and law, it is easy to be unsurprised by how even "Indian studies" might regard the Indigenous female. To speak accurately about American Indian women and their powerful, egalitarian role in Indigenous cultures would bump into a double prejudice of the traditional Eurocentric mind-set—one against "Indians" and the other against women. In this chapter Barbara Mann contrasts the remarkable visibility of Indigenous women with the glaring omission of them in virtually any meaningful discussion about the Indigenous. In most Indigenous cultures, the role of men was to protect the woman's power to give and nurture life and to maintain community harmony. Women "owned" all but those items men needed for hunting or defense. Even today on reservations throughout the United States, when serious issues face the nation, women often emerge as the primary leaders. Yet even the less hegemonic American Indian Studies programs at the university level tend not to fully address the place of the woman in traditional Indigenous culture. In this shocking exposé, Dr. Mann explains why.

Barbara Alice Mann, PhD, lives, teaches, researches, and writes in Ohio, the homeland of her Seneca ancestors for the last fifteen hundred years. She is the author of Iroquoian Women: The Gantowisas *(2000) and* Native Americans, Archaeologists, and the Mounds *(2003); editor of and contributor to* Native American Speakers of the Eastern Woodlands *(2001); and co-editor and main contributor of* Encyclopedia of the Haudenosaunee (Iroquois Confederacy) *(2000). She has also authored numerous journal articles and book chapters, including "Euro-forming the Data" (1985) and "A Sign in the Sky" (1997). She is currently a Lecturer in the English Department at the University of Toledo.*

***

In 1757, the great Cherokee speaker and chief Atagulkalu (Attakullakulla) arrived at a meeting in Charles Town, South Carolina, but he hesitated to conduct business with its all-male European council. Prodded by the Europeans to get busy, he turned impatiently to Governor William Henry Lyttelton and demanded, "But where are your women?"[1]

This remains a good question for Western commentators, popular and scholarly alike. Women are missing-in-action in nearly all studies of Native America, whether historical, social, or anthropological. I believe this is because westerners are still reacting to the panic that European patriarchs felt upon discovering Turtle Island chock-full of self-directed, articulate, and confident Native women, all demanding to be dealt with as equals. The initial Euro-male horror was frank and obvious in first-contact records, and, although it might have gone underground in more recent treatments, the recoil remains, skewing discussion. In particular, to reestablish their comfort zone, Euro-American scholars industriously erased women from the memory of Native American cultures, in the same way that they had long since "disappeared" women from their own memory traces.

Consequently, in the often fractious discussions of the extent of Native American contributions to modern Euro-American culture, the glaring omission of women continues almost utterly unaddressed. Despite their importance to Native cultures—particularly in the eastern woodlands and the desert Southwest, where women are vital elements of economic, political, social, and spiritual life—they are nowhere to be found in Western discussions. Women's policies, words, and concerns may loom large on their own cultures' agendas, and female representatives may hold important, decision-making offices in their own communities, but one is hard-pressed to guess as much from Western discussions of Native America.

This being the twenty-first century, it is well past time for scholars to stop treating Native American history as though only men saw, thought, acted, and spoke. Women saw, thought, acted, and spoke, too—and a crying scandal it was to their European interlocutors. In 1632, the Dominican missionary Gabriel Sagard clucked his tongue over the amount of free time Wyandot women enjoyed and positively glowered that, as their own bosses, they used this leisure to feast, party, and gamble.[2] Such behaviors put a European woman on the fast track to hell. With the perfect wife of the Bible a perfect slave to her family (see Proverbs 31: 13–27), Christian men "saved" Christian women from Christian hell by leaving them no free time whatsoever, while simultaneously ensuring that they went nowhere on their own. The Wyandot example of free women doing as they pleased, when they pleased, could only make a missionary's blood run cold.

Worse, from the European perspective, was the level of political clout wielded by woodlands women. The sixteenth-century Spaniards in La Florida (the whole American southeast) were nonplussed by matrilineage and the *cacicas* (female chiefs) with whom they were forced to deal, especially among the Gaules, staunch resisters of invasion. Spanish frustration was not a little focused on Guale females, who undermined patriarchal tampering with Guale culture. Indeed, the gutsy Guale Revolt—which successfully threw off Spanish rule for an unheard-of four years, from 1597 to 1601—was occasioned specifically because the missionaries were attempting to reformat Guale matrilineal institutions, especially marriage and inheritance, to follow the patrilineal model of Europe. Although Spanish primary sources all speak as though only Guale men objected, the primary losers, the women, were not only front and center for the revolt, but also participants, helping to hold fast the rebel capital of Yfusinique. This was why, upon finally conquering Yfusinique in October 1601, the Spaniards punished the rebel women of the city by forcing them to scalp their own sons, husbands, fathers, and brothers.[3]

In 1724, the Jesuit missionary Joseph François Lafitau recorded in astonishment that Haudenosaunee women were "the soul of the councils" in whom "all the real authority" resided.[4] The men were no more than their functionaries, for *by law*, the men's Grand Council could not consider a matter that the Clan Mothers' Council had not sent forward.[5] In fact, Iroquois League law was careful to stipulate that *men* had the same civil rights as *women*.[6] This perhaps needed clarifying, since women, alone, nominated both male and female officials of the League, while women, alone, retained the right to impeach—and did impeach—any officials errant in their duties.[7] A high crime certain to bring on impeachment was conversion to Christianity, a fact to consider in light of Christian misogyny.[8] None of this information aided patriarchal digestion.[9]

Judicial affairs so entirely belonged to women that any woodlands man who wished to become a jurist or a negotiator had first to have been "made a woman" in order to be qualified for the job.[10] Rendering judgments and untangling affairs was likened to pounding out the corn, reducing the hard kernel of a dispute to powder, easily blown away by the breath of reason. Consequently, all judges carried cornpounders. Early colonial Europeans were often quite rattled to see men striding purposefully into the treaty councils, proudly wearing their skirts and carrying their cornpounders. Failing to grasp the distinction between Native American gendering of tasks and European sex-role stereotyping of people, early chroniclers concluded that such men had (tsk-tsk) to have been "transvestites" or "hermaphrodites."[11] Natives did, of course, have gay and lesbian people—and highly regarded they were[12]—but, unlike the Europeans, they never confused a homosexual orientation with a gendered job assignment.

European culture shock had not abated by 1775, when that erstwhile observer of Cherokee culture James Adair fulminated that the Cherokees had "been a considerable while under petticoat-government and allow their women full liberty to plant their brows with horns as oft as they please, without fear of punishment."[13] Traditionally, civic office in the woodlands was indicated by deer-horn headdresses, so that, even after the period when actual antlers were worn, officers were spoken of as "wearing horns." Thus (for all that, first, horns signified cuckholding in European culture and second, Native women enjoyed complete sexual freedom), what Adair was indicting—with palpable shock that Cherokee men did not join him in fury—was high office-holding among Cherokee women. Since male approval was neither required nor desired in this, Adair's notion that the men ought somehow to have "punished" the women for their civic leadership expresses nothing more than the outraged cultural values of Christian Europeans.

Adair was hardly alone in his grumpy distaste for "petticoat-government." It had been voiced since the first Europeans touched ground in North America, with missionaries at pains to destroy women's power. The seventeenth-century Jesuits of "New France" (Canada), for instance, organized roving gangs of thugs ("Christian captains"), drawn from the outcast element of Iroquoian society, and empowered them with weapons and dispensations to brutalize Clan Mothers and other pesky females, toward the end of extracting from them the same sort of cringing deference that women paid men in Christian Europe.[14] The early nineteenth-century Quakers likewise did their level best to nail women's feet to the floors of their longhouses, although this particular attempt blew up in the missionaries' faces.[15] The nineteenth-century witch hunts later conducted by christianizing and christianized Native "prophets"—notably the Shawnee Tenskwatawa and the Seneca Sganyadaiyoh ("Handsome Lake")—hitchhiked on notions seeded by missionaries regarding the need to control naturally sinful women.[16]

Notwithstanding these efforts to uproot women's rights, honest chroniclers of the nineteenth century continued to point out the freedom and power of Native women. The wildly popular *History, Customs, and Manners* (1820) of Moravian missionary John Heckewelder demonstrated the high status of women among the Lenape and Mahican peoples. In particular, they negotiated international peace conferences. Although they kept and farmed all the land, their lives were not orgies of hard labor, as were the lives of European farm wives. Masters of their own time, Lenape and Mahican women saw to it that their tasks were light. They also called and ran women's funerals, a type of recognition not even accorded queens in Europe, where female-led religious ceremonies were unthinkable.[17] Early secondary sources, such as Lucien Carr, ruefully admitted the truth of such accounts, moaning that the men had been emasculated by the women, who "exercised an influence but little short of despotic" in social and political life.[18]

Such revelations were pills too bitter for Western men to swallow—so they fixed up the record.

Native Americans have long lambasted the way that westerners skew the record to suit their ends. Ohio Natives have traditionally called this tactic "pen-and-ink witchcraft,"[19] that is, making the written record (which westerners promote as the *only* record) say something completely different from what the living record said at the time and what oral tradition said afterward. We knew that it was not at all uncommon for colonial and later U.S. "translators" deliberately to misstate what was afoot during councils, to adjust meeting minutes to reflect something quite other than what had been presented, or to misrepresent the contents of a treaty to ensure that it was signed.[20] Such well-worn tactics of pen-and-ink witchcraft came in handy for arranging the documentary disappearance of anything Western officials found annoying.

They certainly found Native women annoying, so they plied their pen-and-ink witchcraft against them. The missionaries started with women's spirituality, which, continent-wide, featured females as the progenitrices of creation. A favorite tactic here was simply to excise women from creation traditions. The Lynx (also called Hanging Flowers), the daughter of Sky Woman in Iroquoian tradition, was almost entirely erased by the missionaries—in a process continued by later anthropologists![21] Ultimately she was reduced to little more than a womb for birthing the male Twins, in replication of the Mary-as-womb story favored by Europeans. In the original story, the Lynx actually gave birth to quadruplets, the male Direction of the Sky (the east-west axis) and the female Split Sky (the north-south axis).[22] However, once the missionaries had mutated the male Twins into counterparts of their own god and devil,[23] they discarded the female Twins altogether as worthless, so that it is almost impossible to hear of the girls today.

Sky Woman, for whom the water animals made Turtle Island in the first place, remained, but ignominiously. Her accidental fall (most Native

WHERE ARE YOUR WOMEN?

creation stories feature accident as the precipitating cause of creation) was transmuted into an Eve-like error, replete with a fall from sky-born grace. Under the massaging of the missionaries, Sky Woman was turned from Hard Luck Woman into Evil Grandmother. Meantime, her great services in the creation of life on earth were sidestepped, with credit given in later, missionary-mangled traditions, to her grandson, Sapling, so that modern Longhouse traditionalists actually refer to him as *the* "Creator."[24] The results of such tinkering did give early missionaries like Sagard pause to wonder at God's having a Grandmother, but, by the nineteenth century, anthropologists paid too little attention to Sky Woman even to notice this hitch anymore.[25]

Another handy strategy, often employed by early anthropologists, was simply to declare the female progenitrix a male progenitor. The Raven of the Pacific Northwest underwent a DNC (dusting 'n cleaning), reemerging as emphatically male by the time John Reed Swanton got around to writing up Tlingit stories in 1909,[26] while the best that Michael Dorris could manage by way of restoration in 1994 was to present her as androgynous.[27] In another instance, the Cherokee Corn Mother, Selu, was diminished in favor of her husband, Kanati, the Lucky Hunter. The original female lead of the Cherokee cosmological drama, Selu was shunted aside, and her mate casually promoted to the status of "Creator."[28]

The machinations to arrive at such switches were particularly egregious and, consequently, obvious in the case of the Shawnee Star Woman, Kokomthena. Not a shadow of a doubt exists in authentic Shawnee oral tradition that Kokomthena is female, the spiritual Grandmother.[29] Her personal names, so ancient as to be untranslatable, explicitly contain the female particle *h\si*, and all traditional references are to her as female.[30] Nevertheless, in 1829, when Charles Christopher Trowbridge spoke with the "prophet" Tenskwatawa and the chief Cathecassa, taking down their traditions, he freely interposed a male "Great Spirit" into their accounts, even when it was obvious that Cathecassa was merely speaking of a Sky vision guide.[31] Given such capricious, nineteenth-century interpolations, by 1944 Charles and Erminie Voegelin were hot on the trail of a major anthropological find: that the Shawnee creator had always been male, and that it was only the degenerative effects of contact with the Iroquois that had turned Kokomthena female![32] A little nip here, a big tuck there, and voilà, she's a he.

Outrageous misrepresentations of women's medicine did not abate as the twentieth century wore on, but instead culminated in the insulting sort of mumbo-jumbo masquerading as Native spirituality that gave rise to Disney's *Pocahontas* and "her" laughable colors of the rainbow. The true and agonizing story of Pocahontas' selfless sacrifice of personal freedom to obtain the fleeting safety of her people was warped into a silly romance (true love being the only "proper" topic of female discourse) capped by some shuck-and-jive minstrelsy about rainbows—but why should a mere movie studio be held to higher standards of accuracy than a professor of Religious Studies at the University of Colorado at Boulder?

In 1987, said professor, Sam Gill, had the ethnic arrogance to come out with *Mother Earth: An American Story*, and the University of Chicago Press had the lack of standards to publish it. The primary contention in Gill's *American Story* is that Mother Earth is a wannabe, not Native at all. No, indeedy, the idea of Mother Earth was entirely supplied by Europeans, pressed by missionaries, and taken up with zeal by over-wrought New Agers. In a way, it is hardly surprising that Gill might have reached such a conclusion, since his self-confessed method of research was to ask non-Natives, mainly students, their thoughts on the subject.[33]

It is clear that Gill could not have asked any actual Natives, for then he would have learned, through countless traditions in every nation, that Mother Earth lives, whether or not she has federal recognition. Among the Iroquois, she is the daughter of Sky Woman, who, upon death, per-manently reincarnated as Mother Earth, with all the staple crops instantly sprouting from her body.[34] To the Cherokee, she is Selu, who pushed up corn from her own guts until her death, at which time she instructed her son and Wild Boy how to safely plant in her, now as Mother Earth.[35] In the Southwest, home of Yellow Woman, she is Iyatiku of the Keres.[36] Farther south in Mexico among the Aztecs, she is Tonacaygohau, literally translating as "she feeds us," or Centeotl, the Earth Mother.[37]

Indeed, Mother Earth traditions abound in every nook and cranny of Turtle Island, and always in the company of crops that were utterly unknown to the Europeans until after their arrival. For heaven's sake, the woodland planting mounds were consciously construed as the "breasts" of Mother Earth, while farming was conventionally referred to as "sucking the teat of Mother Earth."[38] Mother Earth and the Three Sisters (corn, beans, and squash) were traditionally known to women and carefully cul-tivated from Mexico to Maine, the female farmers of Turtle Island having long since discovered that the co-planting of crops, particularly corn and beans, revitalized rather than depleted the land.[39]

Given that the oldest ideas of any cultural continuum are exactly those enjoying the widest geographical spread and the deepest level of con-ventional references—a principle that anthropology has enthusiastically embraced since Edward Sapir first articulated it in 1916[40]—Mother Earth is clearly among the *most ancient* of Native ideas. Notwithstanding Euro-scholarship's own rules, however, academic fluff like Gill's regularly replaces Native truth, and I find myself having to defend such fully Native ideas as Mother Earth to doubting Western scholars, who then patronize my need to create ethnic fantasies in a pathetic act of self-validation.

Westerners take Native women to task on the secular side, as well. Powerful women, central facets of historical traditions, are simply written out of the record. The founding of the Iroquois League, an absolutely historical—and datable[41]—event was the *joint* effort of the Peacemaker, the Peace Queen, and Hiawatha. Nineteenth-century anthropologists out "collecting" tradition were, however, all men, so they heard only the men's versions of the tradition of the Great Law. The upshot today is that Western accounts lavish praise on the Peacemaker and Hiawatha but remain silent on the Peace Queen, that Mother of Nations, the Jigonsaseh, even though she was the pivotal leader of the Corn Way, whom the Peacemaker had perforce to seek out as his first step in lobbying for peace. Without her alliance, he would have had no movement. It was she who stumped tirelessly for the Great Law of Peace and she who provided the ultimate solution to the last thorny set of problems blocking ratification of the Constitution. Once established, the first men's Grand Council could not meet until after she had lain the horns of office on its male representatives, that is, until after she had appointed and sworn them in.[42] "Her word was law," says tradition,[43] but Western scholars are as oblivious of the Jigonsaseh, Head Clan Mother of the League, as they are of her Clan Mothers' Council, which controlled the agenda of the League.

Far from recognizing the strong civic roles of woodlands women, early nineteenth-century scholars began flatly contradicting the evidence of the primary sources, instead pumping out nonsensical stereotypes of Natives as lazy hunters in male-dominated cultures that oppressed women as slave labor.[44] By the mid-nineteenth century, prestigious scholars like Lewis Henry Morgan were falsely claiming that Native women saw themselves as inferior to men.[45] At the turn of the twentieth century, anthropologists such as Alexander A. Goldenweiser were claiming that Native women only held power by virtue of the primitiveness of their cultures, and by the mid-twentieth century, scholars including Elisabeth Tooker were ridiculing as poor scholarship the notion that Native women had ever held any "exceptional power."[46]

By the same token, women's economic power was downplayed until it was not there at all. Native women were the farmers, producing yields uniformly staggering to westerner observers, including the seventeenth-century Marquis de Denonville and the eighteenth-century General John Sullivan, both sent to destroy those yields, the better to rid the land of Natives in favor of Western settlers.[47] In 1687, Denonville reported that the fields produced in such amazing abundance that, all told, his men destroyed 1.2 million bushels of corn.[48] A century later, in 1779, Sullivan's men recorded excited journal entries noting corn stalks eighteen feet high and individual cobs a foot-and-a-half long.[49] Major Burrowes, one of Sullivan's officers, described the women's lush fields as "almost incredible to civilized people."[50] Sullivan's men, farmers themselves, eagerly brought back seeds that Native women had kept hidden from them: sweet corn, as opposed to the white flint corn, which was all that Native women had, up to that point, shared with the European invader.[51]

The better to distract scholarly attention from the authors of these wondrous fields, the large-scale agriculture of Native women was demoted in Western historical lore to mere "hoe horticulture."[52] To this day, I know of no work devoted to Native women's agriculture, despite the women's numerous and significant innovations, including the use of natural pesticides (tobacco) and fertilizers (fish heads), as well as their discovery of such things as the efficacious depths and spacing of seed planting; conservation (mound) tillage; and village (as opposed to crop) rotation.[53]

In the service of pooh-poohing women's stunning advances in farming techniques, Lewis Henry Morgan carefully categorized woodland farmers as "savages" and low-level "barbarians" in his *Ancient Society, or Researches in the Lines of Human Progress from Savagery through Barbarism to Civilization* (1877). The abject prejudice that animated Morgan's "study" might have toned down by the late twentieth century, but, by way of trade-off, the women managing Native agriculture had become invisible. In his 1983 *Changes in the Land*, a look at European versus Native land-use practices, William Cronon acted as if Native women did not exist, much less develop the crops that today would account for two-thirds of the world's vegetable sustenance.

The consequence of two centuries' worth of sustained pen-and-ink witchcraft is a phonied-up picture of Native America, pared down to faceless male "warriors" (the actual term is "young men") and a handful of visionary statesmen. Notwithstanding very clear oral traditions *and* historical primary sources documenting the centrality of both peaceful relations and female officials, leaders, and innovators in Native American cultures, the full half of the Native world that was female is relentlessly assumed to have been the same, silent, passive observer that she was forced to have been in Western European culture.

Even in modern works, such as Daniel Richter's *Ordeal of the Longhouse* (1992)—which posits women's war duties—the picture that is rendered chunks women's roles categorically, isolating one power, the right to call war, from women's extraordinary authority in all other aspects of society. Because only warfare is considered, Richter's woodlands women ultimately come off looking like the shrieking, gore-happy banshees of settler propaganda. Nowhere to be seen are the industrious planting chiefs, the sensitive funeral directors, the vision-quest mentors, the inventive chefs, the elaborate quill and bead workers, the nurturing parents, the articulate judges, the knowledgeable herbalists, or the brilliant counselors. All but the war women disappear in the narrative's rush to battle.

In the twenty-first century, it is incumbent upon (especially Native American!) scholars to rectify the Western obliteration of women from the record, surely the most unconscionable of the many misrepresentations that have been foisted upon Native America by Euro-America. In the like-minded company of other Native female scholars, I have labored as mightily as I can to reinstate Native women into the record of Native America, but this handful of us cannot alone salvage the situation—especially when we experience the academic double whammy: ghettoization for reasons of both sex and race. We need the strong arms of our brothers reinforcing us in the effort.

NOTES

1. John Phillip Reid, *A Law of Blood* (New York: New York University Press, 1970), 69.
2. Gabriel Sagard, *The Long Journey to the Country of the Hurons*, ed. George M. Wrong, trans. H. H. Langton (1632; Toronto: The Champlain Society, 1939), 101.
3. Maynard J. Geiger, *The Franciscan Conquest of Florida (1513–1618)*, Studies in Hispanic-American History, vol. 1 (Washington, D.C.: Catholic University of America, 1937), 121. For a full discussion of the Guale Revolt, see Barbara Alice Mann and Donald A. Grinde Jr., "'Now the Friar Is Dead': Sixteenth-Century Spanish Florida and the Guale Revolt," in *Native American Speakers of the Eastern Woodlands: Selected Speeches and Critical Analyses*, ed. Barbara Alice Mann (Westport, Conn.: Greenwood Press, 2001), 1–33.
4. Joseph François Lafitau, *Customs of the American Indians Compared with the Customs of Primitive Times*, ed. and trans. William N. Fenton and Elizabeth L. Moore, 2 vols. (1724; Toronto: The Champlain Society, 1974), 1: 69.

5. Pierre de Charlevoix, *Journal of a Voyage to North America*, 2 vols. (1761; Ann Arbor, Mich.: University Microfilms, Inc., 1966), 2: 26; Lafitau, *Customs of the American Indians*, 2: 295.

6. Arthur C. Parker, *The Constitution of the Five Nations, or The Iroquois Book of the Great Law* (Albany: University of the State of New York, 1916), 55.

7. Parker, *Constitution of the Five Nations*, nomination, 27, 97; impeachment, 46. Charlevoix, *Voyage to North America*, 2: 24.

8. For impeachment of converted female official, see Reuben Gold Thwaites, ed., *The Jesuit Relations: Travels and Explorations of the Jesuit Missionaries in New France, 1610–1791*, 73 vols. (1896–1901; New York: Pageant Book Company, 1959), 54: 281; for impeachment of converted male official, see the entry for Albert Cusick in Carl Waldman, *Who Was Who in Native American History: Indians and Non-Indians from Early Contacts through 1900* (New York: Facts on File, 1990), 91.

9. For a thorough look at the powers and rights of Iroquoian women, see Barbara Alice Mann, *Iroquoian Women: The Gantowisas* (New York: Peter Lang, 2000).

10. John Heckewelder, *History, Manners, and Customs of the Indian Nations Who Once Inhabited Pennsylvania and the Neighboring States*, The First American Frontier Series (1820; 1876; New York: Arno Press and The New York Times, 1971), 56–58.

11. Lafitau, *Customs of the American Indians*, 1: 57–58.

12. Many studies of Native gay, lesbian, transgender, and bisexual people's roles have been done, but for a sampling, see Sabine Lang, *Men as Women and Women as Men: Changing Gender in Native American Cultures* (Austin: University of Texas Press, 1998); Lisa Frink, Rita Shepard, and Gregory A. Reinhardt, eds., *Many Faces of Gender: Roles and Relationships through Time in Indigenous Northern Communities* (Boulder: University Press of Colorado, 2002); and Sue-Ellen Jacobs, Wesley Thomas, and Sabine Lang, *Two-Spirit People: Native American Gender, Identity, Sexuality, and Spirituality* (Chicago: University of Illinois Press, 1997).

13. James Adair, *History of the American Indians*, ed. Samuel Cole Williams (1775; Johnson City, Tenn.: Watauga Press, 1930), 232. For a close look at the rights and powers of Cherokee women, see Theda Perdue, *Cherokee Women: Gender and Culture Change, 1700–1835* (Lincoln: University of Nebraska Press, 1998).

14. For "Christian captains," see Karen Anderson, *Chain Her by One Foot: The Subjugation of Women in Seventeenth Century New France* (New York: Routledge, 1991), 219–220. For the full course of horrifying abuses to which the Jesuits subjected Iroquoian women, try the whole book.

15. Diane Rothenberg, "Erosion of Power: An Economic Basis for the Selective Conservatism of Seneca Women in the Nineteenth Century," *Western Canadian Journal of Anthropology* 6.3 (1978): 106–122.

16. For Tenskwatawa's witch hunts, see Alfred Cave, "The Failure of the Shawnee Prophet's Witch Hunt," *Ethnohistory* 42.3 (summer 1995): 445–475; for Sganyadaiyoh's witch hunts, see Mann, *Iroquoian Women*, 317–323.

17. Heckewelder, *History, Manners, and Customs*, e.g., women as peace-makers, 57–58; easy life of women, 154, 155, 157; funeral of important woman, 268–276. See also Anthony F. C. Wallace, "Women, Land, and Society: Three Aspects of Aboriginal Delaware Life," *Pennsylvania Archaeologist* 17.1–4 (1947): 1–36.

18. Lucien Carr, "On the Social and Political Position of Women among the Huron-Iroquois Tribes," Peabody Museum of American Archaeology and Ethnology, *Reports*, 16 & 17, 3.3–4 (1884), 211.

19. [Alexander McKee], "Minutes of Debates in Council on the Banks of the Ottawa River (Commonly Called the Miami of the Lake), November, 1791," pamphlet (Philadelphia: William Young Bookseller, 1792), 11.

20. United States, *Report of the Select Committee to Investigate Matters Connected with Affairs in Indian Territory Hearings November 11, 1906–January 9, 1907*, Fifty-Ninth Congress, 2nd Session, Report 5013, parts 1 and 2, vol. 2 (Washington, D.C.: Government Printing Office, 1907), 2: 1247.

21. Barbara A. Mann, "The Lynx in Time: Haudenosaunee Women's Traditions and History," *American Indian Quarterly* 21.3 (1997): 425.

22. J. N. B. Hewitt, "Iroquoian Cosmology, Second Part," *Forty-Third Annual Report of the Bureau of American Ethnology to the Secretary of the Smithsonian Institution, 1925–1926* (Washington, D.C.: Government Printing Office, 1928), 468.

23. Mann, *Iroquoian Women*, 305–312.

24. For a discussion of the Christianization of Iroquoian tradition under Handsome Lake, see Mann, *Iroquoian Women*, 299–312.

25. Sagard, *The Long Journey*, 169.

26. John R. Swanton, *Tlingit Myths and Texts* (Washington, D.C.: Government Printing Office, 1909), 3–21.

27. Michael Dorris, *Paper Trail: Essays* (New York: HarperPerennial, 1994); raven story, 154; whole chapter, "Discoveries," 145–162.

28. For the documented, original Selu and Kanati tradition, along with a discussion of its skewing, see Barbara Alice Mann, *Native Americans, Archaeologists, and the Mounds* (New York: Peter Lang, 2003), 222–223.

29. Thomas Wildcat Alford, "Shawnee Story of Creation," *Indians at Work* 2.18 (1935): 7–8.

30. Charles F. Voegelin, "The Shawnee Female Deity," *Yale University Publications in Anthropology* 8–13 (1936): 4.

31. C[harles] C[hristopher] Trowbridge, *Shawnese Traditions*, ed. Vernon Kinietz and Erminie W. Voegelin (1829; Ann Arbor: University of Michigan Press, 1939), 2–3. See my discussion of this tradition in Mann, *Native Americans, Archaeologists, and the Mounds*, 123–124.

32. Charles F. Voegelin and Erminie W. Voegelin, "The Shawnee Female Deity in Historical Perspective," *American Anthropologist* 46 (1944): 370–375. Here, Charles Voegelin was contradicting his own earlier, primary source research for Yale. See note 30, above.

33. Sam Gill, as quoted in Ward Churchill, "A Little Matter of Genocide: Colonialism and the Expropriation of Indigenous Spiritual Tradition in Academia," in *From a Native Son: Selected Essays on Indigenism, 1985–1995* (Boston: South End Press, 1996), 323–324.

34. Jacob Thomas, "Creation," Jake Thomas Learning Center, pamphlet, print no. 3 (n.d.); Mann, *Iroquoian Women*, 186; William N. Fenton, ed., *Parker on the Iroquois* (Syracuse: Syracuse University Press, 1968), 37.

35. James Mooney, "Myths of the Cherokee," *Nineteenth Annual Report of the Bureau of American Ethnology, 1897–1898*, part 1 (Washington, D.C.: Government Printing Office, 1900), 243–244.

36. Paula Gunn Allen, "Kochinnenako in Academe: Three Approaches to Interpreting a Keres Indian Tale," *North Dakota Quarterly* (spring 1985): 97.

37. Fenton, *Parker on the Iroquois*, 27 (note 2).

38. Ibid., 36.

39. Vine Deloria Jr., *God Is Red* (New York: Dell, 1973), 269.

40. Edward Sapir, *Time Perspective in Aboriginal American Culture: A Study in Method* (Ottawa: Canada Department of Mines, Geological Survey, 1916), 17.

41. Barbara A. Mann and Jerry L. Fields, "A Sign in the Sky: Dating the League of the Haudenosaunee," *American Indian Culture and Research Journal* 21.2 (1997): 105–163.

42. For a documented discussion of the role of the first Jigonsaseh, see Mann, *Iroquoian Women*, 124–134.

43. Arthur C. Parker, *The Life of General Ely S. Parker: Last Grand Sachem of the Iroquois and General Grant's Military Secretary* (Buffalo: The Buffalo Historical Society, 1919), 46.

44. See, for instance, Lewis Cass, "The Indians of North America," *North American Review* 22 (January 1826): 53.

45. Lewis Henry Morgan, *League of the Haudenosaunee, or Iroquois*, 2 vols. (1851; New York: Burt Franklin, 1901), 1: 315.

46. Alexander A. Goldenweiser, "Functions of Women in Iroquois Society," 1914, reprinted in *Iroquois Women: An Anthology* (Ohsweken, Ontario: Iroquois Publishing and Craft Supplies, Ltd., 1990), 51, 52; Elisabeth Tooker, "Women in Iroquois Society," in *Iroquois Women: An Anthology* (Ohsweken, Ontario: Iroquois Publishing and Craft Supplies, Ltd., 1990), 199, 200.

47. E. B. O'Callaghan, ed., "Letter from M. de Denonville to the Minister [of France]," in *Documentary History of the State of New York*, 4 vols. (Albany: Weed, Parsons, & Col., Public Printers, 1850), 1: 147; Alexander C. Flick, "New Sources on the Sullivan-Clinton Campaign in 1779," *The Quarterly Journal of the New York State Historical Society* 10.4 (October 1929): 308–309.

48. O'Callaghan, "Letter from M. de Denonville to the Minister [of France]," 1: 147.

49. Frederick Cook, *Journals of the Military Expedition of Major General John Sullivan against the Six Nations of Indians in 1779* (1887; Freeport, N.Y.: Books for Libraries Press, 1972), 27, 45, 99.

50. Ibid., 44.

51. Lyman Butterfield, "History at the Headwaters," *New York History* 51.2 (1970): 135.

52. Joan M. Jensen, "Native American Women and Agriculture: A Seneca Case Study," in *Unequal Sisters: A Multicultural Reader in U.S. Women's History*, ed. Ellen Carol DeBois and Vicki L. Ruiz (New York: Routledge, 1990), 51, 63 (note 2).

53. Mann, *Iroquoian Women*, 220–223.

Chapter 8

PEACEFUL VERSUS WARLIKE SOCIETIES
IN PRE-COLUMBIAN AMERICA:
WHAT DO ARCHAEOLOGY AND
ANTHROPOLOGY TELL US?

James DeMeo

Perhaps the ultimate price we all pay for diminishing the female's power and position in society is war, the great corporate money-machine and ideological tool of fascism. This chapter reveals the relationship between patriarchal culture and war. Discussion of this relationship has typically been suppressed in one of two primary ways. The previous chapter addressed the first way: simply curtail any discussion about the power of Indigenous women in peaceful, traditional Indigenous society. The second way is to re-create history so as to make the world believe that Indigenous cultures were not at all peaceful in the first place.

The latter has been a primary occupation for a number of authors for some time. For example, in 2003, St. Martin's Press published Harvard archaeologist Steven LeBlank's book, Constant Battles: The Myth of the Peaceful, Noble Savage, *co-authored with Katherine E. Register. Like a number of other academic books, such as those referred to in the introduction, this one attempts to demonstrate that warfare today is far less prevalent than it was in "primitive" cultures. It argues that the assumptions and the actions of early Indigenous People resulted in patterns of violence throughout the world, and that awareness of these patterns in concert with recognizing the advantages of modern technology increases the ability for humans to avoid war in the future.*

An admirable goal, but their anecdotal evidence contradicts larger bodies of evidence about war in pre-contact cultures. In fact, their "evidence" simply replicates the self-authorizing mythology in which the majority of Americans have been thoroughly steeped. From images of the caveman dragging his mate into a cave after crushing the head of an opponent with a club to memories of Saturday morning television programs depicting blood-thirsty savages, Americans do not need "more awareness" about Indigenous violence. As previous chapters have shown, popular literature, Hollywood movies, and school textbooks have done an ample job of getting the average person to see ancient cultures as having been prone to violence and war.

A large body of research, however, opposes claims that war and belligerence were very prevalent in Indigenous cultures. A day spent looking at the Human Resources Area Files demonstrates this clearly. HRAF, an internationally recognized organization in the field of cultural anthropology founded in 1949 at Yale University, publishes scholarly materials arranged by geographic region. Its large data base in archaeology and cultural anthropology clearly shows that warfare, religious conflict, genocide, and massive civilian morbidity and mortality from social wars were rare in most Indigenous societies relative to European ones.

In this chapter, one of the foremost researchers on the subject, James DeMeo, presents a summary of his painstaking research, which further supports the conclusion that "pre-contact" American Indian cultures were oriented more toward peace than war. Although he does show a number of exceptions to this rule, he demonstrates that they are examples of "isolated patristic violence amid a background ocean of matristic and peaceful social conditions."

Knowing that our Indigenous ancestors had a way of living cooperatively can give us hope that there is at least one human model that may help us end the increasingly horrific wars so prevalent in our dominant cultures today.

James DeMeo received his doctorate in geography from the University of Kansas, where his research corroborated various aspects of Wilhelm Reich's controversial social and biophysical discoveries. DeMeo has been on the faculty of geography at Illinois State University and the University of Miami. He has published over 150 articles on a range of issues—energy resources, health, cultural history, environmental problems, and experimental life-energy research—as well as the following books: The Orgone Accumulator Handbook *(Natural Energy Press, 1989, now in seven languages),* Nach Reich: Neue Forschungen zur Orgonomie *(co-editor, Zweitausendeins, 1994),* On Wilhelm Reich and Orgonomy *(editor, Natural Energy, 1993),* Saharasia: The 4000 BCE Origins of Child Abuse, Sex-Repression, Warfare and Social Violence *(Natural Energy, 1998),* Heretic's Notebook: Emotions, Protocells, Ether-Drift and Cosmic Life Energy *(editor, Natural Energy, 2002). He is also editor of the journal* Pulse of the Planet. *In 1978, he founded the Orgone Biophysical Research Laboratory, of which he has remained the director to this day.*

***

*When people come to trouble, it is better for both
parties to come together without arms and talk it
over and find some peaceful way to settle it.*

—SPOTTED TAIL, BRULE' LAKOTA, 1876

This chapter will address the question posed in its title, from the findings in my global cross-cultural and archaeological-historical research, summarized in the book *Saharasia: The 4000 BCE Origins of Child-Abuse,*

Sex-Repression, Warfare and Social Violence, In the Deserts of the Old World,[1] and in a subsequent study.[2] This work, a combined geographical and cross-cultural analysis of global human behavior with many maps, is hardly known outside of a handful of specialists, though it remains one of the most thoroughgoing and systematic studies on the origins of violence which has ever been undertaken. This work was not focused upon any given culture, but rather, contrasted levels of violence and violence-correlated social institutions and behaviors across a group of 1,170 different Indigenous cultures around the world, on every continent. The results showed that violence was neither randomly nor evenly distributed around the world, but rather existed at its highest levels within specific geographical regions, while being at much lower levels in others. The geographical patterns were hidden within the standard anthropological literature, overlooked until the 1980s when I drafted the first world maps of human behavior. I additionally spent several years reviewing the standard archaeological literature and discovered a similar geographical pattern, correlated to what was demonstrated in anthropology. Through geographical methods, human violence was traced back in time to several specific and isolated regions from which it first developed, and from which it spread over millennia to infect other world regions. The mechanism of this spreading of violence involved mass migrations, invasions and conquest, contact diffusion of culture, and long-distance voyages of exploration and colonization. Over the centuries, the more peaceful Indigenous Peoples of nearly every world region were assimilated, displaced, or wiped out by the more violent invader cultures. My work either directly demonstrates, or strongly implies, that the human species was originally characterized by generally peaceful and cooperative social conditions, with only the most rare and isolated examples of violence or warfare. This was particularly the case in the Americas, prior to the arrival of invaders from the Old World.

My behavior maps, constructed from standard ethnographic and anthropological data, oppose the claim of any widespread or predominant violent condition among pre-Columbian Native Americans, and also goes against the denigrating and dismissive attitude toward First Nations that this text addresses. When the claims of a number of "academics" are reviewed critically, using a systematic, cross-cultural, and geographical approach involving plotting the cultural data on maps and viewing them historically, their limitations are exposed, and an even stronger foundation for the opposing claim emerges. In fact, Indigenous Peoples in the Americas prior to Columbus, in most regions of the New World, enjoyed a peaceful and socially cooperative existence without the chronic patterns of warfare and conflict which infected, and continue to afflict, the Old World.

THE FINDINGS

My research proceeded from the *sex-economic theory* of the radical psychiatrist Wilhelm Reich,[3] which places a strong emphasis upon the treatment of infants and children, and upon the basic human need for sexual gratification and love-fulfillment in the creation of human character structure and society. Reich also argued that state structure was *determined* and *predictable* from family structure, where social institutions played a central role. The findings of Reich are too complex to summarize here, but it can be noted they were rooted in, but eventually diverged from, Freudian psychoanalysis in the 1930s. Reich's writings on the social and psychosexual considerations underlying political fascism (of both left- and right-wing variants) suggested to me that they were universal factors to be found in all patriarchal authoritarian and violent cultures.

Using Reich's writings and confirming them with cross-cultural findings of James Prescott's "Body Pleasure and the Origins of Violence,"[4] I constructed two dichotomous categories of human social variables, which would define the extremes of violent and peaceful culture.[5] These were:

1. *Patrism*, characterized by harsh, pain-inflicting, and rough treatments for infants and children (i.e., genital mutilations, prolonged swaddling, beatings for "obedience training"); extreme sexual repression of girls, boys, and women; high levels of pedophilia; severe taboos regarding female sexuality (breast-feeding, virginity, childbirth, menstruation); severe punishments against taboo violators; patriarchal domination of marriages, childbirth, descent, and inheritance rules; high levels of child abuse and spousal abuse; high levels of social hierarchy, with emphasis upon class, castes, and slavery; strong religious authority; a dominant military caste; and emphasis on group superiority and the need for conquest. Both males and females, it should be noted, become willing participants in the entire system of patristic culture. At its fundament, patrism works to destroy maternal-infant and male-female sexual bonding, and out of this destruction comes the sadistic and violent impulses later organized for socially approved discharge through various social institutions. Patrism is incorporated into belief systems and traditions, and therefore rationalized by ordinary people

and carried forward, generation after generation, in spite of the social turmoil and deadly consequences to its own advocates. An example of the most extreme patristic culture would be the Wahhabi Islamic Bedouins, who later formed the misogynistic and violent nation of Saudi Arabia.

2. *Matrism*, characterized by gentle, pleasure-oriented, and indulgent treatment of babies and children; equal status for women, who control their own marriage and fertility decisions; an absence of pedophilia; sexual freedom for the unmarried and for women as well as men; matrilineal descent and inheritance rules; absence of child or spouse abuse; lack of significant social hierarchy; absence of castes or slavery; lack of religious extremism; a part-time and purely defensive military structure; and low levels of violence. Matrism appears directed, at its fundament, toward protecting and preserving maternal-infant and male-female sexual bonding, thereby supporting nurturing, cooperative, and pleasure-directed impulses which generate a genuinely civil and peaceful society. Examples of the most extremely matristic culture would be the Trobriand Islanders of Melanesia,[6] the Musou of Southwestern China,[7] and the Muria of India.[8] These societies were sexually free, but not pornographic; nor were they attracted to the kinds of sexual distortions seen among the repressed patrist cultures around the world (i.e., fetish-driven "sexual swingers" and pedophiles). Also, the prejudicial suggestion that such cultures were intellectually retarded as a consequence of genuine sexual freedom needs to be challenged. They were not some kind of "cultural black hole" in history, but instead the creative innovators and geniuses of history, just as the more matristically inclined individuals within any culture are more likely to be the creative inventors, architects, writers, musicians, and so forth. The ancient Anasazi culture of the southwestern United States, the Harappa of the Indus Valley, the pre-Dynastic Chinese villages, and the ancient Minoan society of the eastern Mediterranean are cases in point. In all those cases, culture and daily life were characterized by artistically rich and technologically innovative conditions, with a free mingling of the sexes; relatively equal wealth distribution; an absence of significant war weaponry, fortifications, or temple architecture; and an absence of big-man rulers or slaves, as determined through examination of graves. They also lacked skeletal evidence for wife beating or within-group violence. From all indications, they appear to have been matristic, overwhelmingly peaceful, yet creative, artful, productive, and inventive. The reader is referred to my original writings for clarification on these essential points.

We may then correctly view the matristic peoples of the world as the truly civilized ones, who were progressively exterminated, transformed, pushed aside, or assimilated, in a 6,000-year-long global epidemic of patristic violence.

CROSS-CULTURAL EVALUATIONS

With the above definitions in hand and supported by many real-world examples, from my readings and fieldwork, I undertook a standard cross-cultural review of a regionally balanced selection of 400 different native aboriginal world cultures, using 63 different social variables indicative of patrist culture taken from Textor's *A Cross-Cultural Summary*.[9] Of these 63 variables, 95% were shown to be *positively correlated* with each other, with moderate to very high levels of statistical significance (where p ~.05 to p ~.001). The three negatively correlated variables were shown to be the consequence of miscoding or other factors which made them completely understandable from within the context of Reich's theory. This was substantial confirmation for my approach, and the same cultural data were then evaluated regionally.

Several histograms of regional behaviors were constructed, first from the data of Textor, and second from the larger *Ethnographic Atlas* database of George Peter Murdock,[10] which encompasses 1,170 different native aboriginal cultures. These data, from both Murdock and Textor, did not include modern European-derived cultures, such as Canada, the United States, Mexico, Brazil, and so on. For Africa, Asia, Oceania, and the Americas, the data used in my study reflect pre-European, precolonial conditions as closely as possible. Each of the 1,170 cultures was evaluated separately for the percentage of 15 different cultural variables that could be classified as either "patrist" or "matrist" in character. The methodology and list of 15 variables are given below. This percentage figure, for each individual culture, was then organized into regional histograms; these are given in Table 8.1 and clearly show a geographical pattern where the peoples of the Old World show higher levels of patristic authoritarianism and violence than the peoples of Oceania, North America, and South America.[11]

Table 8.2 gives the average *percent patrist* values for the different regions indicated in the Murdock histograms, as well as the number of cultures which appear in the upper and lower third of the percent patrist categories, respectively.

These data indicate that the Old World regions of Africa, Circum-Mediterranean, and Eurasia contain more than 95% of all the world's

TABLE 8.1. NUMBER OF CULTURES WITH A GIVEN PERCENT PATRIST CULTURE (BASED ON MURDOCK DATA, WITH 1,170 CULTURES AND 15 VARIABLES)

		Africa	Circum Mediter.	East Eurasia	Insular Pacific	North America	South America
Extreme Patrist	94						
	92						
	90	2	4		Number of cultures with a given percent patrist value		
	88	5	9	1			
	86						
	84	5	19	1	= mean value		
	82						
	80	10	12	3			
	78	17	17	6	2		
	76						
	74	51	14	5	2	1	1
	72						
	70	57	19	5	1		
	68	72	15	10	6		1
	66						
	64	50	8	10	4	2	2
	62						
	60	34	5	11	8	1	1
Percent	58	41	4	8	8	5	1
Patrist	56						
Behavior	54	24	3	8	11	2	1
	52						
1170	50	16	5	9	12	13	7
Cultures	48						
	46						
	44	9	2	3	13	17	4
	42						
	40	4	5	6	19	21	5
	38	1	1	1	10	23	4
	36						
	34	2	2	1	9	19	7
	32						
	30	1	5	3	9	27	12
	28		1	4	8	26	9
	26						
	24	3	2	4	2	25	10
	22						
	20		2	2	2	19	12
	18		1	2	8	26	7
	16						
	14	1	1		2	15	4
	12						
	10			2		20	5
	8					5	2
	6						
Extreme	4					3	1
Matrist	2						
	0						

TABLE 8.2. PERCENT PATRIST VALUES AND AVERAGE NUMBER
OF CULTURES FALLING WITHIN UPPER AND LOWER THIRDS
OF PERCENT PATRIST SCALE, BY REGION

Region	% Patrist Values	Upper Third Extreme Patrist	Lower Third Extreme Matrist
Africa	65%	219	5
Circum-Mediterranean	67%	109	12
East Eurasia	55%	26	17
Insular Pacific (Oceania)	41%	11	31
North America	29%	1	166
South America	30%	2	62

"extreme patrist" cultures (those found in the upper third [~66%] of the Table 8.1 regional histograms). By contrast, Oceania and the Americas held around 87% of all the world's "extreme matrist" cultures (those found in the lower third [~66%] of the Table 8.1 histograms).

Another set of histograms was also developed from the 400-culture sample of Textor, using a database of 63 different social variables. This second set of histograms, while not reproduced here, yielded results nearly identical to those in Table 8.1. These findings alone are a blow against the idea that Native Americans, or the Islanders in Oceania, were "just as violent and authoritarian" as those from the Old World. Clearly they were not, and this point was underscored even more dramatically once the various data were mapped.

As mentioned above, each of the 1,170 different cultures in the Murdock data were evaluated in terms of 15 different variables to construct the Table 8.1 histograms of regional behaviors. These variables are given in Table 8.3.

GEOGRAPHICAL EVALUATIONS: THE WORLD
BEHAVIOR MAP

Each of these 15 variables, along with a few others (i.e., infant cranial deformation and swaddling, female genital mutilations) was individually plotted on world maps, showing nearly identical geographical distributions. A composite map was also constructed, in the following manner. Latitude

TABLE 8.3. FIFTEEN VARIABLES USED TO EVALUATE
THE 1,170 DIFFERENT CULTURES

Variable	Present/Absent
Female premarital sex taboo	Present
Postpartum sexual taboo	Present
Segregation of adolescent boys	Present
Male genital mutilations	Present
Bride price	Present
Class stratification	Present
Caste stratification	Present
Slavery	Present
Belief in a high god, active in human affairs	Present
Polygamous family organization	Present
Patrilocal family organization	Present
Patrilineal descent	Present
Patrilineal land inheritance	Present
Patrilineal movable property inheritance	Present
Cognitive kin groups (which erode patrilineality)	Absent

and longitude values were obtained for each of the 1,170 cultures, allowing their placement on the world map. All computations and plotting were eventually undertaken by computer methods, using a special program I wrote for the procedure. If a culture tested "yes" on all 15 of the Table 8.3 variables, it received a maximum (100%) patrist designation. If "no" on all 15, it received a minimum (0%) patrist designation. In practice, and as shown in Table 8.1, cultures within any given region were distributed over a spectrum of values, from low to high, but with clear regional differences. Once each culture could be located on the world map, all cultures falling within a region bounded by a 5° × 5° block of latitude and longitude then had their percent patrist values averaged together. Those 5° × 5° block averages were then mapped, and from this came the World Behavior Map.

WORLD BEHAVIOR MAP

The World Behavior Map identifies various regions according to their relative levels of percent patrism, as defined above. This map shows a core region of high percent patrism, or patriarchal-authoritarian cul-

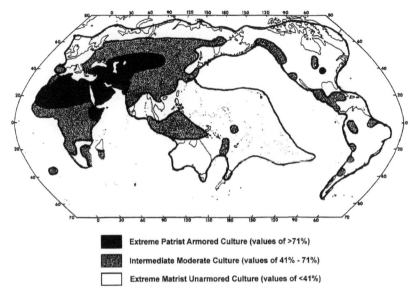

Extreme Patrist Armored Culture (values of >71%)

Intermediate Moderate Culture (values of 41% - 71%)

Extreme Matrist Unarmored Culture (values of <41%)

FIGURE 8.1. *The World Behavior Map. For the period roughly between 1840 and 1960, as reconstructed from aboriginal cultural data given in Murdock's* Ethnographic Atlas *(1967), with minimal historical interpretation.*

ture, across the large desert belt of North Africa, the Middle East, and into Central Asia. This geographical region, characterized both by a high degree of patrist culture and a harsh desert environment, was given the name Saharasia. The map also shows that as one moves away from Saharasia, human culture becomes more matristic. Saharasia proper is surrounded by a belt of intermediate human culture, roughly halfway between the extremes of patrism and matrism. Finally, in Oceania and the New World, one finds a larger background of more generally matristic culture, as detailed in Table 8.2. The same is true for the southern tips of Africa and India, for Southeast Asia and Island Asia—except for Islamic regions—and for the high Arctic fringe of Asia. Islands of intermediate and occasional high levels of patrism are found in Oceania along trade routes, and in the New World along or within close proximity to the coasts, as well as at interior locations along navigable rivers.

By any standard, this is a highly structured, nonrandom geographical pattern that reflects historical epochs of mass migrations, outward expansions, and military conquests, as well as progressive contact diffusion of culture as mechanisms for the spreading of violent patrism, from its original starting places within Saharasia proper, after c. 5000–4000 BCE. A full discussion of these historical processes has already been given in my other publications, and is not the focus of this paper. But cultural conditions in the New World, I believe, can only be understood from this perspective.

POINTS FOR CONSIDERATION REGARDING THE WORLD BEHAVIOR MAP

Importance of Historical Context

Given the problem of cultural mixing within Europe by the early twentieth century, Murdock's European data includes only selected culturally isolated European villages and a few historical reconstructions. This isolated and reconstructed European cultural data does not reflect conditions at the beginning of the bloody twentieth century, but is suggestive of a more peaceful social condition in Europe at some much earlier time, prior to the widespread wars of empire and conquest which devastated the continent (but bypassing and sparing the isolated groups). This certainly gives the World Behavior Map an artificially low patristic value for Europe and emphasizes the importance of viewing the maps in their historical context.

The Centrality of Climate Change

Paleoclimatic evidence indicates that most of Saharasia was, prior to c. 4000 BCE, a relatively moist and well-watered grassland-savannah, with large rivers and huge freshwater lakes. It teemed with animal life, including giraffes, elephants, hippos, crocodiles, birds, mollusks, and other browsing and aquatic creatures. Bones and petroglyphs of such creatures are abundant across regions of Saharasia which are today totally dried up and lacking in all but the most meager and scarce plant and animal life. Human cultures also inhabited this large region, first as bands of hunter-gatherers then as agricultural, fishing, and pastoral communities, and still later as nomadic pastoralists who were, as the land progressively dried up in the course of massive desert formation, forced from cattle to goat and camel herding. A few early human settlements developed toward city-states within this large Saharasian region during the last stages of its wet period. Examples are Altyn Depe in Asia, Sumer and Ur in Mesopotamia, the Decapolis cities of the Levant, and both Egyptian and Garamantian regions of North Africa. All villages and cities of the Saharasian region finally succumbed to the dramatic effects of this massive climate change, either with the drying up of their water resources, leading to famine and mass migrations toward moister regions, or, if they had secure water resources from large rivers (i.e., the Nile and Tigris-Euphrates), they were eventually overwhelmed by an influx of increasingly violent and patristic peoples from surrounding drying desert regions. This period featured the most significant climate change and human mass migration to occur since the end of the Pleistocene Ice Age some eight millennia earlier, and it had dramatic consequences for emerging human cultures of the Old World. I have already provided evidence on how harsh, repeating, generations-long drought, desert spreading, famine, and starvation—with the attendant mass deaths, forced migrations, and social discord—would destroy the original nonviolent matristic social conditions and progressively drive a culture toward violent patrism.

High Matrism before Desert Spreading

My systematic review of archaeological and historical materials strongly suggested that prior to the onset of desert spreading within Saharasia (starting in Arabia, the Middle East, and Central Asia around 5000–4000 BCE), there were generally peaceful social conditions across most of the world, Old and New. Only isolated examples of human social violence and warfare exist in the archaeological record prior to that date, as evidenced in unambiguous destruction layers in settlements, war weaponry, fortification architecture, and human skeletons showing war wounds and violent deaths.

I have already summarized the major examples of pre-Saharasian archaeological evidence of violence, such as that found in Jebel Shabah, Jericho, Talheim-Schletz-Ofnet, and southeastern Australia. All the examples involve either a harsh early phase of desert/drought conditions or specific migratory paths of peoples who had abandoned such early deserts.

High Patrism and Old World Contact

Geographical distributions of behavior in North and South America show clear consequences of these Old World events, with the strong suggestion of pre-Columbian contacts to Old World cultures of high patrism. Figure 8.2 reproduces in larger scale the New World portions of the World Behavior Map. From this map, one can readily observe that matrism is the predominant behavioral characteristic, as one might expect from massive waves of early peaceful human groups arriving from an equally peaceful and matristic Old World at the close of the Pleistocene Ice Age, after c. 15,000 BCE. Peaceful migrations of matristic peoples would have continued, but increasingly after c. 4000 BCE, any such migrations would have shown a patristic and violent quality. In the Americas, patrism is shown to have existed in isolated clusters or regions, mostly along coastal regions, as one might expect from its being "transplanted" into the Americas after c. 3000 BCE by the arrival of more violent warrior-caste Ocean-navigating cultures from the Old World. In most cases, these warrior-invaders do not appear to have come in sufficient numbers to overwhelm or completely replace the preexisting cultures, but they surely would have arrived with superior weapons and the will to use them against other human beings, establishing themselves as the ruling castes, intermarrying and adopting many preexisting Native American cultural aspects in the process, while injecting a considerable dose of their own patrism. While controversial, there is a very large and growing body of evidence to support pre-Columbian contacts to the Old World states of kingship and empire. The evidence includes artifacts as well as artistic, architectural, and linguistic similarities, including correlated legends and myths on opposing sides of the Pacific and Atlantic Oceans. There are parallels between this artifactual and linguistic-artistic evidence, used to support pre-Columbian contacts, and my World Behavior Map. Some specific examples include the following:

1. Along the Pacific Northwest coast, social institutions such as cranial deformation, slavery, and other aspects of hierarchy and caste are known to have existed well before the arrival of Europeans, along with artistic motifs suggestive of early Dynastic Chinese influences. Large stone anchors, as used by Dynastic Chinese ships, have also been found off the Pacific coast of the Americas.
2. The large central-state empires of Mesoamerica and Peru show some of their earliest large settlements at coastal locations, with little or no cultural similarities to earlier or surrounding native populations. Early cities showing the earliest war weapons, with temples, fortifications, cranial deformations, human sacrifice, and other trappings of extreme patrism and violence, as well as an emphasis upon shipbuilding and fishing, contrast dramatically with earlier peaceful villages of hunter-gathering or early agriculture, lacking in such elements of violence and patrism. Pyramid building also appears as a part of this transplanted *Saharasian cultural complex*, which extends deep into the Mississippi River Valley, and always seems to carry with it, on both sides of the

ocean, the connotation of kings, warfare, social violence, and human sacrifice.

These and many more examples identified in my research are prima-facie evidence for the long-distance transoceanic transplantation of patristic violence into the New World, even during the centuries prior to Columbus. Columbus and all those who followed afterward certainly brought their own brands of patristic violence and cruelty into the New World, but it does not appear that they were the first to do so. Some of the more "grand constructions" of the New World were stimulated by early emigrants from the Old World—but the construction of large pyramids upon which human hearts were chopped out should rightfully force us to rethink their meaning, no less than Europeans should rethink the meaning of massive cathedrals, which up until the time of Napoleon were centers of political and military power, and sadistic cruelty directed against women and heretics, who most certainly perished in far greater numbers in auto-da-fés than did captives upon the Aztec pyramids. In my opinion, such pyramids and cathedrals are a testament to the human "edifice complex," which too often gravitates toward mass murder and domination, and are not necessarily something any culture should be proud of. They appear as historical monuments to old slave-empires, where the god-kings meant everything, and the ordinary person meant nothing. Indeed, mainstream history and archaeology too easily celebrate the "gold of the gods" and the glittering treasures and grave-goods of the ancient butcher-kings, with scant attention paid to those cultures which did not build huge stone monuments to dictators, nor mass armies to wage giant wars, for the poets to record heroically.

In a similar vein, this neglect by archaeology and history of ordinary people, and especially of women and children, parallels the overall neglect and too-often denigrating view of Indigenous Peoples of North America, almost in direct proportion to their more life-positive and peaceful attri-butes. Honest study of the more gentle and matristic elements of human history will require us to discard this emphasis on pyramids, gold, gods, and kings.

The ruins of the North American Anasazi, or "ancient ones," are more suggestive of a genuine High Culture and civilization, by comparison. Like the ancient Minoa and Harappa, such peaceful groups as those that built the Chaco Canyon complex were genuine innovators, architects, artists, workers, and organizers. But they appear to have been displaced by more aggressive and warlike patristic invader groups moving south within the desert Great Basin, a story which is repeated elsewhere in the New World, though not in such a widespread or systematic nature as seen in the Old World. Even the most aggressive and warlike of the Native American empire-building cultures (i.e., the Aztecs) never came close to the systematic murder and destruction seen at the hands of various Saharasian butcher-kings (e.g., Attila the Hun, Genghis Khan, Ivan the Terrible, Josef Stalin, Adolf Hitler, Mao Tse-Dung, Pol Pot, etc.). In fact, the overwhelming percentage of New World Native Peoples, even after all the trauma and destruction which followed Columbus, maintained significant elements of their original peace-oriented matristic cultures, all the way into the 1800s.

ARCHAEOLOGICAL EVALUATIONS

The major New World sites of violence and warfare, based on archaeological data and shown in Figure 8.2, reinforce the conclusions suggested by the World Behavior Map, which is based solely on anthropological data. The numbers in Figure 8.2 correspond to sites known to show clear and unambiguous evidence for pre-Columbian warfare and violence in the Americas:

1. *Southeastern Michigan, Riviere aux Vase, c. 1000–1300 CE.* Collection of several hundred skeletons showing signs of conflict and violence, predominantly against women.[12]
2. *Illinois, Norris Farms, pre-Columbian.* Substantial intergroup violence.[13]
3. *South Dakota, Crow Creek, c. 1300 CE.* Site of a tribal massacre of around 500 men, women and children, but with a deficit of reproductive-age females.[14]
4. *La Plata River Valley, Four Corners, c. 900–1300 CE.* Substantial nonlethal interpersonal violence, especially against females.[15]
5. *Santa Barbara Channel, Southern California, c. 1490 BCE or earlier to 1804 CE.* Collection of 753 remains, demonstrating healed nonlethal cranial vault fractures in 128 (17%), with a similar high percentage of projectile point injuries and deaths.[16] Males were more affected than females, children, or the elderly, suggestive of combative roles.
6. *Central Southern Mexico, sites at Tetelpan, San Luis Potosi, and Mexico City, c. 500 BCE–1521 CE.* Substantial interpersonal and intergroup violence with organized warfare, human sacrifice, and possible ceremonial cannibalism.[17]
7. *Western Tennessee Valley, primarily late Archaic, c. 2500–500 BCE, possibly earlier.* Collection of several hundred skeletons showing signs of violent death and trophy taking.[18]

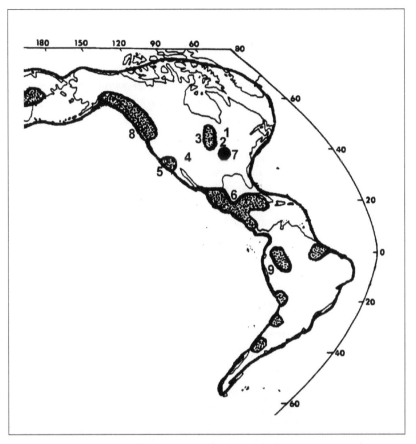

FIGURE 8.2.   *Major New World Sites of Violence and Warfare.*

Key: Shaded areas indicate relatively high patrist culture; numbers 1–9 indicate specific archaeological sites evidencing ongoing interpersonal or even extreme intergroup violence. See text for details.

8. *Southeastern Alaska, British Columbia, Northwest Pacific Coast, c. 3000 BCE–900 CE.* Substantial interpersonal violence with nonlethal skeletal injuries amplified eventually into organized warfare, defensive villages, especially after 1500 BCE.[19]

9. *Peru, coastal zone, Nasca and Ostra sites, c. 3000–1500 BCE.* Ostra Site: Early (c. 3000 BCE) ambiguous evidence of stone weapons which might as easily have been used for other purposes.[20] Later unambiguous Nasca artwork and mortuary evidence (c. 1500 BCE) of warfare and head-hunting, including mummified heads in a manner similar to later Jivaro and other head-hunting groups in adjacent regions.[21]

The map in Figure 8.2 demonstrates a close geographical correspondence and correlation between the archaeological sites for violence and warfare and the identified anthropological regions of intermediate or high patrism. New World archaeology thereby confirms anthropology by identifying isolated islands of violence within a larger ocean of peaceful conditions.

In Brian Ferguson's review of archaeological evidence of violence and warfare around the world, he notes a general absence of evidence of violence or warfare within many large collections of skeletons, including many from the Americas, which cover very long time periods.[22] Save for the examples mentioned above, available evidence suggests the Americas were a region of *generally* peaceful social conditions.

CONCLUSIONS

This evidence, drawn from history, archaeology, and anthropology, speaks clearly: The New World prior to Columbus was a far less violent place than the Old World. And it can be argued that, in spite of many terrible events which followed after Columbus, the New World remained a less violent place all the way down through the centuries because of its geographical isolation from the more violent Saharasian empires. And is not this overarching condition of relatively easygoing social relations and peaceful conditions exactly what was recorded by most of the early immigrants to the New World from Europe, including Columbus? While some of the Spanish chroniclers who came with the conquistadors in the early 1500s recorded violent patrism preexisting in Mesoamerica, others remarked on the innocence and gentleness of the early inhabitants, who were more often than not quickly taken advantage of. Modern American cultural myths, however distorted, record the generosity of the early Native American cultures, as in our Thanksgiving rituals, even if Manhattan was subsequently obtained for a box of trinkets, and even if some of those Indigenous Peoples eventually fought back against the creeping exploitation and loss of their lands. The democratic structures of the Iroquois made an indelible impression on Ben Franklin, whose thinking on the American Constitution developed from both European-reformist and Native American ideals. European emigrants very often took "American Indians" for their wives or husbands, blending the two great cultures in ways that today are an integral aspect of the American cultural experience. And while some of the European migrants moving West did often encounter exceedingly hostile receptions from patristic Native American groups, more frequently the western migrations were not harassed, and as experienced by Lewis and Clark, Europeans made their way West across the continent often with the help of Native Americans—at least during the initial period.

North and South America are littered with place-names which are a testament to Native People who subsequently vanished from modern existence: Massachusetts, Connecticut, and other matristic Indian names are now mixed with ancient Saharasian Old World place-names: Philadelphia, Athens, Troy. Predominantly, those Native Americans who had some preexisting patristic cultural elements, who obtained the horse and gun from the Europeans, who were familiar with battle tactics and could fight back, are the ones who survived the European onslaught after c. 1500, so that their descendants can still be found today. This is a situation which roughly parallels the history of the Old World and Oceania as well, where history and anthropology record remnant peaceful cultures only deep within the rainforests (e.g., Mbuti Pygmy, Muria of India), tucked away in remote mountain valleys (e.g., Musou in China), or on islands (Trobrianders) far removed from trade routes or regions of empire. The New World was the ultimate example of isolation from the warrior cultures of Saharasia.

This summary suggests the general vindication of the vast majority of Native American values and peoples as standing on the peace-making side of history. Certainly, not all Indigenous American cultures fit the peaceful images given in *Dances with Wolves*, but it is not an exaggeration to say that the majority did. If members of the "white man's culture," which has been far more patristic and violent, ridicule this assessment, they risk dismissing the more peace-oriented and democratic, egalitarian aspects of their own cultural history.

The debt of modern American society to the Indigenous Peoples of this land is large, and a more scientifically grounded appreciation of their culture—which reveals the largest region of Planet Earth where the larger percentage of humans lived peacefully so late into the historical period—can only make the world a better place.

NOTES

The epigraph to this chapter is drawn from the *Report and Journal of the Commission to Obtain Certain Concessions from the Sioux Indians*, 44th Congress, 2nd session, Senate Executive Document 9, #1718, p. 38.

1. James DeMeo, *Saharasia: The 4000 BCE Origins of Child Abuse, Sex-Repression, Warfare and Social Violence, In the Deserts of the Old World* (Ashland, Ore.: Natural Energy, 1998).

2. James DeMeo, "Update on Saharasia: Ambiguities and Uncertainties in *'War before Civilization,'" Pulse of the Planet* 5 (2002): 15–40.

3. Wilhelm Reich, *The Mass Psychology of Fascism* (New York: Orgone Institute Press, 1946).

4. James W. Prescott, "Body Pleasure and the Origins of Violence," *Futurist* (April 1975): 64–74.

5. DeMeo, *Saharasia*, 5, 51–68.

6. Bronislaw Malinowski, *The Sexual Life of Savages* (London: Routledge & Kegan Paul, 1932).

7. H. Göttner-Abendroth, *Matriarchat in Südchina* (Stuttgart: Kohlhammer Verlag, 1998).

8. Verrier Elwin, *The Muria and Their Ghotul* (Bombay: Oxford University Press, 1942).

9. R. Barry Textor, *A Cross-Cultural Summary* (New Haven, Conn.: HRAF Press, 1967).

10. George Peter Murdock, *Ethnographic Atlas* (Pittsburgh: University of Pittsburgh Press, 1967).

11. DeMeo, *Saharasia*, 73.

12. Richard G. Wilkinson, "Violence against Women: Raiding and Abduction in Prehistoric Michigan," in *Troubled Times: Violence and Warfare in the Past*, ed. Debra Martin and David Frayer (New York: Gordon and Breach, 1997), 21–43.

13. Ibid.

14. Ibid.

15. Debra Martin, "Violence against Women in the La Plata River Valley, A.D. 1000–1300," in Martin and Frayer, 45–75.

16. Patricia Lambert, "Patterns of Violence in Prehistoric Hunter-Gatherer Societies of Coastal Southern California," in Martin and Frayer, 84, 93–98; Philip Walker, "Wife Beating, Boxing and Broken Noses: Skeletal Evidence for the Cultural Patterning of Violence," in Martin and Frayer, 164.

17. Carmen Ma, Pijoan Lory, and Josefina Lory, "Evidence for Human Sacrifice, Bone Modification and Cannibalism in Ancient Mexico," in Martin and Frayer, 217–239.

18. Maria Ostendorf-Smith, "Osteological Indications of Warfare in the Archaic Period of the Western Tennessee Valley," in Martin and Frayer, 241–265.

19. Herbert Maschner, "The Evolution of Northwest Coast Warfare," in Martin and Frayer, 321–355.

20. John R. Topic, "The Ostra Site: The Earliest Fortified Site in the New World," in *Cultures in Conflict: Current Archaeological Perspectives*, ed. Diana C. Tkaczuk & Brian C. Vivian (Calgary: University of Calgary, 1989), 215–228.

21. Donald Proulx, "Nasca Trophy Heads: Victims of Warfare or Ritual Sacrifice," in Tkaczuk and Vivian, 73–85.

22. R. Brian Ferguson, "Violence and War in Prehistory," in Martin and Frayer, 332–334. Also see P. Gabriel, *The Culture of War: Invention and Early Development* (New York: Greenwood Press, 1990), 20–21.

ECOLOGICAL EVIDENCE OF
LARGE-SCALE SILVICULTURE
BY CALIFORNIA INDIANS

Lee Klinger

The previous chapter raises some serious questions. If we are not necessarily by our Indigenous nature a warring people, or if most of the original people of the Americas managed to live in relative peace, then why are we led to believe the opposite through literature, film, the academy, and popular discourse? Is it because we then are more likely to acquiesce to the existence of wars, trusting our leaders to decide which ones are for liberty or democratic ideals?

If such a design exists, then indeed cultural/educational hegemony is operating. Whether we are learning false histories about Indigenous People; or that Columbus was a hero; or not learning that true heroes like Helen Keller or Martin Luther King Jr. were avid antiwar activists, we tend to use this "knowledge" in ways that cause a blind form of common sense to support the policies of those in power. The current Iraq war may be a classic example of the ultimate effect.

In this chapter we are reminded that there is another war that profits those in power and also seems to benefit from a false history of Indigenous People and their ways of seeing the world. I refer to a war against the natural systems of the planet. For example, during just the first few years of George W. Bush's administration, hundreds of environmental protections were dissolved and some of the worst corporate polluters were placed in key environmental protection positions.[1] In supporting the claim that pre-contact Indigenous People devastated their natural environment, we are left to again trust that because of technology and American leadership, we have no reason to question the dominant worldview. Yet how difficult is it to see the corporate/government profit motive behind such hegemony? Robert Whelan expresses the dominant view in his book Wild in Woods: The Myth of the Noble Eco-Savage: *"The opposition of native wisdom to market forces is as familiar as it is wrong. Thus, in the cases where native peoples did practice sustainable use of resources it was because they had developed the institutions of private property and the market, often as a result of contact with white settlers."[2]*

In this chapter, Dr. Klinger gives us one of many examples revealing that the Indigenous perspective is in line with preserving our Earth for future generations. (Note: Although he refers to the distant past, there are also many examples of how Indigenous People today are working against great odds to stop the corporate, military, and government policies that are unnecessarily killing life on this planet, such as the Duwamish River Cleanup project, whose goal is to fix one of the most toxic sites in the nation in Seattle and King County.)

LUMINOUS Project Director Dr. Lee Klinger has worked in the fields of ecology, complexity, and Gaia for more than twenty years and is recognized as one of the world's leading scholars in earth systems science. His recent work at the Institute of Noetic Sciences has helped to expand human consciousness through revelations about the profound ecological wisdom of Indigenous People. His studies have taken him to all the major ecosystems of the earth, from arctic Alaska to central Africa, where the key stories of Gaia's metabolism are told. Dr. Klinger also helped to found the Gaia Society (now a part of the Geological Society of London) and served for several years as its Vice-Chair. He has held scholarly appointments at the National Center for Atmospheric Research, the University of Colorado, the University of Oxford, and the University of East London. He is currently a Senior Visiting Scholar with the Chinese Academy of Sciences, and serves on the Graduate Faculty of Eco-psychology at Naropa University.

The fieldwork here was supported, in part, by the Institute of Noetic Sciences and by the National Center for Atmospheric Research.

***

The Earth does not belong to us. We belong to the Earth.

—CHIEF SEATTLE

The native trees of California are famous for being among the oldest, largest, and tallest creatures in the world. Besides their great age and size, these trees possess various idiosyncrasies in their arrangements and shapes that are revealed in ecological surveys. Indeed, some characteristics, such as the extremely narrow and disjunct distribution of the giant Sequoia groves, appear to defy basic principles of population biology. When taken together, the odd features of California's ancient trees and forests present an anomalous situation that cannot be explained using our current ecological understanding of old-growth forests. It seems that unknown forces are at work in the older forests (those greater than 200 years in age) that defy the normal tendencies of nature. In this chapter I describe several abnormalities of California trees and forests recorded during ecological surveys in the Sierra Nevada foothills and Coast Ranges in 1997 and 2003. The described features are all plainly visible, expressed as gross variations in the appearance and distribution of the dominant trees and surrounding soils. In the search for a plausible and parsimonious explanation of these anomalies, I am drawn by previous experiences to consider the potent wisdom and ways of the Indigenous People.

THE SEQUOIA GROVES

The most massive of any tree species, the giant sequoia *(Sequoia giganteum)* is a California endemic found only in a handful of sites in the western foothills of the Sierras. For such a massive and dominating species, its narrow range (totaling only 14,410 ha) and highly disjunct distribution[3] are quite remarkable, especially if one considers that it is a pioneer species that reproduces best after fires.[4] In June and September of 2003 I investigated several giant sequoia sites in the Sierra Nevada foothills and observed that the trees grew in isolated, mono-dominant clusters (groves) separated by several kilometers of mixed conifer forest within which was seen not a single sequoia individual, seedlings and saplings included. The populations of trees in Muir, Giant Forest, Redwood Mountain, Grant, and Tuolumne Groves were all seen to be comprised almost solely of very large sequoia individuals each on the order of a thousand years or more in age. It has been shown that this kind of lop-sided demographic represents a population which, following a long period of proliferation in most of its current locales, now lacks sufficient recruitment of younger trees needed to maintain a viable population.[5] Despite the evidence from fire scars of many historical fire events,[6] it is puzzling that the regeneration of this fire-adapted species has been nearly absent for the past several hundred years in and around most sequoia groves.

Perhaps even more puzzling are the circular and semicircular arrangements of giant sequoias that were found in Muir and Redwood Mountain Groves. Whereas the many circles or "rings" formed by the coast redwood *(Sequoia sempervirens)* are attributed to the stump-sprouting behavior of that species, the giant sequoias are known to reproduce only from seed. Given the lack of a plausible mechanism for how a natural population of trees growing from seed could establish and maintain themselves in this way, the occurrence of tree circles and other orderly formations of *S. giganteum* is highly problematic. Even among the coast redwoods, stump-sprouting behavior cannot explain the many *large* circles (>10 m diameter), as no remnants of any massive former stumps can be found inside these circles.

The shapes and orientations of fire scars on many giant sequoias present another dilemma. In sloping terrain, fire scars typically form at the uphill base of a tree, places where fires smolder for extended periods due to fuels moving downslope and piling against the trunk.[7] In June of 1976 while fighting a large fire on Comforter Mountain near Boulder, Colorado, and again in June of 1979 while fighting a smaller fire near Brown's Lake on the Kenai peninsula of Alaska, I indeed noticed that fires tended to linger and smolder on the uphill sides of the larger trees. Yet, observations last year of giant sequoia trees on slopes revealed that downhill-side fire scars, which are rare or absent in other forests, were fairly common in the sequoia groves, and often with little or no sign of uphill scarring. Furthermore, many of these scars were huge (>10 m high) and bore evidence of multiple large fires, each of which burned only the downhill side of the trunks. This odd pattern of fire scarring was observed, as well, in coast redwoods at the Mill Creek, Esalen, and Samuel Taylor State Park sites (Table 9.1).

Most curious of all are the findings from Redwood Mountain Grove in September of 2003, where soils within a meter or two from the bases of several giant sequoia were found to contain a thin, white mineral horizon approximately 1 cm thick. The horizon was situated either within the O horizon or between the O and A horizons at depths of 10 to 20 cm. This white mineral horizon was not found in the soils located 10 m or so away from the trees. Similarly, white mineral layers were observed around several coast redwood trees in October of 2003 at Mill Creek and Esalen sites in Big Sur (Table 9.1). Here the layers were comprised of crushed shells, bones, and limestone. The origin of these lime-rich horizons cannot be explained by any known depositional sources or processes of soil genesis.

OAK SAVANNAS

The oak savannas of California are a dominant and defining feature of the state's landscape, characterized broadly as a scattering of trees, mostly oaks, throughout the native grasslands. The oaks occur as individual large trees or in clusters of a few, with broad canopies and thick trunks that indicate the trees are centuries old. Open grasslands adjacent to the oaks are in certain places distinctly terraced, especially on steeper slopes and in draws. Young trees are notably few or absent in oak savannas. As in the case of the giant sequoias, a predominance of old trees and a lack of regeneration means that the population of trees in these savannas is not sustainable, nor has it been sustainable for several hundred years. This abnormality in age structure is a concern, for instance, in the blue

TABLE 9.1. STUDY SITE COORDINATES AND VEGETATION TYPES

Site	Veg. Type	Obsv. Period	Latitude	Longitude	Elev. (m)
Sierra Foothills					
Muir Grove	Giant sequoia forest	June 2003	36°38.0'N	118°50.1'W	2080
Giant Forest	Giant sequoia forest	June 2003	36°45.1'W	118°45.6'W	2050
Grant Grove	Giant sequoia forest	Sept. 2003	36°44.9'W	118°55.0'W	1850
Redwood Mountain Grove	Giant sequoia forest	Sept. 2003	36°42.5'N	118°55.0'W	1850
Tuolumne Grove	Giant sequoia forest	June 2003	37°45.9'N	119°48.7'W	1860
China Garden	Oak-pine savanna	Sept. 2003	35°32.1'N	118°38.9'W	650
Latrobe Road	Oak savanna	June 1997	38°33.5'N	120°59.1'W	250
Coast Range					
Olompais[a]	Oak savanna	July 2003	38°10.5'N	122°36.4'W	170
Olompais	Oak-bay savanna	July 2003	38°10.6'N	122°36.5'W	110
Samuel Taylor State Park	Redwood forest	Aug. 2003	38°01.9'N	122°44.6'W	100
Esalen	Tan oak-redwood forest	Oct. 2003	36°08.6'N	121°39.2'W	30
Mill Creek	Redwood forest	Oct. 2003	36°00.2'N	121°28.2'W	650

[a]Designated as Mt. Burdell on modern maps.

oak savannas, where a problem of regeneration in the oaks is reported to be widespread.[8] On top of this is the concern lately that many of the larger oaks are experiencing elevated levels of mortality (e.g., sudden oak death). In the Sierra foothills, oak savannas dominated by interior live oak (*Quercus wislizeni*), valley oak (*Q. lobata*), and blue oak (*Q. douglasii*) were studied at the Latrobe Road site in June of 1997 and at the China Garden site in September of 2003. Coast Range oak savannas dominated by coast live oak (*Q. agrifolia*), valley oak (*Q. lobata*), and black oak (*Q. kelloggii*) were examined in July of 2003 at Olompais (Table 9.1). At all three sites the populations were comprised mostly of very old oaks (~300+ years) around which were observed little or no regeneration, indicating that the population of oaks in the savannas is clearly not being sustained. Unlike other savannas and woodlands that I've studied, where in the course of succession oaks are eventually replaced by pines or other evergreen species,[9] succession at these sites appears to be arrested at the oak stage. A recurring wildfire regime could account for the maintenance of oaks in the savannas by creating conditions that favor the early-successional tree species (e.g., oaks). Still, the lack of regeneration, as well as the presence of bay laurel (*Umbellularia californica*), Pacific madrone (*Arbutus menziesii*), Monterey cypress (*Cupressus macrocarpa*), and several species of pines (*Pinus* spp.) seems to rule out genetics as a cause.

Upon closer inspection, more oddities appear in the oak savannas, like scatterings of seashells under the trees. A cursory examination of soils beneath several large oaks at Olompais turned up a fair number of shell fragments, mainly in the upper 15 cm, though no obvious layers of shell material appeared in the soil. Also, on the trunks of several large valley oaks and coast live oaks at Olompais were observed peculiar white crusts covering the bark. Not to be confused with certain whitish-colored crustose lichens, these white crusts are curious in that no mosses, liverworts, or other such acid-loving organisms grew on them, even when found on the north sides of the trees. The distribution of these white crusts revealed that, in places, they were slowly being dissolved by waters flowing down the trunk. Positive tests for reaction using a 1 M solution of HCl indicated the crusts were, curiously, rich in lime.

NATIVE AMERICAN AGRICULTURE

The interpretation of these unusual features of sequoias, oaks, and other ancient trees of California presents a formidable problem as they cannot be explained using our current ecological knowledge of natural processes and forces. This assumes, of course, that the unusual distributions, shapes, and behaviors of the trees are mainly the result of "natural" influences (i.e., those not involving humans). On the other hand, we know that throughout the Americas people have for thousands of years been heavily engaged in the care and cultivation of their lands.[10] In a comprehensive work on the topic of presettlement agriculture in North America, Doolittle presents clear evidence that the indigenous people engaged in a number of traditional farming and gardening activities.[11] Fields and plots were burned, drained, mounded, terraced, tilled, weeded, fertilized, and mulched; canals and aqueducts were built for irrigation; crops were sown, thinned, and transplanted; and orchard trees were pruned and coppiced. Therefore, it is prudent to consider here the possibility that the anomalies reported above are the result of intentional and purposeful cultivation practices by California tribes over many centuries. It is well established that the California Indians employed fire in the management of their lands.[12] Grasslands were regularly burned in order to remove brush cover and to encourage the growth and regeneration of the native grasses and forbs used by the Indians for both food and fiber.[13] Besides burning, the people employed a variety of other agricultural techniques, including irrigating, pruning, selective harvesting, sowing, terracing, tilling, transplanting, and weeding. Knowledge of this comes from documentary, ethnographic, and archeological evidence found in published works on the Cahuilla, Chumash, Kamia, Kumeyaay, Miwok, Paiute, and other California tribes.[14] With regard to the practice of plant husbandry, the California Indians were considered "masters."[15]

This challenges the conventional notion of native peoples being primarily hunter-gatherers: many of the major tribes in California were clearly well engaged in agriculture and silviculture. Therefore, if we consider that all the native people of the state probably had access to the knowledge and skills of agriculture and so likely practiced agriculture to some degree, then perhaps we should ponder how an array of traditional cultivation techniques may have affected the California landscape. In doing so we quickly see that many of the ecological anomalies described above can be attributed in a sensible way to the recent secession of age-old agricultural activities by the native peoples. With the understanding that the harvest of acorns was what largely fed the people, the curious gnarly forms of the oaks and other nut-bearing trees should perhaps be viewed and appreciated as the culmination of seven generations or more of caring acts.[16]

The age-related dimorphisms of oaks and other "crop" trees are explainable, as well, by certain plant husbandry practices of the local Indians. The crooked and many-boled forms of older oak cohorts, with large spreading branches and with bent and trailing boles, are probably the result of coppicing, pruning, and training (altering stem growth using ropes and stakes) by native people mainly for the purposes of maximizing the size of the tree canopy and, thus, the production of acorns. The low, lateral-tending branches also would have greatly facilitated the gathering of the acorns. Oak cohorts established since white settlement were not traditionally tended and so have taken on normal, more upright and unbranched growth forms. The individuals of the older cohorts that still thrive today should plainly reveal these two modes of land management in their architecture, an earlier cultivated phase expressed as highly branched and lateral-tending forms, and a recent, nonmanipulated phase seen as more normal, upward forms attributable to the cessation of plant husbandry at the time of white settlement. It would seem that both the cohort-related and the developmental dimorphic features described here can be explained by the shift in land management practices that occurred with white settlement.

Many of the anomalies seen in the giant sequoia and redwood groves also appear to be attributable to manipulations by the native people, though in this case perhaps not for agricultural purposes. While tannins extracted from the giant sequoia were used in the tanning of hides, and the bark of the redwood was used in the construction of lodges, these tall trees may have served more of a ceremonial or ritual purpose. The circular and semicircular arrangements of the giant sequoias, and in some cases coast redwoods, are strongly indicative of intentional planting by the native people. Perhaps instead of building them, the Miwok decided several thousand years ago to grow their temples, by planting and tending sequoias and redwoods in sacred groves. The downhill-side fire scars as well as the excessive size of these scars indicates that the use of fire in tending these groves included the setting of virtual conflagrations at the bases of many sequoias. It seems strange, at first, why the native people would have intended to scar these sacred trees severely and repeatedly in the same place on the trunk. But in noticing how the trees respond to scarring, by growing thick stocks of scar tissue on either side of the fire scar, one can see that this regrowth around the base would help to stabilize the trunks, thus preventing the tall sequoias and redwoods from being knocked over by winds or by falling trees. Furthermore, after repeated burning, certain trunks are seen to become hollow, allowing access to the center or "heart" of the tree. These fire-carved cavities at the base of the sequoia and redwood trees served, and continue to serve, as sacred places for native rituals and initiations.

The above explanations rest on the assumption that the California tribes possessed, collectively, the knowledge, tools, and abilities necessary to alter many thousands of trees in the landscape in a prescribed way. In my view there is good circumstantial evidence indicating that this assumption is quite plausible, though not enough to say it is probable. The probability that this assumption is correct depends on whether evidence exists for landscape-scale agriculture by California Indians. In the search for that evidence let me consider carefully the latest theories and findings in the field of landscape ecology, then return to the questions regarding seashells and white crusts.

GAIA THEORY AND FOREST HEALTH

The connection of native people with the anomalous shell fragments appears to be profound, but it only becomes obvious in the light of a holistic understanding of the complex behaviors of ecosystems. The holistic or *systems* approach in ecology is grounded in a solid body of theory that is ultimately tied to the well-known concepts of complexity and Gaia.[17] The idea that the earth and its ecosystems are living systems, which is the main tenet of Gaia theory, represents fundamentally the same view that indigenous people in the Americas and elsewhere have long held—that all of nature is alive.[18]

The large volume of studies on lime treatments of declining forests together indicate that that addition of lime-rich minerals clearly improves the health of trees,[19] improves root and mycorrhizae growth,[20] improves soil fertility,[21] reduces levels of toxic metals in soils,[22] and reduces moss cover.[23] In short, remineralization appears to slow or arrest the aging process in ecosystems. The native people could well have known this by observing how the ash from fires accomplished this, and so applied the knowledge in ways that benefited the many edible plants and trees. However, could they also have known that, in lieu of fire, one can effectively ameliorate systemic acidification and maintain a healthy soil through the periodic application of lime-rich minerals?

MORTARS, MOUNDS, AND MIDDENS

It may not be obvious at first, but if we assume that the answer to the above question is *yes*, then immediately a whole host of long-standing problems involving bedrock mortars, shell middens, and the association of these with large trees begins to make perfect sense. The first step in seeing the ecological wisdom of the ancients is to recognize that the many types of refuse mounds and middens, including shell middens, bone middens, and rock middens originate not from the gradual accumulation of the waste products of daily living, such as food remains, ashes from cooking fires, and broken pots and tools, but rather from the intentional stockpiling of gathered or recycled lime-rich materials for use as mineral fertilizers. Strategically located for the purposes of access and trade, these middens are to be found in those regions of the world where the trees were heavily tended. A village of considerable size would have had to flourish for most of the 2,500 years of the mound's existence in order to generate so much refuse. Yet, no evidence of such a village has been uncovered at or anywhere near the site. Nelson also found evidence that the mound had periodically been excavated or reworked during its formation, and that much of the substructure of the mound was likely "not in the place of its original deposition."[24]

An important question that keeps arising about shell middens is: *Why were the native people consuming so much mollusk meat?* The nutritional value of mussels is not particularly high,[25] and it is not uncommon for mollusks to become toxic at certain times of the year. It has been suggested that rather than eating them all, the native people of the California coast may have smoked the mussels and traded them with interior tribes.[26] Similar to other sites containing shell middens, the Emeryville excavations have produced very little in the way of vegetal matter such as seeds, grains, husks, and other kinds of crop food refuse. This scarcity of plant refuse is a key reason why archaeologists conclude that the native people here and elsewhere, whose diets and habits the middens are thought to reflect, were simple hunter-gatherers. The apparent lack of plant foods in their diets is interpreted to mean that the native people either had no knowledge of agriculture or, having had the knowledge, chose not to conduct it. This assumes, of course, that the middens are indeed refuse piles.

The Emeryville mound is only one of hundreds of shell mounds recorded in and around San Francisco Bay on lands formerly occupied by the Ohlone. The Coast Miwok, too, built many shell mounds in the bay area. Along Miller Creek several kilometers south of Olompais are found six shell middens of significant size comprised of shell and bone fragments, charcoal, and heat-fractured rock.[27] Mortar fragments were reported to be common, while clusters of whole mortars were found at sites adjacent. Another midden located a short distance north of Olompais was found to be closely associated with several bedrock mortars.[28] This midden was comprised mainly of mollusk shell fragments, splintered mammal bones (including fragments of human cranium), chert and obsidian flakes, pieces of quartz, various stone, bone, and shell artifacts, and a single plant remain (a carbonized pinenut). Shellfish species in the midden were reported to be "out of place in this habitat."

CONCLUSION

Drawing from the observations of odd shapes and distributions of old-growth trees, from the findings of shells and shell layers in the surface soils around the largest of these trees, and from the many published reports on related activities and practices of the native people, I conclude that the California Indians of the Sierra Nevada and Coast Ranges were not simple hunter-gatherers, but, instead, were sophisticated farmers who practiced sustainable silviculture that involved the cultivation of oaks, buckeyes, bays, pines, and other nut-bearing trees in vast orchards. Besides cultivating the trees, one can see that the native people terraced many of the hillsides to prevent erosion and increase water infiltration, and gathered shells and quarried rocks to stock the various middens with the materials needed for making mineral fertilizers. Standing as convincing testimony to the cultivation skills of the native people are the mighty coast redwoods and the giant sequoias, the largest trees in the world, which were apparently planted many thousands of years ago and have been carefully tended ever since. Today this ancient wisdom casts new light on a promising cure for sudden oak death and many other tree decline syndromes simply by improving mineral nutrition and, thus, growing healthier trees able to resist attacks by pests and diseases.

ACKNOWLEDGMENTS

The author wishes to express a sincere thanks to those who assisted me in the field, including Ava Klinger, Sonya Klinger, Chris Geron, Bill Baugh, Jennifer Zabel, Clarke Bugbee, Ariana DeToro-Forlenza, Daniel Brooke, Charlene Farrell, Ralph Zingaro, Kerri Ewald, Erika Pedersen, and Leigh Noë, as well as to Dr. Steve Emerman and Dr. Joel Kreisberg for comments on the manuscript.

NOTES

1. Robert F. Kenney Jr., *Crimes against Nature: How George W. Bush and His Corporate Pals Are Plundering the Country and Hijacking Our Democracy* (San Francisco: HarperCollins, 2004).

2. Robert Whelan, *Wild in Woods: The Myth of the Noble Eco-Savage* (London: Institute of Economic Affairs, Environment Unit, 1999), 37.

3. C. Phillip Weatherspoon, *Giant sequoia*, www.na.fs.fed.us/spfo/pubs/silvics_manual/volume_1/sequoiadendron/giganteum.htm. Accessed July 5, 2004.

4. Nathan L. Stephenson, *Long-Term Dynamics of Giant Sequoia Populations: Implications for Managing a Pioneer Species*, USDA Forest Service General Technical Report PSW-151, 1994.

5. Philip W. Rundel, "Community Structure and Stability in the Giant Sequoia Groves of the Sierra Nevada, California," *American Midland Naturalist* 85 (1971): 478–492; Stephenson, *Long-Term Dynamics of Giant Sequoia Populations*.

6. Tim W. Swetnam, R. Touchan, C. H. Baisan, A. C. Caprio, and P. M. Brown, "Giant Sequoia Fire History in Mariposa Grove, Yosemite National Park," in *Yosemite Centennial Symposium Proceeding—Natural Areas and Yosemite: Prospects for the Future* (Denver, 1990).

7. Richard P. Guyette and M. A. Spetich, "Fire History of Oak-Pine Forests in the Lower Boston Mountains, Arkansas, USA," *Forest Ecology and Management* 180 (2003): 463–474; M. A. Finney, *Development of Fire Scar Cavities on Old-Growth Coast Redwood*, www.cnr.berkeley.edu/~jleblanc/www/redwood/rdwd-developm.html. Accessed July 5, 2004.

8. Tedmund J. Swiecki and E. Bernhardt, "Understanding Blue Oak Regeneration," *Fremontia* 26 (1998): 19–26.

9. Lee F. Klinger, Q.-J. Li, A. B. Guenther, J. P. Greenberg, B. Baker, and J.-H. Bai, "Assessment of Volatile Organic Compound Emissions from Ecosystems of China," *Journal of Geophysical Research* 107.D21, 4603 (2001).

10. R. Douglas Hunt, *Indian Agriculture in America* (Lawrence: University Press of Kansas, 1987); W. M. Denevan, *Cultivated Landscapes of Native Amazonia and the Andes* (Oxford: Oxford University Press, 2001).

11. William E. Doolittle, *Cultivated Landscapes of Native North America* (Oxford: Oxford University Press, 2000).

12. Kat Anderson, "Native Californians as Ancient and Contemporary Cultivators," in *Before the Wilderness: Environmental Management by Native Californians*, ed. T. C. Blackburn and K. Anderson (Menlo Park: Ballena Press, 1993), 151–174; J. Timbrook, J. R. Johnson, and D. D. Earle, "Vegetation Burning by the Chumash," in Blackburn and Anderson, 117–150.

13. Henry T. Lewis, "Patterns of Indian Burning in California: Ecology and Ethnohistory," in Blackburn and Anderson, 55–116.

14. Robert F. Heizer and Albert B. Elsasser, 1980. *The Natural World of the California Indians* (Berkeley: University of California Press, 1980); Anderson, "Native Californians"; H. W. Lawton, P. J. Wilke, M. DeDecker, and W. M. Mason, "Agriculture among the Paiute of Owens Valley," in Blackburn and Anderson, 329–378; F. Shipek, "Kumeyaay Plant Husbandry: Fire, Water, and Erosion Control Systems," in Blackburn and Anderson, 379–388; M. K. Anderson and M. J. Moretto, *Native American Land-Use Practices and Ecological Impacts. Sierra Nevada Ecosystem Project: Final Report to Congress, Vol. II, Assessments and Scientific Basis for Management Options* (Davis: University of California, Centers for Water and Wildland Resources, 1996).

15. Doolittle, *Cultivated Landscapes of Native North America*, 462.

16. Helen McCarthy, "Managing Oaks and the Acorn Crop," in Blackburn and Anderson, 213–228.

17. James Lovelock, *The Ages of Gaia* (New York: Norton, 1995); Lee F. Klinger, "Gaia and Complexity" (chapter 16), in *Scientists Debate Gaia: The Next Century*, ed. S. H. Schneider, J. R. Miller, E. Crist, and P. J. Boston (Cambridge: MIT Press, 2004), 187–200.

18. Lee F. Klinger and Q.-J. Li, "Gaia in China," *Gaia Circular* (winter 2001/spring 2002): 13.

19. Timothy R. Wilmot, David S. Ellsworth, and M. T. Tyree, "Base Fertilization and Liming Effects on Nutrition and Growth of Vermont Sugar Maple Stands," *Forest Ecology and Management* 84 (1996): 123–134.

20. Andrew P. Coughlan, Yolande Dalpe, Line Lapointe, and Yves Piche, "Soil pH-Induced Changes in Root Colonization, Diversity, and Reproduction of Symbiotic Arbuscular Mycorrhizal Fungi from Healthy and Declining Sugar Maple Forests," *Canadian Journal of Forest Research* 30 (2000): 1543–1554.

21. A. Hindar, F. Kroglund, E. Lydersen, A. Skiple, and R. Hogberget, "Liming of Wetlands in the Acidified Lake Roynelandsvatn Catchment in Southern Norway: Effects on Stream Water Chemistry," *Canadian Journal of Fisheries and Aquatic Sciences* 53 (1996): 985–993.

22. J. H. Graham and D. P. H. Tucker, "Role of Calcium in Amelioration of Copper Phytotoxicity for Citrus," *Soil Science* 155 (1993): 211–218.

23. Lief Hallbacken and L. Q. Zhang, "Effects of Experimental Acidification, Nitrogen Addition and Liming on Ground Vegetation in a Mature Stand of Norway Spruce (Picea abies (L.) Karst.) in SE Sweden," *Forest Ecology and Management* 108 (1998): 201–213.

24. Nels C. Nelson, "Shellmounds of the San Francisco Bay Region," *University of California Archeology and Ethnology* 7 (1909): 361–426.

25. Evan Peacock, "Shellfish Use during the Woodland Period in the Middle South," in *The Woodland Southeast*, ed. David G. Anderson and Robert C. Mainfort Jr. (Tuscaloosa: University of Alabama Press, 2002), 444–460.

26. Heizer and Elsasser, *The Natural World of the California Indians.*

27. Charles Slaymaker, *The Material Culture of Cotomko'tca, a Coast Miwok Tribelet in Marin County, California*, MAPOM Papers No. 3, Miwok Archeological Preserve of Marin, San Rafael, 1977.

28. Thomas Fulling King, *Excavations at Site CA-SON-392, near Petaluma, California*, www.californiahistory.com/reports01/repo012.html. Accessed June 28, 2003.

Chapter 10

PRESERVING THE WHOLE:

PRINCIPLES OF SUSTAINABILITY IN

MI'KMAW FORMS OF COMMUNICATION

Trudy Sable

Reinforcing Dr. Klinger's silvicultural research, Trudy Sable shows, through an analysis of Mi'kmaw dances and stories, how Indigenous cultures revere the sacred relationship between Mother Earth and humanity, a relationship central to most Indigenous worldviews and one that makes the concept of sustainability a logical imperative. In describing the Mi'kmaw relationship to the environment through their dances and stories, Trudy underscores the idea that Indigenous cultures embraced no dualism between humans and other life forms and recognized consciousness in all. Considering that even the most progressive reforms in education, such as constructivism or critical pedagogy, all but ignore this interconnectedness by maintaining an overly anthropocentric view of the world, there is much to learn from this piece about how we are part, and not master, of universal processes and cycles.

Dr. Sable is the Director, Labrador Project, Gorsebrook Research Institute at Saint Mary's University Halifax, Nova Scotia, a collaboration between the Innu Nation of Labrador and Environment Canada, whose goal is to investigate incorporating both Innu and Western scientific perspectives into research. Since 1989 she has dedicated her work to First Nations and Inuit issues and to the development of a cross-cultural dialogue in the teaching of science. She has published extensively on issues of Indigenous Knowledge, teaches in the Department of Anthropology at Saint Mary's University, and sits on committees for the University of the Arctic. She has written extensively on her research with the Mi'kmaw.

***

It has always intrigued me that so much of what is written on pre-contact, oral cultures is based on what was previously written. Alternatively, it could be based on archaeological interpretations of the remnants of material culture. These artifacts can offer a gold mine of information, but only on what is found, and based on interpretations made from another faraway time and place. My own research into Mi'kmaw[1] culture began this way, in the early missionary documents, digging through archival research, anthropological and archaeological studies, meeting with scholars of the culture. And then, I leapt. I began visiting reserves, sitting around kitchen tables sipping tea, sitting in smoky bingo halls, dancing at powwows, doing sweats, and walking and traveling through the landscape with Mi'kmaw friends. This is where I came to understand that history is not just about words, but about contexts and relationships, and it is about rhythms.

As I researched the dances and legends of the Mi'kmaq of Eastern Canada, I began to discover a worldview based on the recognition of the connectedness and interdependence of all things in the natural world. Today, we might call this the fundamental view of ecology, the basic foundation for environmental sustainability. It is embedded in Mi'kmaw language, dances, songs, and legends. As with so many oral cultures, these expressive forms act as "libraries," hidden within the memories of elders, in features of the landscape as it is recalled and as it still exists. These "libraries" were not immediately evident to me as a Western researcher. If one leaves the history books and looks toward other means of knowledge storage, one can begin to appreciate that the Mi'kmaw language, dances, stories, and songs are a warehouse of valuable information. They are probably the closest anyone can come to understanding the biophysical environment of the Atlantic Provinces of Canada as it existed in pre-contact and early contact periods. At the same time, this "scientific" information is embedded in a larger narrative about how the Mi'kmaw reflected, perceived, and acted in the world, a world they did not experience as separate from themselves. Their sense of identity, at the collective and individual level, was bound up with the landscape.

This chapter will describe a different way of knowing the world that can greatly enrich a westerner's knowledge of the environment. It will present examples of how different cultural media were used to communicate knowledge about interdependence and insure sustainability. This knowledge extends beyond what traditional Western science might consider valuable or useful, into realms it would dismiss as spiritual or imaginary. This chapter attempts to bridge the gap and extend the horizon of science beyond conventional assumptions.

The Mi'kmaw language reflects a view of the world as interdependent and in constant motion. The nineteenth-century Baptist missionary to the Mi'kmaq, Silas Rand, wrote the following description of the Mi'kmaw language:

> The language of the Indians is very remarkable. One would think it must be exceedingly barren, limited in inflection, and crude; but just the

reverse is the fact—it is copious, flexible and expressive. Its declension of nouns and conjugation of verbs are as regular as the Greek, and twenty times as copious. The full conjugation of one Micmac verb will fill quite a large volume; in its construction and idiom it differs widely from the English ... The verb is emphatically the word in Micmac. Whole sentences, and long ones too, occur constantly, formed wholly of verbs. All adjectives of the animate gender are real verbs, and are conjugated through mood and tense, person and number ... Even the numerals are verbs, and any noun can assume the form and nature of a verb without difficulty.[2]

One of the most distinguishing factors about the Mi'kmaw language, as noted by Rand, is that it is verb based, not noun based, as in the English language. The verb is the focus of the language, with prefixes and suffixes added to determine gender, tense, plurality, animacy, and inanimacy. This focus on the verb, and the "copious" suffixes that can be added to it, allows for extraordinary adaptability, breadth, and creativity of expression. The nature of the Mi'kmaw language reflects the nature of the universe as being in a continuous state of flux, ever-changing and non-static. This implies the relative nature of any particular form, and its interdependent relationship with all other forms.

Linguist Doug Smith, who worked extensively in the 1970s with Bernie Francis to develop a new and more precise Mi'kmaw orthography (the Smith/Francis orthography), described the difference between the Mi'kmaw and English languages as follows:

> The verb-like quality noun-centred languages which objectify the world; they turn the world into objects which can then be analyzed. They can be gotten hold of, taken apart, put back together and treated as things as opposed to movements. In the Mi'kmaw language, there is an inherent dynamism or movement that Mi'kmaw speakers them-selves are always aware of, whereas in English, we tend to be more aware of nouns. We are a thing-oriented society, rather than a move-ment oriented society.[3]

The fluid nature of Mi'kmaw reality can be seen through the many Mi'kmaw words for "creator," including *kisu'lkw, ankweyulkw, jikeyulkw,* and *tekweyulkw.* None of these words are nouns that connote one central being as a source of creation; they are transitive verbs conveying differ-ent *processes* of creation. They can be conjugated four hundred different ways, and can move and change constantly. Furthermore, these terms are all present-tense indicative, meaning that "creator" or "God" is ongoing.

You cannot speak of Creator as something that has already happened, such as "When God created the world . . ." "God" is a process, a continuously manifesting, creative force.[4]

The holophrastic nature of the language allows the speaker to compress a multitude of meanings into a single word. An image that might take many sentences in English to write out can be expressed in one word or one movement. There may be implicit meanings that might not be conveyed in the literal translation of the word.[5] Eleanor Johnson, in a lecture given at the Gorsebrook Institute in Halifax on Mi'kmaw oral tradition, described how frightening it was to be told that she had to write a one-thousand-word essay for a class she was taking at University College of Cape Breton. She said, "I come from a one-word language where one of my words is a whole sentence in our language. Can you imagine how it felt to write trying to think out 1,000 words?"[6]

This means that the profundity of Mi'kmaq is often lost when translated into English. Furthermore, the conventional assumptions of objective and subjective experience are inherent in English, and so translation distorts the dynamic and interdependent worldview offered by the Mi'kmaw language. There is no absolute split between the "inner" and "outer" worlds, or the spiritual and physical in the Mi'kmaw worldview. Things appear in intimate relation to one another.

This relational and nondualistic quality of the language extends to the Mi'kmaw relationship to the environment. A simple demonstration occurs in the words for colors. Except for the four colors red, black, white, and yellow, all colors are associative, or "analogised," as Francis terms it.[7] For example, the color terms mean "like the sky" (blue) or "like the fir trees" (forest green).[8] Thus there is no way to describe the color of blue and green rocks, or even a dream of blue and green rocks, without ascribing to them a connection, or relation, to the sky and fir trees. Even the four main colors are thought to have derived from Proto-Algonquian words that associate them with blood (red), light/sunlight/dawn (yellow and white), and ash (black). All the colors are intransitive verbs that can be conjugated. The translation of *maqtew'k* (black) means "in the process of being black," inferring that there is no fixed state of blackness, but rather a stage in a process that could change.[9]

The intimate relation between the Mi'kmaq and their physical world can also be seen in the extension of kinship terms to animals, stars, and other beings. All animate beings are, or have the potential to be, one's relatives and can take human shape. A Kluskap story recounted by a Mi'kmaw, Jerry Lonecloud, and documented in the 1920s, demonstrates this:[10]

On the Island Sighignish, Glooscup's [Kluskap's] niece (they, the animals and birds, were human then) was in the woods w(ith) bow and arrow shooting small game, such as squirrels, rabbits, animals for their prey, and other small animals. When she returned she found the people in the encampment had left in their canoes to go to the mainland when Glooscup [Kluskap] required them. She didn't know how to get to the mainland. Finally, she saw a whale passing by. She said to the whale, "Uncle, will you be so kind as to take me to the mainland? I am here all alone." So he said, "Yes, I will take you but I can't take you on dry land." But, she said, "Well take me as near as you can."[11]

In another legend retold by Silas Rand, "The Two Weasels," two sisters inadvertently, by choosing their favorite stars while lying awake one night, cause the stars to transform into humans and become their husbands. This demonstrates the interchangeability of energy, the shape-changing quality of the world, seen throughout Mi'kmaw legends and language. Humans commonly shape-changed into animals, birds, plants, rocks, and other than human beings, and vice versa. Birds and animals were said to come from the stars. Plants, rocks, mountains, thunder, and many geographical features were conscious beings that could change shape unpredictably and at will.[12] People also had "animal helpers" or personal alliances with animals, whom they could call upon for assistance, protection, or guidance. Their spirits were interchangeable and inseparable in essence. Whatever happened to one affected the other, so if the moose leg was broken, the man's leg also broke.

The landscape of the Atlantic Provinces and part of Québec where the Mi'kmaq traditionally lived is imbued with their culture and history. Place-names in Mi'kmaq not only tell of features of the landscape, historical events, and important resources, but also act as a mnemonic device to remind people of how to live correctly. There are numerous legends where animals and people are transformed, or transform themselves, into stones, trees, mountains, and islands. Certain rocks, generally large and anomalous in shape, termed "Grandmother" and "Grandfather" rocks, have been documented throughout the Maritimes, and are also associated with legends. They acted as guideposts or landmarks for travelers, and were regarded as conscious beings or as having power, and offerings were made to them out of respect and in supplication.

Creation myths abound regarding the various landscape formations of the Maritimes. For example, the creation of Moose Island in the Bay of Fundy was formed by Kluskap during one of his hunts, according to one legend. The story as told by Jerry Lonecloud to Clarissa Archibald Dennis is as follows:

> He [Kluskap] says to his dogs, "Now we will have a moose chase." They chased the moose, he calculated to kill the moose but didn't and the dogs chased him in the water of Advocate Harbour and the moose was swimming out toward Isle Haut or Spencer's Island. And when Kluskap came to shore, he says to the moose, "I am going to leave you here for a landmark. You turn to stone, Moose." And there was, until twenty years ago, a stone island a perfect shape of a moose, but twenty years ago the head of the moose disappeared owing to storms, etc.[13]

The story reminded people of their connection with the world of creation, and the powers (what we might term supernatural) at play. Additionally, I have speculated that these stories acted as maps, telling travelers of the geography and resources of an area.[14]

Thomas Andrews, in conducting research into the significance of place-names in the Dene culture, stated:

> Place names provide a "hook" on which to structure the body of narratives, and in doing so become an integral part of the narrative itself. This is particularly evident in myths and legends recounting the travels and exploits of mythical heroes, which list in great numbers places relevant to the story line. Place names are therefore mnemonic devices, providing a mental framework in which to remember relevant aspects of cultural knowledge . . . It is clear from the previous discussion that within many societies possessing rich oral traditions, landscape may be viewed as a collection of symbols which record local knowledge and meaning, and where place-names become memory aids for recalling the relevance of a "message" encoded in associated narratives. Physical geography is transformed into "social geography" where culture and landscape are fused into a semiotic whole. In essence, one cannot exist without the other.[15]

Andrews cites a number of examples from various cultures, for instance, the songlines of the Australian aborigines and the work of Keith Basso among the Cibecue Apaches and the Roti of Indonesia, to name a few, all of which demonstrate the inextricable union between these cultures and the land.

In conducting research into traditional land-use practices of the Mi'kmaq and Maliseet for the Canadian Parks Service (CPS, now Heritage Canada), I spoke with several Mi'kmaq who suggested that place-names be integrated into any interpretation of the land. It became apparent during this research that where CPS was looking for in situ, visible evidence of land use within park boundaries, the Mi'kmaq and Maliseet put much more emphasis on the oral traditions associated with various regions. For instance, at the time, the Bay of Fundy National Park had produced little archaeological evidence of First Nations presence. However, a strong oral tradition exists regarding the use of the land, which is valid evidence of First Nations presence for the Mi'kmaq.[16]

The notion that narrative tradition is rich in place-names that become mnemonic devices, providing a framework in which to remember relevant aspects of cultural knowledge, does not seem so different from European cultures. This fact alone would not justify the claim that traditional Mi'kmaq held, and still have, a different "worldview." It is the *power* of the stories and the *consequent significance* of the place-names to individuals within the cultural community that gives us a glimpse into what can be termed another worldview. The Mi'kmaw culture, essentially, is inseparable from the land of the Maritimes.

The following story, documented by Stansbury Hagar in 1900 (italicized) with commentary by Bernard Hoffman (not italicized), provides an example of the richness of information embedded in the legends. Hagar's work, in conjunction with legends provided by Silas Rand and Jerry Lonecloud, illustrates the mirroring of events in the sky and the earth common to many Mi'kmaw legends:

> *These stars and constellations are so arranged in the sky that the Bear is represented by the four stars in the bowl of what we call the Dipper. Behind are seven hunters who are pursuing her. Close beside the second hunter is a little star. It is the pot which he is carrying, so that, when the bear is killed, he may cook the meat therein. Just above these hunters a group of smaller stars form a pocket-like figure—the den from where the bear has issued . . .*

The activities of these celestial characters were integrated by the Micmac in a legend which not only explained their relative positions in the sky, but also contained the motif of annual death and resurrection. In this case the celestial bear emerges from her den in the spring of each year, to be spotted and chased by the seven (the Micmac magic number) hunters. The chase goes on throughout the summer, and finally, in mid-autumn, the hunters who remain overtake their prey and kill her. Robin becomes covered with her blood in the process and attempts to shake it off, which he does except for a spot on his breast. The blood which he shakes off however,

spatters far and wide over the forests of earth below, and hence we see each autumn the blood-red tints on the foliage; it is reddest on the maple, because trees on earth follow the appearance of the trees in the sky, and the sky maple received most of the blood. The sky is just the same as the earth, only up above, and older.

After dancing around the fire and offering their thanks to the "Universal Spirit," the chickadee, the moose bird, and the robin feasted on their catch.

But this does not end the story of the bear . . . Through the winter, the skeleton lies upon its back in the sky, but her life-spirit has entered another bear who also lies upon her back in the den, invisible, and sleeping the winter sleep. When the spring comes around again this bear will again issue forth from the den to be again pursued by the hunters, to be again slain, but again to send to the den her life-spirit, to issue forth yet again, when the sun once more awakens the earth . . . And so it is, the Micmacs say, that when a bear lies on her back within her den, she is invisible even to those who might enter that den. Only a hunter with great magic power could perceive her then . . .

[The Micmac] . . . say that they know the Celestial Bear never dies, because she is always in sight, and that is why her earthly descendants never die of natural causes, but only fall asleep each autumn and come to life again in spring. For all earthly animals are the descendants of the ancestor animal in the sky, and their appearance and habits are but reflection of hers. In all things as it was and is in the sky, so it is on earth . . .[17]

In this story, we see the earth mirrored in the sky, and vice versa. The interconnectedness between the movement of the stars, the changing of seasons, the hunt of the bear, the robin, and the other birds, the trees, and the celebration and honoring of all of this is embedded in this one story. Earth, stars, seasons, birds, animals, trees, and men move in synchronization—they are all related.

The story also mirrors the scientific knowledge of the bear as we know it today. The black bear, *Ursus americanus,* begins its preparations for hibernation in September, when it begins to gain weight and collect leaves and tree branches, which it drags into its den. About a month later, as the snows begin to fall, the bear goes into hibernation, where it remains for up to six months. It is during the latter part of hibernation, usually in January, that the sows (female bears) give birth to their offspring.[18] As Hagar's account of the story says, "Through the winter, the skeleton lies upon its back in the sky, but her life-spirit has entered another bear who also lies upon her back in the den, invisible, and sleeping the winter sleep."[19] This probably is an allusion to the sow giving life to her embryonic cubs. The bear referred to in Hagar's rendition is a she-bear.

The same mirroring quality can also be seen in the dances. Dance, whether formal or informal, suffused Mi'kmaw culture of Eastern Canada in the prehistoric, protohistoric, and early contact periods. As with the legends of the Mi'kmaq, many of these dances were a storehouse, or an embodiment, of multiple layers of information and meaning encapsulated in particular body movements and choreography. Within the dances of the Mi'kmaq, extensive knowledge of the world was conveyed, one's relationship to the world was reaffirmed, and, in essence, the world was danced into existence.

The Serpent Dance provides one of the most stunning examples of the multiple layers of meaning embodied in some of the dances.[20] My research into this dance revealed that the dance acted as an effective and powerful form of communication and, like the legends, carried practical information about the environment and also about a particularly powerful medicinal plant, *meteteskewey*. This particular dance brought together a web of processes that occurred simultaneously—the changing of seasons, probably linked to the appearance or position of a constellation in the sky; the time of snakes molting, an indicator for the ripening and picking of *meteteskewey*. The *jipijka'm*, a horned serpent that lived underground and was featured in many legends, was the essence or protector of medicine. It was possibly the spirit ally of the *puoin*, the most powerful medicine man or woman. Ultimately, the dance was seen as protecting the well-being of the people themselves.

The dance also exhibited the mirroring of one thing in another, the microcosm reflecting the macrocosm. It mirrored the sound of the medicinal plant (a rattling or tapping sound), the coiling and uncoiling of the literal snake awakening from hibernation and shedding its skin, and it also served as a way to evoke or tune in to the power of the medicine in the form of the *jipijka'm*. The male and female dancers were possibly a reflection of male and female *jipijka'maq* associated with male and female medicinal plants.

Finally, the dance illustrates the Mi'kmaw relationship to the world as part of universal processes and cycles. The dance was a means to help effect the changing of seasons and channel the energy appropriately so that medicine would be powerful and effective. Dance was a way to reflect and come to know the world, embody and communicate its rhythms and its stories, and reestablish one's relationship to and within a shifting reality again and again.

Mi'kmaw chants mirrored the rhythms and sounds of the natural world in much the same way as the dances. There is a snake song, a wind song, a pine needle song, an eagle song, a toad song, and many others. However, chants and songs held a power far beyond mere mimicry. They were a means of communicating with the natural world, as can be seen in the following account by Frank Speck of Penobscot men canoeing across Penobscot Bay:

> The magic power of song syllables was thought to have a quieting influence upon the forces causing rough water, and also to strengthen the canoe men. A number of years ago an informant (Charlie Daylight Mitchell) was crossing from Deer Island to Eagle Island in Penobscot Bay during a heavy sea. He was in a small canoe in the company of an old man who chanted . . . all the way across. The singer tempered his voice to follow the pitching of the canoe as it mounted wave after wave. He said that the boat rode the waves much more easily while the old man was singing.[21]

As this excerpt clearly shows, the Mi'kmaq did not view their environment as an inanimate, unconscious object. It was sentient, and they mirrored it and communicated with it through various forms of cultural expression. At the same time, what westerners would view as "practical information" was embedded inseparably within this supernatural communication.

The mirroring motif so common in legends and chants can also be seen in the importance placed on their repetition. Orin Hatton in his *Power and Performance in Gros Ventre War Expedition Songs*, discusses the role of repetition as a re-creation of a paradigm mirroring the act of creation. He writes, "The act of creation involves transformation . . . The initial transformation has been completed, and transformation is replaced by repetition. Repetition is a source of power in that it extends the initial creative act."[22]

This type of re-creating creation is seen vividly in the "songlines" of the Aboriginal people of Australia. Songlines, invisible to anyone outside the culture, crisscross the Australian landscape. They hold the story of creation, which is continually sung into being by the people. During what is termed "dreamtime," totemic ancestors are said to have traveled throughout the country scattering a trail of words and musical notes along the lines they walked. These dreaming tracks lay across the whole

Australian landscape, connecting various tribes. Human beings who knew these songs could find their way in distant territories.[23]

Some skeptics might question how coherent and accurate the information contained in legends, songs, and dances remains as it is passed down through generations. Some anthropologists have looked into this question, concluding that legends are not fantasy, nor a free-for-all improvisation, but are open to interpretation by the storyteller and the audience. Eric Havelock, in his research on Greek oral traditions, noted that the stories were not "inventive," nor were they fiction as we understand it. With the bards of ancient Greece, Havelock states:

> It's not the creation of a free mind, it is a bard all the time responding to and telling his tale according to what his people also want and expect to hear. The tale may entrance them, but they don't want people to act out of line without getting it. And they don't.[24]

This observation is in keeping with the following account, taken down from Jerry Lonecloud, in which he describes how the older generation monitored the storyteller. In this case, Lonecloud stated that it was the Chief Medicine Man who related the historical legends:

> When I was a young boy, the Chief Medicine Man would gather the children, boys and girls, into his camp and tell them stories. Some old people would be there also listening (judges like) to see if he told them correctly. Every word has to be put in proper place. People there knows the stories as good as him but they're not to be told by them, only by the Chief Medicine Man. Supposed to be not one word out of the way—same as scripture. Often time by making mistakes they lose chiefship. Then he is put away and a new chief elected. It is not very often this occurs but this is what happened when it did occur.[25]

This account highlights the importance of accuracy in storytelling and the role the audience plays in monitoring and ensuring the accuracy of the stories as they are passed down to the younger generations.

The quality of transmission through generations was put to the test by Tom McFeat's experiments with small group cultures in the 1960s and 1970s. McFeat enlisted three different control groups, to which he gave a body of text to be memorized and subsequently passed to new generations of people who were introduced to the initial group at intervals. In his experiment, McFeat monitored three aspects of knowledge transmission: the actual content as memorized from the original text (to which the group no longer had access once initial memorization took place), interpretation, and innovation. Although each group related differently to each of these three, giving greater or lesser emphasis to each one, what became apparent was that choices were made regarding whether or not to interpret and innovate, and if interpretation were to take place, the group had to accept or dismiss interpretations. Those accepted would be integrated into future transmissions to the newer generations, either as part of the corpus of knowledge or as possible alternatives. Constant in all groups, however, was the retention of the accuracy of the original text, which was monitored by the group as a whole.[26] But, we also have to think beyond the text to the meaning conveyed through context.

If we expand our thinking about Mi'kmaw communication of knowledge as moving beyond the text itself, and include different modes of expression—dance, chants, and music—we can see there is a kind of mirroring taking place. The medium of a particular person, animal, rock, or river reflects and embodies rhythms, the movements of nature, and the processes of creation on a larger scale. I like to use the image of a mirror because every "thing" appears to reflect the whole, not just appear as an isolated part, but as an embodiment of the whole. What was experienced in the cycles of people's lives was mirrored in the stars, embedded in landscape features, which in turn was reflected in the many forms of expression that stored that knowledge. Each dance, chant, and song holds the changing moment in the light of the whole of space and time. An examination of all Mi'kmaw modes of communication reveals an extraordinary awareness and reflection of the physical properties of the world as inseparable from the whole, much as a mirror and its reflections cannot be separated. Everything was related.

All cultures create ways through a variety of media—story, song, dance, pictorial art, language—to make experiences of the many forces at play in the world understandable and communicable. The language and methods of Western science have tended to exclude other ways of knowing.[27] In this chapter, I have tried to illustrate how, by expanding our approach to the study of Indigenous cultures to incorporate other ways of understanding, communicating, and storing knowledge, we can see how principles at the foundation of sustainability were the foundation of these alternative knowledge systems.

NOTES

1. "Mi'kmaw" is the singular and adjectival form of "Mi'kmaq" (plural) according to the Smith/Francis orthography. "Micmac" was a commonly used

spelling in many publications, as seen in some of the references cited in this chapter.

2. Rev. Silas Tertius Rand, *Legends of the Micmacs* (New York: Longmans, Green, and Co., 1891; New York: Johnson Reprint Corporation, 1971), xxxviii, xxxvii.

3. Doug Smith, videotaped interview with Bernie Francis, September 30, 1994.

4. Bernie Francis, personal interviews, July 27 and August 30, 1995, and March 14, 1996.

5. Ibid.

6. Eleanor Johnson, Lecture on Mi'kmaw Oral Tradition, Gorsebrook Research Institute, Saint Mary's University, Halifax, Nova Scotia, November 11, 1994.

7. Bernie Francis, personal interviews, July 27, 1995, and August 30, 1995.

8. Bernie Francis and Margaret Johnson, personal interviews, July 27, 1995; Doug Hewson, personal communication, 1996; Ruth Holmes Whitehead, *Micmac Quillwork: Micmac Indian Techniques of Porcupine Quill Decoration: 1600–1950* (Halifax: The Nova Scotia Museum, 1982), 71.

9. Bernie Francis, personal communication, July 23, 1994.

10. This translation is unedited and the Mi'kmaw terminology has not been transposed into the Smith/Francis orthography.

11. Clarissa Archibald Dennis, *Journals of Clarissa Archibald Dennis*, Public Archives of Nova Scotia, 1923, MG1, vol. 2867, notebook #2, 11.

12. Ruth Holmes Whitehead, *Stories from the Six Worlds: Micmac Legends* (Halifax: Nimbus Press Limited, 1988), 12.

13. Dennis, *Journals of Clarissa Archibald Dennis*, notebook #1, 135–238.

14. Trudy Sable, "Another Look in the Mirror: Research into the Foundations for Developing an Alternative Science Curriculum for Mi'kmaw Children" (master's thesis, Saint Mary's University, Halifax, Nova Scotia, 1996), 207–220; oral presentation, "Mi'kmaw Legends as Maps," Sixteenth Annual Archaeology in Nova Scotia Workshop, Nova Scotia Museum of Natural History, July 26, 2001.

15. Thomas D. Andrews, *Yamoria's Arrows: Stories, Place-Names and the Land in Dene Oral Tradition* (N.P.: National Historic Parks and Sites, Northern Initiatives, Canadian Parks Service, Environment Canada, Yellowknife, NWT, 1990), 3, 8.

16. Trudy Sable, *Traditional Sources Study*, report prepared for Canadian Parks Service, Atlantic Region, Halifax, Nova Scotia, 1992; and Joe Knockwood, personal interview, December 16, 1991.

17. Bernard Gilbert Hoffman, "The Historical Ethnography of the Micmac of the Sixteenth and Seventeenth Centuries" (PhD diss., University of California, 1954), 252–254.

18. Nicholas Denys, *Descriptions and Natural History of the Coasts of North America (Acadia)* (New York: Greenwood Press [originally published as Champlain

Society Publication II], 1968), 363; Susan Wernert, ed., *North American Wildlife: An Illustrated Guide to 2000 Plants and Animals* (Pleasantville, N.Y.: Reader's Digest Association, Inc., 1982), 64; Wildlife Education, Ltd., "Bears," in *Zoobooks* (San Diego, n.d.), 3–4.

19. Hoffman, *Historical ethnography*, 253.

20. Trudy Sable, "Multiple Layers of Meaning in a Mi'kmaw Serpent Dance," in *Papers of the Twenty-Eighth Algonquian Conference*, ed. David H. Pentland (Manitoba: University of Manitoba, 1998), 329–340.

21. Frank Speck, *Penobscot Man: The Life History of a Forest Tribe in Maine* (New York: Octagon Books, 1976), 167. Also see Nicholas Smith, unpublished manuscript on Penobscot songs and dances (n.d.).

22. Orin T. Hatton, *Power and Performance in Gros Ventre War Expedition Songs*, Canadian Ethnology Service, Mercury Series Paper 114, Canadian Museum of Civilization, 1990, 16.

23. Bruce Chatwin, *The Songlines* (New York: Elisabeth Sifton Books-Viking, 1987), 14.

24. Eric Havelock, Canadian Broadcasting Corporation, "Ideas" transcripts, 1988, 3.

25. Dennis, *Journals of Clarissa Archibald Dennis*, notebook #2, 114.

26. Tom McFeat, *Small Group Cultures* (New York: Pergamon Press, 1974),177.

27. Vine Deloria, "Ethnoscience and Indian Realities," *Winds of Change* (summer 1992): 12–18.

	THE LANGUAGE OF CONQUEST AND
Chapter 11	THE LOSS OF THE COMMONS
	Chet Bowers

In contrast to the deep knowing embedded within the Mi'kmaw forms of communication, even the most progressive environmental movements of Western culture are superficial. Few can point out this shortcoming as conclusively as Dr. Chet Bowers. In this chapter, he shares his succinct and thought-provoking ideas about how K–16 education, the misuse of so-called liberal and conservative political discourse, the "myth of technology as a tool," and about how uninvestigated language itself is destroying the commons at a frightening rate. Without even mentioning Indigenous People, who continue to absorb the worst that loss of the commons entails, or the Indigenous perspective per se, it is too easy to see that if our vicious cycle of "progress"—which ignores traditional Indigenous wisdom emphasizing a more community-centered and less money-dependent life—continues, we may soon see a lost of "commons" such that only the wealthy will be able to afford clean air and water.

Chet Bowers has been on the faculty of the University of Oregon and Portland State University. He has been invited to give talks at twenty-nine foreign universities and is the author of eighteen books, including Culture of Denial, Let Them Eat Data, Educating for Eco-Justice and Community, Revitalizing the Commons: Cultural and Educational Sites of Resistance and Affirmation, *and* Mindful Conservatism. *His approach to education is shaped by the view that the fundamentals of academia need to change: that there needs to be a shift in the present paradigm from a mechanistic society to a whole-systems approach similar to that of traditional Indigenous People.*

***

Most people, including college students and their professors, continue to be socialized to think within the traditions of inquiry and knowledge accumulation that are based on cultural assumptions that do not take account of the ecological crisis. The study of environmental issues, whether from the social sciences and humanities or from the hard sciences, does not provide people with the knowledge and values that enable them to recognize the cultural alternatives to living a less consumer- and technology-dependent lifestyle. People may be aware of the need to recycle some throwaway products of mainstream industry, or of the need to purchase more energy-efficient technologies, but personal economic considerations are probably more responsible for such choices than a deep understanding of the consequences.

On the whole, most of us join the vast majority, who are happily dependent upon the industrial approach to health care, processed food, entertainment, and leisure. The core cultural assumptions that influence thinking and values are unlikely to be reconciled with environmental issues and values, even in college-level environmental classes. These are sweeping generalizations of course, but asking people what they understand about the nature of the commons or how the idea of the commons is paramount in indigenous worldviews can assess their accuracy. Questioning them about the commons as well as about how various technologies are undermining the intergenerational knowledge that might help people to live less environmentally destructive lives might lead people to realize the power of hegemony that continues the destruction.

Traditional Indigenous worldviews make a vital contribution to the reforms that are now necessary in thinking about the environment, but in this essay I am not suggesting that reform should be based on a preferred ideological orientation. Rather, I am saying that reform is *required* as a matter of survival because of the fundamental changes now occurring in the Earth's ecosystems, by recent technological developments that are contributing to the global spread of poverty, and by the growing influence of market liberalism in globalizing a consumer- and technology-dependent lifestyle. Global warming, now recognized as contributing to reductions in the yield of rice and other staple crops, as well as other cultural developments that are contributing to the depletion of the world's fisheries, the growing scarcity of potable water, and the spread of deserts and the loss of topsoil, is now affecting daily experience of people around the world. Such experiences might cause people to question for the first time the long-held myth that the continual quest to create new technologies is the best guarantee for increasing their material security and overall well-being.

In light of these accelerating global changes, it might seem foolish to suggest that addressing the influences that silence the important narrative we all should be having, especially college students, on these subjects might reverse the trends that put us at risk. However, the evidence suggests that the eco-management approach in the environmental sciences and the limited environmental perspective acquired in the social sciences and humanities, and certainly in the popular literature and media, all fail to introduce people to the traditions of thinking and living that can be traced back to origins of humankind—to our Indigenous ancestors who once lived in relative harmony with Earth's rhythms. The silence resulting from our inability to awaken to this wisdom prevents people from recognizing non-monetized activities, patterns of mutual support, and intergenerational knowledge that represent everyday alternatives to the increasingly degrading impact of a consumer- and technology-driven culture.

The commons, as historically understood and as they exist today in a more attenuated condition, represent the aspects of the physical environment and symbolic world that are shared in common—that is, shared in the sense that they have not been privatized and monetized. Indigenous wisdom honors the commons to the point where it was difficult to conceive of how Europeans began "owning" the land. The air we breathe, the water we drink, the forests and oceans we depend upon, the topsoil we rely on, are still part of the commons—just as the language, narratives, artistic traditions, food preparation, and so forth were and still are part of the commons. All of these aspects of the commons are now being rapidly enclosed. That is, they are being privatized by individuals and corporations—and thus are becoming increasingly unavailable to those who do not have the means to participate in a money economy.

The biases in universities and public schools against studying the traditions of different cultures that have had or have a smaller ecological impact leaves students vulnerable to the consciousness-shaping power of the media, which continually promotes the importance of relying upon expert knowledge and the market as the source of happiness and way of communicating social status and success. The importance of intergenerational knowledge, which varies from culture to culture, to attaining greater personal and community-centered self-sufficiency in such areas as food preparation, health care, entertainment, craft knowledge, and traditions of moral reciprocity and civil rights, is thus being ignored.

Even assumptions that equate critical reflection with living a more emancipated and progressive existence lead to overlooking the many approaches to knowledge and intergenerational renewal that are essential to sustaining the commons. Equating critical reflection with changes that, in formulaic fashion, are assumed to be progressive in nature can lead to overlooking that critical reflection should also help clarify which traditions should be conserved and built upon. For example, the traditions of habeas corpus, separation of church and state, an independent judiciary, legal protection of workers, environmental legislation, trial by a jury of peers, craft knowledge, mentors and cultural elders, are just a few of the traditions of the commons in the West that are now being threatened by the growing dominance of market liberalism. There are few university professors or public schoolteachers who have their students examine how critical reflection and the cultural assumptions that lead to viewing it as the one true source of knowledge are also the basis of technological innovation and the current process of economic and technological globalization. Critical reflection, along with other approaches to knowledge, are essential to the traditions of local democracy that are now being undermined by the modern forms of enclosure, but we must go far enough to include an examination of the enclosure of the commons.

The following questions should guide the focus of inquiry that applies traditional Indigenous wisdom to current affairs:

1. What are the general characteristics of the commons that are shared by different cultures?
2. How do Western science, technology, and neoliberal policies undermine (enclose) the world's diverse commons?
3. To what extent do the commons still exist within home communities?
4. What are the connections between the enclosure of the symbolic and natural commons and the spread of poverty?
5. How does the enclosure of the commons undermine the conservation of biodiversity?
6. What is the history of ideas in the West that have legitimated the enclosure of the commons, and what is the history of ideas that have helped people understand the importance of the commons?
7. How does the language of modernization and progress reproduce the patterns of thinking that further the expansion of industrial culture that is undermining the commons?

If these questions are to be taken seriously within the context of these different disciplines, other aspects need to be addressed. These include aspects of culture that now are either misrepresented or relegated to the realm of silence. Until we are introduced to a more complex and accurate account of these aspects of culture, the assumptions that underlie the thinking of most educators and business leaders will continue to shape the expectations of students and the public at large. We will remain unable to recognize how dependent we are upon what remains of the commons. In not being able to recognize the networks of interdependence with the natural and symbolic commons they are part of, people will be less inclined to participate in the political discourse that defends the commons from the economic and political forces that have as their goal the further enclosure of the commons. The following is a brief overview of the resulting misunderstandings and "silences" and how they need to be rectified.

MISUSE OF LIBERALISM AND CONSERVATISM IN POLITICAL DISCOURSE

In spite of the tradition of philosophic conservatism that extends from Edmund Burke and James Madison to Robert Bellah, including environmental writers from John Muir, Aldo Leopold, Wendell Berry, and Vandana Shiva to Gregory Bateson, most people continue to relate conservatism with such prominent individuals as William Buckley Jr., Rush Limbaugh, and President George W. Bush and their followers. On the other hand, those who tend to oppose these folks, including environmental activists and university professors and public schoolteachers, reproduce a similar set of conceptual errors when they label themselves as liberals.

The result of this intellectual confusion is that the word "conservative" is now used to refer to the promoters of capitalism, a survival of the fittest form of individualism, and policies that further degrade the environment, while ignoring Indigenous wisdom, which stands for generosity and equality, a symbiotic form of community, and traditional practices that maintained the environment. The irony is that this misuse of political labels may prevent even those who address social justice and environmental issues from recognizing that they are contributing to the enclosure of the commons. By identifying themselves as liberals, they are inadvertently aligning themselves conceptually with the liberalism that has its roots in the thinking of John Locke, Adam Smith, and John Stuart Mill. A shared characteristic of these founders of modern liberalism is that they all assumed that their ideas were universal truths that should be imposed on the "backward cultures" of the world, that the environment should be viewed in economic terms and privately owned, and that all traditions should yield to the needs of the self-made individual. What is being overlooked is that their ethnocentrism, which is now being repeated in the globalization policies of market liberals and faux conservatives, totally marginalizes the question that should be central to sustaining the commons: What do we want to conserve in this era of ecological uncertainty that will contribute to more ecologically and socially just communities?

If this question were raised, given the policies of the current Bush administration, students and faculty might identify the need to conserve and even to recover the full range of civil liberties, the gains of the labor movement, the separation of church and state, the need for an independent judiciary, programs that benefit the economically marginalized, and so forth. An equally conservative agenda would be expressed by environmentally oriented citizens that would include preservation and renewal of habitat, conservation of the diversity of species, conservation of nonrenewable sources of energy, conservation of topsoil and old growth forests, and so on. Because the market liberals, neoconservatives, and extremist talk-show hosts have succeeded in representing their classical liberal agenda as conservative, people who are concerned with environmental and community renewal issues continue to misrepresent themselves and thus help to ensure continued confusion about our most basic political vocabulary.

In other words, if people are going to be introduced to the diverse history of the commons, which includes Indigenous wisdom and worldviews, they will need to use a political vocabulary that more accurately represents what needs to be conserved and what needs to be changed—what contributes to the well-being of the commons. This will require expanding the political vocabulary so that what people stand for is clearly represented—such as being an extremist, a reactionary, a fascist, a traditionalist, a religious conservative, an environmental conservative, a market liberal, an ethnocentric and messianic liberal, and so forth.

DESTRUCTIVE WORDS AND PATTERNS OF THINKING

The above discussion of how words carry forward the misunderstanding and silences of earlier generations is just part of the evidence that challenges the widespread misrepresentation that language is a sufficient conduit for successfully transmitting ideas, objective data, and information between autonomous individuals. If we consider the interpretative frameworks that are encoded in the language used in our educational systems, churches, and in business, such as patriarchy, anthropocentrism, mechanism, change as progress, individualism, evolution, and so on, we can easily see how they have influenced the modern approach to such diverse areas as agriculture, medicine, industrial production, genetic research, education, architecture, and so forth. The myth that language is a conduit is essential to maintaining several other myths that are reinforced within the educational establishment, including the myth of autonomous and rational individuals who are uninfluenced by their culture's deep assumptions and the myth of objective information and data. These two myths help to marginalize an awareness of students' ethnocentric patterns of thinking—which will likely lead in later years to their support of colonizing foreign policies. But the myth of being an autonomous individual, which the conduit view of language helps to support, has other consequences that relate directly to undermining the viability of the local commons as well as that of the other cultural commons.

The lack of awareness that language encodes the deepest and most taken-for-granted assumptions about culture further marginalizes the awareness that other cultures are based on different assumptions—and that some of these cultural ways of understanding human nature account for their smaller ecological footprint.

Unfortunately, the language reinforced in public schools, universities, and the media carries forward past ways of thinking that see Indigenous cultures as evolving from primitive (and thus backward) to the advanced stage of culture development represented by Western thinking and teaching. This has the effect of making it appear irrelevant or as the expression of romantic thinking to learn about how other cultures renew their commons and how they resist the Western model of enclosing the commons. If we consider the dominant root metaphors or interpretative frameworks embedded in individualism, progress, a human-centered world, mechanism, evolution, markets, and so on, we find a lack of words that are needed to name and to make explicit both the natural and cultural commons that are part of the taken-for-granted world. In being taken-for-granted, dependence on what remains of the commons is not recognized. The language of the commons will not be part of the industrially oriented vocabulary, nor will the word "tradition" have any standing other than as a word that designates what is irrelevant and in need of being overturned.

For the classical liberal thinkers, tradition was understood as the source of oppression and backwardness. Today the word is still associated with whatever stands in the way of progress and greater freedom of individual expression and self-discovery. Within the context of corporate culture, traditions represent what has to be replaced with expert systems and new consumer products. Because the viability of the commons is dependent upon intergenerational knowledge (traditions) that represents alternatives to being dependent upon consumerism and expert systems, it is important that people be able to discriminate between traditions that are essential to personal and community empowerment and social

THE LANGUAGE OF CONQUEST ‖ 187

justice, and traditions that undermine the sustainable characteristics of the commons. This ability is undermined when both intergenerational knowledge and traditions are reduced to abstract phrases and words that have only a negative meaning.

The influence of taken-for-granted patterns of thinking can be seen in how past achievements in establishing the separation of church and state, in labor legislation, in civil liberties, and in achieving greater equity in gender and race relations are understood as expressions of progress, rather than traditions that need to be conserved and built further upon. The point is that hard-won gains in social justice that have become part of the legacy of past generations are still not view by most people as examples of traditions. The way of thinking that identifies social justice gains as expressions of progress, which is associated with liberalism, still dominates the pattern of thinking that contributes to the silence about asking what needs to be conserved. The effect is that social justice advocates continue to identify themselves with the political label that more accurately encodes the deep cultural assumptions that promote, in messianic fashion, the enclosure of the world's diverse commons.

Thus, "progress" and "tradition" should not be understood as categorical opposites. Rather, they need to be evaluated in terms of different cultural contexts and in terms of specific examples. There is a further need to adjust our language in a way that takes account of how any cultural pattern that is reenacted over four generations is more accurately understood as a tradition, and how these traditions support or destroy the commons.

HOW SCIENCE AND SCIENTISM INFLUENCE THE COMMONS

Few people understand the difference between science and scientism, and how in their different ways they contribute to the enclosure of the world's commons. Scientific knowledge has benefited humankind in many ways, and it is especially useful now in adding to our understanding of the changes occurring in natural systems. However, science as a mode of knowing and thus as a source of new knowledge has a Janus face in that it has also been a major contributor to the process of enclosure of the commons by bringing more life-forming processes under the control of private ownership and corporate control. Scientific knowledge created the possibility of patenting gene lines and genetically engineering seeds. These are just two of the recent examples of how the commons is being further incorporated into the industrial systems of production and consumption.

The scientism of E. O. Wilson, Richard Dawkins, and others who are attempting to explain how cultural beliefs and practices ("memes") are subject to the same laws of natural selection as the biological world are making predictions and providing explanations that cannot be justified in terms of scientific evidence. Their supposedly scientifically grounded explanations and futuristic predictions provide what can easily be interpreted by the uninformed as supporting the survival-of-the-fittest economic principles of the market liberalism that is now the centerpiece of American foreign policy. This example of scientism contradicts the assumptions of most Indigenous worldviews and creates the illusion of a science-based ideology that justifies the enclosure resulting from economic and technological colonization as the better adapted cultural memes prevailing over the less well adapted ones, such as those that come from traditional indigenous cultures.

People need to be able to recognize when science is being used to strengthen the commons, when it is being used by corporations to transform more of the commons into market opportunities, and when scientists are using their achievements to make predictions and value judgments that have no basis in terms of scientific evidence. In this era of globalization, it is essential that people acquire a more complex understanding of the limits and possibilities of science, and when it is being used to further enclose the commons. Without this understanding, people cannot participate in the democratic decision-making process about appropriate uses of science, a requirement for being a citizen of the commons.

THE MYTH OF TECHNOLOGY AS A TOOL AND AS CULTURALLY NEUTRAL

University reform should also focus on recognizing the difference between technologies that help to sustain the commons and technologies that undermine both the cultural and natural commons. Currently, most people think that technologies are culturally neutral; at the same time, people believe that technologies manifest positive progress. How different technologies undermine intergenerational knowledge that might reduce dependence upon consumerism currently is not understood, and thus there is a lack of awareness of the need to democratize decisions about the introduction of new technologies. In the case of introducing computers into classrooms, for example, it was the experts who represented the interests of the computer industry who explained what the educational gains would be—which recent studies have found to be grossly overstated.

A number of issues should be central to any in-depth study of technology and its impact on what remains of the commons. These include how different technologies either marginalize or facilitate the traditions of craft knowledge, how they contribute on a global scale to new forms of dependencies on a money economy, how they progressively reduce the need for workers and de-skill those that can still find work, how they influence social relationships and ways of thinking, and how they alter the values, language, and thus ways of thinking within different cultures. Learning about the influence of different technologies on the commons would help to overcome one of the major silences that is maintained through the educational systems of the West. The myth that technology is simply a tool and that the major educational challenge is to create more efficient technologies continues to go unchallenged in public discourse, public schools, and Western universities.

IMPLICATIONS FOR SCHOOL CURRICULUM

Because these subtopics of ideologies, language, scientism, technologies, silencing the narrative, and Indigenous wisdom have a direct impact on the world's diverse commons and cut across many academic areas of study, it should be evident that a single course would provide only a superficial overview. Schools need to integrate the focus on studying cultural practices that contribute to sustaining or destroying the commons into every class as much as possible. The willingness among educators to agree upon curriculum that lacks conceptual and moral coherence and that fails to address the most critical issues we face today is no longer acceptable.

The politics of establishing curriculum today has not been influenced by those who are aware of how rapidly natural systems are being degraded, but rather by those corporate forces that continue to profit by this degradation. Current university training, regardless if it varies across universities, does not provide the basic understanding of how cultural beliefs and practices are contributing to the rapid changes now occurring in the natural systems upon which we all depend. This now needs to be made the basic priority. It will require a commitment to addressing the challenges we face in revitalizing our own commons and in avoiding the destruction of the commons of other cultures. Such a commitment will be served by awakening to the wisdom of traditional Indigenous cultures and to the illusions of education, media, politics, and public discourse that deny such wisdom.

Chapter 12

OVERCOMING HEGEMONY IN NATIVE STUDIES PROGRAMS

Devon A. Mihesuah

Chet Bowers called for drastic curriculum reform in education, one that embraces not a new ideology, but a more authentic way of viewing ourselves in the world. Throughout this book we have attempted to show that this authenticity exists in the ways traditional Indigenous People understand the relationship, and we have posited that this understanding may be such a challenge to the dominant culture's materialistic, militaristic, paternalistic, and corporate goals, that hegemonic efforts to deflect Indigenous thinking insinuate themselves throughout society.

Dr. Devon Mihesuah agrees, and in this chapter she explains that only through frank discussions about colonization and decolonization can future generations begin to awaken from cultural hegemony. Furthermore, she discloses that the place one might assume anti-Indian hegemony would not appear, in university-level American Indian Studies programs, is not immune to the shadow of colonization. As a result, even future Indigenous scholars and teachers may not, in such programs, be able to recover traditional Indigenous wisdom and be able to move beyond stifling historical trauma and hegemonic influence.

Also in this chapter, Devon offers classroom-tested examples for teaching Indian students in ways that can be successful. Her suggested approaches for effective teaching, however, do more than offer practical tips. They also expose the various levels of educational hegemony, from a dualistic history to a colonized diet, that plague "Indian education" and cultures today, and they show the extent to which we must begin to engage in authentic "political" conversation if we are to avoid the negative effects of anti-Indian hegemony on Indian and non-Indian people today and in the future.

Devon A. Mihesuah (Oklahoma Choctaw) is professor of Applied Indigenous Studies at Northern Arizona University in Flagstaff. She is the editor of the American Indian Quarterly, *for which she won the Wordcrafters Circle of Native Writers' Award as the 2001 Journal Editor of the Year. She is the award-winning author of ten books, including* American Indians: Stereotypes and Realities; Natives and Academics: Researching and Writing about American Indians; Indigenous American Women: Decolonization,

Empowerment, Activism; *and co-editor (with Waziyatawin Angela Wilson) of* Indigenizing the Academy: Transforming Scholarship and Empowering Communities. *She has also published a novel,* The Lightning Strikes.

***

Throughout education there are obstacles to teaching topics dealing with Natives. Even university programs in Indigenous Studies usually exist within a colonialist structure. As a teacher, you may have problems with colleagues who expect you to teach in a certain fashion in order for you to receive tenure and promotion. Problems that Native students face in modern universities are similar to what Natives faced at federal boarding schools. Unless professors are well versed in tribal happenings, they usually will be unconcerned with the troubles Native students face on or off campus. For them, it is "business as usual," and the students who cannot "cut it" are left behind to drop out or fail. Until they get to know you, many Native students will indeed expect you to behave in the same prejudicial manner.

One of the major problems is that professors concerned about proper teaching also have to deal with university bureaucracy. Many universities are eager to advertise their Native programs. The problem is, just because a university has a "Native Studies" department or major as part of its curriculum does not mean that program benefits Natives. It sometimes doesn't mean much even if the professors are Native. Unless those Native professors are knowledgeable about and dedicated to decolonization, you may as well have a non-Native representative of the status quo in there. Indeed, a Native who behaves just like the colonizers can actually be worse than a white colonizer. I've witnessed situations in which Native professors were staunch advocates of fighting anyone who had a desire to help students with decolonization and empowerment strategies. They epitomize those Natives who have found a comfort level in their roles as token minorities in a white system.

As Tewa educator Gregory Cajete has said, "The money an Indian individual, tribe, school, or organization gets depends not only on how well you have learned to play the game, but how many compromises of spirit and authenticity you are willing to make to appease the political, bureaucratic, and industrial controllers of the game."[1] Vine Deloria Jr. concurs: "Professors stand more chance of getting their ideas accepted if they are immensely popular with their peers than if they actually have something to contribute."[2] On top of that, many AIS and NAS programs have become "dumping grounds" for those professors and instructors who, because they cannot succeed in their home departments, are allowed to join an AIS department (often because the home department wants to get rid of them). As a result, some students receive an inferior education.

An administration that pretends to admire tribes' cultures by incorporating many classes about Natives into the curriculum does not mix well with the reality of academic racism and ignorance, which is why we see so many potentially useful programs fail. Many professors are so caught up in theorizing about Natives that they have no idea what life was, or is, like for Natives.

We have read much about the importance of retaining cultural knowledge. We also know that mainstream education does not promote that goal. Many universities want window dressing, that is, Native faculty and staff on display, but they do not want Native ideologies included in the curriculum. This is why we see white professors on many campuses teaching American Indian studies courses who refuse to ask Native scholars on campus to speak in their classes. At my own university, for example, the work of Native scholars is rarely, if ever, used.

Native Studies programs are a boon to the university because they create the illusion of just how "sensitive" and "concerned" the university is to Native people. In reality, many of these schools have no commitment to quality; their only concern is to have numbers in the classroom. If they can fool grant-giving agencies into giving them money so they can perpetuate the programs, then so much the better. These programs exist because they cater to those professors who need jobs and to students who want to know a little bit about Natives' history, literature, and religion, what Yuchi educator Daniel Wildcat refers to as "educational tokenism."[3] If these Native Studies programs cannot fit Native students' needs and wants into the western discourse, then we have nothing more than the same old curriculum that does nothing to promote tribes' well-being.

Political intrigue in the academy is complex, and there is not enough space here to explore the various problems in the Ivory Tower. Regardless of the tough realities that Native professors, students, and our allies face, we must keep in mind that Native students are hungry for inspirational words. They want to hear that they have rich histories and cultures and that the mean stereotypes they see and hear everyday are fabrications designed to make the colonizers feel better.

So how can concerned instructors, professors, parents, tribal leaders, and elders help Native students in becoming empowered and inspired to seek out more information about decolonization? The reality is that there is only so much we can talk about in the classroom. We are often handicapped by curriculum committees and departmental regulations. Nonetheless, students can be taught that tribal histories and cultures are unique, rich, and diverse. They can be taught how to look for author bias and how research should and should not be conducted. They can be taught ways to recognize stereotypes and bias in writings and conversations, including their own, and appropriate methods to use when writing about peoples of other cultural, racial, and gender groups. They can be given enough information so they can consider how to mesh their tribe's needs with their own.

I tell my Native students that even if they do not agree with the versions of history they read, or if they do not like a certain professor, they are still gathering knowledge. Nothing is wasted. After reading a variety of works, they will be more capable of discussing topics with authority and having points of departure for their arguments. They should be made aware of not only the topics of author bias and manipulation of information, but also how historical events put them in the situations they are in today.

There are certain topics that I discuss in every class I teach, whether it be about politics, literature, or history. One is that all the various areas of Native Studies—policy, indigenous rights, identity, health, literature, history, religion, philosophy—are intertwined, and I tell students at the outset that there is no way that I can see to discuss one area without bringing in aspects of the other areas. I also discuss the effects of colonization and decolonization strategies. All of these topics are appealing to Natives, but using this strategy opens the eyes of non-Natives who thought they knew everything there is to know about Indians from watching "Dances with Wolves" and reading Tony Hillerman novels. And, they are topics complex enough to be discussed throughout the semester in a variety of lectures.

After teaching Native and non-Native students for many years, I believe that if we're going to teach about indigenous histories and cultures, we must be honest and provocative, and what we teach must be useful and relevant to our students. Very few people can tolerate listening to a professor who drones on about dates and places. The human factor is what people like to hear about and that is what they can relate to.

Hearing only negatives about the past and present doesn't get us anywhere, either. Hawaiian behavioral health services director Poka Laenui says that "some people are happy to go no further than mourning, finding sufficient satisfaction in long-term grumbling. People can be 'stuck in the awfulizing' of their status as victims. Some build careers on it."[4] So, our goal should not be to focus exclusively on negative events and histories. We need to get to work to solve problems that face us today.

The ideas outlined here are designed to build self-confidence, to inform students about their contributions to society and to place them on the path to find more knowledge in order to assist their tribes. In the process, students gain inspiration to help themselves. We should strive to create survivors, not victims who depend on others to bail them out of tough situations.

What follows is not a true course syllabus. Lists of reading materials, test schedules, and so forth, are omitted. What I have collected here are the highlights that I have culled over ten years of teaching, both in terms of what to teach and how to teach it. No matter what courses I teach, whether it be history, methodology, writing, women's studies, policy, or a general Applied Indigenous Studies introductory course, I always integrate the following themes. Some of these issues are courses in themselves, but all of them can be molded to fit into a given course topic. It is important to remember Daes' comment:

> Victims of oppression not only lose interest in self-preservation but also find it difficult to maintain their relationships as parents, friends, and neighbors. If you have been made to feel irrelevant, you cannot understand why anyone could possibly love you, and you anticipate betrayal from anyone who tries.[5]

It is up to us to help students respect themselves so they in turn can assist their communities.

Professors who teach courses on minority issues may not always have minorities in their classes. In those cases, it is crucial that the teacher take great pains to treat every student with respect. Hopefully, we're all doing this already, but keep in mind that many white students become immediately defensive when any topic of racism, oppression, or injustice arises. Many students will believe that you are picking on them regardless of how even-handed you are. Some actually hope that you really do insult them so they can take you to task.

I've talked with many professors who teach Native history and culture courses who complain about how white students treat them with disrespect and bash them on end-of-semester evaluations. They say that no matter how careful they are not to say that "whites are guilty," some students insist that this is the message. In the past ten years, however, I have run into only a handful of such students; typically, they have an agenda and they are intent on making a point. Often, they enrolled in the class with a defensive mind-set that remains intact.

Being inclusive is the best strategy for teaching classes that contain volatile lecture material and white enrollment. Learn everyone's name. Call on all students, not just the Natives. Don't assume that non-Natives are racist or that Natives are all victims. Making assumptions about their values, motivations, and intelligence will only get you into deep trouble. Be positive, not negative, and you'll win over the hardest hearts.

INTRODUCE YOURSELF AND PURPOSE OF THE COURSE

Most professors introduce themselves and tell the class their office hours and how their grades will be calculated. Instructors who work with Native students must do more than this. Native students are used to hearing racist and stereotypical information from teachers and they want to know from the start where your allegiances are focused. If you are a member of a tribe, then introduce yourself as such.

Many professors believe that politics should stay out of the classroom, but with Native courses, especially those populated by Native students, politics *is* the classroom. I would say that anyone teaching "minority" courses, especially, needs to make it clear from the first day that all students—regardless of race and gender—are welcome and that the instructor wants to thoroughly educate the class on the course topics. Students must be made aware that included in the canon of the field is much work that does indeed "bash" white men—and women. There is a growing literature about how history and culture have been written and how Natives are treated by those with little concern for tribes' well-being. One way to get the point across is to present a brief exposé on that first day of stereotypes of Natives and make it clear that Natives have been forced to deal with these images for hundreds of years.

Included in your introduction should be a statement about the responsibilities of Native scholars. Tell them how you perceive yourself and why. Are you an activist? Then tell them what you teach and write about. Among the comments that one can include are the price of doing nothing to empower oneself and tribe, the duties Natives have to tribe, self, and family, and the realities of tribal life. I tell my students about the university structure and how courses are approved (and disapproved), the statistics of how many Indians are scholars and professors, what many of us believe are our responsibilities, statistics of Indigenous peoples in school, and dropout factors.

You also can include a few comments about American Indian Studies as a discipline and the politics surrounding who studies American Indians and why. I want students to understand that social, political, religious, and economic aspects of Indigenous life are interconnected and that tribal histories and cultures cannot be understood without an awareness of the fields under the heading of Native American or Indian Studies. This introduction sets up the context of the class and lets students know about the complexity of Native studies. This also gives racist, close-minded students an opportunity to leave your class and your life.

POLITICS OF NAMING

Names are identifiers. Naming and labeling is political and students must know the controversies over the term "Indian." Explain to the class why it is that you use "Indian," "Native," "Native Americans," "First Nations," "Indigenous," or whatever. Students also should hear what it is that various tribes call themselves. For example, "Navajos" say "Dineh," "Choctaws" say "Chata," "Winnebagos" say "Ho Chunk," Papagos use "Tohono O'Odham," and so forth. Names can be empowering or insulting to Natives, and teachers must attempt to be respectful. A useful exercise is to write these names on the board and ask the class what they use and why. Most of my students laugh nervously at this exercise because other than saying, "It's the term my parents use," they have no clear reason why they prefer one term or the other. Be sure you tell students why you use the terminology you do. I prefer "Indigenous" or "Native" because both imply that the people of this hemisphere were created here and did not migrate from the Old World. It is an activist statement that directly challenges anthropologists.

Most students have not heard the terms "colonization," "decolonization," "ethnocentrism," or "sovereignty." While they may have heard of empowerment, racism, stereotyping, and Nation-building, they may not know how to define them. Write the terms on the board and ask students what they mean and why they are important words for a Native person to understand and use. For the lecture on labeling, talk to students first about the terms they use, then have them read Michael Yellow Bird's "What We Want to Be Called: Indigenous Peoples' Perspectives on Racial and Ethnic Identity Labels," *American Indian Quarterly* 23:2 (Spring 1999): 1–22, and then ask if the essay has changed their thinking.

CYCLES OF WRITING AND STUDYING
ABOUT AMERICAN INDIANS

A study of almost any topic dealing with Natives involves a look at history. A discussion of the cycles of history is imperative to students' understanding that history is often an authors' creation of stories of past events. Students should be exposed to the current theoretical debates over what constitutes legitimate source materials (such as oral histories and written stories), researcher responsibilities and ethics, and methodologies for interpreting tribal cultures—including gender roles and the benefits of cross-disciplinary inquiry.

Topics to include under this heading might be current trends in studying Natives; how incorrect history damages present-day peoples; the different ways history data is collected; and the politics of historical interpretation. Students need to be aware of these different views of how Native history should be written. There is much racism and territoriality swirling about in the field of Indigenous history. It also is an exclusive field in many respects because those in charge often refuse to use Native voices in their attempts to assess what may have happened in the past. Have students read Angela Cavender Wilson's "Grandmother to Granddaughter" and "American Indian History or White Perceptions of American Indian History?" in *Natives and Academics: Researching and Writing about American Indians*,[6] to stimulate dynamic discussions of the major issues in Native history today.

STEREOTYPES

Within the first two weeks of class I include a slide show of stereotypes of Natives. For my courses on Native women I have a full carousel of slides that focus specifically on stereotypes of females. Discussion of stereotypes teaches several lessons. It reveals how ignorant mainstream American culture is of tribal cultures, and it shows that students have been miseducated in the past because they believe what they see in the movies and on television. It informs students of how damaging stereotypes are to the self-esteem of Natives, especially youth. I have taught entire history courses to great effect by following stereotypes. For basic discussion, I use my *American Indians: Stereotypes and Realities*.[7] Some of the most common stereotypes that never fail to arouse interest (whether laughter or outrage), but that always stimulate good conversations among the students, are that Indigenes

- are all alike
- were conquered because they were weak and powerless
- could have prevented the European invasion if they had banded together
- had no civilization until Europeans brought it to them; Euro-American cultures were and are superior to Indigenous cultures
- arrived in this hemisphere via the Siberian Land Bridge
- were warlike and treacherous
- had nothing to contribute to Europeans or to the growth of America
- did not value or empower women
- have no religion
- welcome outsiders to study and participate in their religious ceremonies
- are a vanished race
- are confined to reservations, live in tipis, wear braids, and ride horses
- have no reason to feel unpatriotic
- get a free ride from the government
- don't have to manage their own affairs, which are taken care of by the BIA
- are not capable of completing school
- cannot vote or hold office
- have a tendency toward alcoholism
- are all fullbloods
- all have an "Indian name"
- know the histories, languages, and cultural aspects of their own tribe and all other tribes
- are stoic and have no sense of humor
- like having their picture taken
- all make money from casinos
- have oral stories that are merely "myths" and "legends"
- are, if they are Indigenous scholars, unable to accurately chronicle their histories and cultures because they are "too close to the topic" and cannot be objective

Each one of these has the potential to branch into numerous other discussions, especially the effects of colonization. A way to facilitate discussion is to ask about the pros and cons of each stereotype and image. For example, my slides on "Indian Maiden Art" show paintings by white artists of Native women in various stages of undress, usually with an animal (wolf, owl, or horse), and they invariably look like white women with dark skin. Some Native students have been furious and insulted at the images, while others see them as "beautiful" and have asked me how they can get one of the paintings. Another issue that students are particularly interested in is a comparison between the Nations, that is, they want to know how tribes differ historically and in the present day in regard to language, religion, gender roles, dress, shelter, economies (food and food procurement), political systems, and so forth. Many Native students have no knowledge about tribes besides their own and even then, they may know little about their own culture.

THE EFFECTS OF COLONIALISM

Because this large heading represents the foundation of the current state of Native America, topics related to colonialism also are the foundation of most of my courses. Native students must learn this information in order to understand how they arrived at their present condition. Those who express interest in Native history and culture need to know it in order to understand why some Natives may appear to be angry and defensive. Topics under this broad heading include

- loss of land
- loss of population due to war, sterilization, disease, policies of genocide, low birth rate as a result of poor health, changing cultures, and removal/relocation
- dependency on material goods that resulted in competition between tribes
- alcoholism and other forms of self-abuse
- competition among tribes for material goods
- degradation of environment—loss of plants and animals
- gender role change because of missionaries who taught that women are inferior to men
- factionalism within tribes, or inter- and intratribal differences that led to "culturalism" and "ethnocentrism"
- extreme change in health conditions (obesity, diabetes, heart disease, etc.) from regressing from a diet of vegetables, fruits, game meats, and an active lifestyle to a processed, fatty, sodium-laden diet and sedentary lifestyle
- dilution of cultural knowledge
- dilution of "indigenous blood"
- depression and other mental problems associated with being disempowered

- internalization of colonial ideologies
- identity confusion
- continued subjugation of Natives because the ideology of Manifest Destiny is still in effect
- loss of intellectual rights to ideas that stem from Indigenous science
- stereotyping
- continued monitoring of tribal governance policies and procedures by the federal government

The colonial power structure stays in power because of all of the above; as a result, Native voices are subsumed, dismissed, and/or devalued in politics, academia, the entertainment industry, and publishing. These aspects of colonialism also meld into each other; for example, discussion of the impact of missionaries leads to discussion of tribal cultural change, the rise of patriarchal thought, the dismissal of women's once-valued place in traditional cultures, and modern-day abuse of females. A discussion about forced education leads to an exploration of what I call the Boarding School Syndrome (BSS), and the historical trauma and distrust of education that stems from it. Discussion of the power structure today leads to talks about who writes history and modern culture, from what perspective, and who is respected as an authoritative voice and, importantly, who is not. The Siberian Land Bridge debate reveals how this theory is used to the benefit of anthropologists who still insist on studying skeletal remains of Natives. And, I have discovered that if you plan on delving into the issue of religion, you must go slowly and be prepared to back off; some Natives in my classes are Mormons with an exalted sense of morality, and no amount of discussion about racism based on skin color can reach them.

EMPOWERMENT STRATEGIES AND RECOVERING
TRADITIONAL INDIGENOUS KNOWLEDGE

Indigenous communities must preserve their social, political, economic, and religious knowledge in order to pass it to the next generations. They also must protect it from misuse by others. A tribe's traditional knowledge defines that community's uniqueness and explains its relation to the world. For Indigenous people, knowledge of the past is crucial for their identity growth and development, pride, problem-solving strategies, and cultural survival. Studying the Native past offers solutions to current problems such as food production, human and animal health, education, natural resource management, understanding treaty rights and land claims, and ultimately, is indispensable to keeping that culture alive. One way to impress upon students the enormity of the topic is to have them log onto http://www.developmentgateway.org/node/130646/, the informative Development Gateway page that provides information about Indigenous knowledge in a global context.

An inclusive view of the past can educate readers about the contributions of Natives to the world. Discovering their contributions to the world's diets, to the arts and sciences, and the U.S. political system is empowering to Natives and can help establish pride and self-esteem. Because the portrayals of peoples and historical events directly impact how their descendents are viewed and treated today, more accurate presentations of the past help to counteract movies, television shows, literature, and cartoons that often portray Natives as savages, buffoons, radical environmentalists, or supporters of colonialism.

Depending on what you are teaching, you can always incorporate aspects of recovering Indigenous knowledge and empowerment strategies to students that they can use immediately. In my classes, for example, students respond enthusiastically to the briefest mention of recovered history. Many students have been waiting for that "lightbulb" to go off that gives them inspiration and a reason to stay in school; others take it further and decide to make careers in policy, environmental science, economic development, or critical writing. Rarely will they not want to learn more.

EGALITARIANISM

Today we see unprecedented abuse of women in tribal communities. One of the strategies used by women's shelters and substance abuse programs is to teach clients about tribal traditions so they can regain pride in themselves and their cultures. By gaining self-confidence and a strong identity, they lose the need to lash out at others. Women tend to be especially enthused during class discussions about females' traditional tribal roles. After teaching two policy courses, two female students declared that they plan on becoming the first female Navajo president (one is in her sixties and the other in her early twenties), and one says she will be the first female Hopi chairwoman. Other females have become interested in politics and have either completed their internships in the Arizona State Legislature and in Washington, D.C., or are planning to.

DECOLONIZING YOUR DIET

The study of how Natives' diets changed from meals of fresh fruits and vegetables and game meats to a diet of processed, sodium-laden, and fatty foods can assist students in understanding why Natives suffer from an epidemic of diabetes, obesity, and all the problems associated with these diseases. A mental exercise for students that can lead to physical action is to ask them to keep a diary of what they eat for one week. Then have them use a nutrition book to make a chart so they can determine how many calories and how many nutrients each item provided them. They also should document how much exercise they get per day and calculate how many calories they use per exercise. This is an intensive assignment and can be confusing, but it gives them a reality check as to not only what nutrients they are and are not taking in, but also how many calories they are ingesting versus how much they expend. I did this for one month in high school—that's over thirty years ago—and I have never forgotten how important it is to keep close tabs on what you eat and drink.

After they have completed their chart, the students should investigate their tribes' traditional diets. For example, the Choctaws of Oklahoma are now suffering from diabetes and obesity and all the problems that result from those illnesses. The tribe traditionally ate a variety of foods: corn, squash, beans, melons, acorns, peas, onions, cherries, plums, pecans, walnuts, potatoes, deer, bear, duck, turkey, fish, rabbit, quail, turtle, and other animals. They now eat a high-carbohydrate, high-fat, and high-salt diet. Trans fat (partially hydrogenated oils that act as the catalyst for artery clogging) has posed a tremendous problem because it lurks in everything from crackers to coffee creamer to Oreos. In combination with a lack of exercise, the "modern lifestyle" has created tribal Nations of overweight and unhealthy Natives who die before their time. Students who consider themselves to be aware of nutrition are still shocked to have this reality brought to their attention.

If students are non-Native, they can research the diets of the tribes closest to them. This assignment sounds daunting. And if you have ever considered your diet or have calculated what you are eating and drinking, it is daunting and humbling (not to mention scary). However, we must take responsibility for our health and for the health of our children and those who cannot make reasonable choices for themselves.

HEALTH CARE

Many Native students have experiences with Indian Health Service hospitals and clinics. What they don't know are overall health statistics within tribal Nations. A discussion about inadequate diets, alcoholism, mental and emotional problems, and the various physical ailments Natives suffer, in addition to the need for more Native health care professionals, can spur students to explore careers in mental or physical health care.

LANGUAGE RECOVERY

Indigenous languages are being lost at an alarming rate. You can encourage students to regain their language. Begin by asking a few uncomfortable questions: If you do not speak your language, why? What are the barriers keeping you from learning? Often, students don't want to learn because they don't think it is important. Suggest ways that they can learn. Tell students that they do not have to become fluent, that learning basic words, greetings, conversational sentences, and prayers can be greatly empowering. If they have no family members or friends who can teach them, they can investigate language programs at their university. Tell them to find out if their tribe has language tapes or books available. The Choctaw language, for example, is available through Internet classes and on a variety of tapes and in books.

TRIBAL POLICY

My students are always intrigued to hear about tribal policy as it relates directly to them (and most policies do). It is helpful for students to hear an overview of traditional tribal politics and why the field of policy is of critical importance to Natives. Give them examples of traditional tribal politics of several tribes to press home the point that tribes are not only different, but they had effective systems of governance prior to colonization. Mention treaty rights that include land, water, fishing, and tribal governance issues. Treaties agreed upon and signed by the federal government and the tribes guaranteed—depending on the arrangement—food, shelter, clothing, lands, and/or education and farming monies. Many of these treaties, however, have been broken and it's up to Natives to fix them.

Most students are surprised to hear about the European intellectual trends that were influential in creating ideologies and policies that were (and still are) applied to the colonized Native peoples. One way of impressing upon students that direct connection between past and present events is to tell them about the Doctrine of Discovery, which has been used by the colonists in this hemisphere since 1492. You recall that in the twelfth and thirteenth centuries the Crusaders swept into the Holy Lands and territories of the Middle East, where they felt they were justified to wage "holy wars" against the "heathens and infidels" (non-Christians) in the name of God. This same ideology is the basis of federal Indian law: that the "discoverers" of this land have a right to develop and refine it according to their culture. Our Founding Fathers acknowledged that Britain was the first discoverer of America, and because those who were to become Americans defeated the British, they inherited that acquisition. Read the Declaration of Independence.

Alfred Taiaiake argues in his *Peace, Power, Righteousness: An Indigenous Manifesto* that an understanding of traditional political processes and values will enable tribes to "restore pride in our traditions, achieve economic self-sufficiency, develop independence of mind, and display courage in defense of our lands and rights."[8] It is crucial that Natives understand treaty rights so they know how laws affect them, their families, and future generations.

ENVIRONMENTAL SCIENCE

Most students are aware of pollution, at least. What they may not be aware of are the impacts of environmental problems (pollution, deforestation, etc.) on tribal lands and on the people who live there. Discuss tribes' responsibilities to the environment (be careful about being stereotypically mystical), the state and federal governments' responsibilities to tribes, careers in environmental science, and specific examples of what tribes are doing currently to protect the environment.

ECONOMIC DEVELOPMENT

While many tribes suffer from what appears to be terminal poverty, other tribes, such as the Oklahoma and Mississippi Choctaws, Potawatomies, and Pequots have found ways to create money in order to take care of their elderly and their children. Many tribes have earned their own money for health care, language programs, environmental protection, housing, and education. A class debate about the pros and cons of casinos never fails to elicit arguments about Natives sponsoring gambling halls.

EMPOWER YOUR STUDENTS

Professors who disallow students to ask questions in class effectively subsume Native voices, which is the same as the racism those students probably face outside the classroom. Numerous students have complained to me for years about those professors who teach Native topics and who sigh loudly when a Native student raises his or her hand, answer curtly, or become angry that a student has challenged their authority. While you cannot allow students to take over the classroom and argue every point you make, it is important that their questions be addressed. You can turn those questions into discussion points so the entire class can learn.

You must keep your cool. I have found that Native students and non-Natives who are truly interested in Native issues are mainly polite and are simply curious. Answering their questions is no problem. Where we run into problems are in the courses on Native history and culture that are composed mainly of non-Natives who want to challenge because they believe we are being "politically correct." Often these types of students want to argue out of spite, racism, and misogyny. It takes a great deal of effort not to become angry, but to become angry is only to the benefit of those racist students who can later use your behavior against you.

Empowering students also means encouraging them to express themselves, to question what they are being taught, and to try and apply what they have learned to a tribal setting. Many non-Natives will resent this, however, so you have to pick and choose your opportunities.

Native students rarely get to hear positive comments about their tribes. Students rarely hear from professors that they have a right to question what is taught to them and that they can challenge, debate, and contribute to class discussions. After more than a decade of teaching Native students from a variety of tribes, I can also attest to the reality that many of them have never heard the term "decolonization," much less a discussion about how colonization has impacted every facet of their lives. Giving them lessons on the above topics can indeed change their lives. Not every Native student will be appreciative of your efforts, but if you can reach only a few each semester, then you have done your job.

NOTES

1. Gregory Cajete, *Look to the Mountain: An Ecology of Indigenous Education* (Skyland, N.C.: Kivaki Press, 1994), 190.

2. Vine Deloria Jr. and Daniel R. Wildcat, *Power and Place: Indian Education in America* (Golden, Colo.: Fulcrum Resources, 2001), 129.

3. Deloria and Wildcat, *Power and Place*.

4. Poka Laenui, "Processes of Decolonization," in *Reclaiming Indigenous Voice and Vision*, ed. Marie Battiste (Vancouver: University of British Columbia Press, 2000), 155.

5. Erica-Irene Daes, "Prologue: The Experience of Colonization Around the World," in Battiste, 7.

6. Devon A. Mihesuah, ed., *Natives and Academics: Researching and Writing about American Indians* (Omaha: University of Nebraska Press, 1998).

7. Devon A. Mihesuah, *American Indians: Stereotypes and Realities* (Atlanta: Clarity Press, 1996).

8. Alfred Taiaiake, *Peace, Power, Righteousness: An Indigenous Manifesto* (Toronto: Oxford University Press, 1999), xii.

THE QUESTION OF
WHITEWASHING IN AMERICAN   *Chapter 13*
HISTORY AND SOCIAL SCIENCE
David N. Gibbs

When one considers how insidious and overwhelming the language of conquest (i.e., cultural hegemony focused on anti-Indianism) has been in academic publications, school curriculum, media, and institutions, and how intensely it has dismissed or disparaged authentic Indigenous voices, perspectives, and contributions, one must consider the ways in which such hegemony stems from the consciousness of the dominant social classes, as well as the degree to which it is intentional. In this chapter, David Gibbs extends Devon Mihesuah's specific argument about the hegemony that exists within universities' Native Studies programs by revealing the close connections between the U.S. intelligence services and academia since 1945. This chapter will not focus on anti-Indigenous hegemony per se, but will instead serve as a case study in how academia has been and continues to be co-opted to serve the interests of the powerful. Consider, for instance, a report I received moments ago about a respected and popular professor at the University of California, Berkeley, who was fired after he published a scientific paper regarding the uncontrolled contamination of irreplaceable native Mexican corn varieties by genetically engineered corn. Dr. Ignacio Chapela, whose article was published in the science journal Nature, *was denied tenure due to pressure from the biotech company Monsanto, in spite of almost unanimous approval (32 to 1) of his department members and tenure recommendations from his department chair and the dean of the College of Natural Resources.*[1] *This is only one of a growing number of such cases across the country where universities pressure faculty to tow the progovernment, procorporate, promilitary agenda, and Dr. Gibb's illuminating piece helps us understand how this can be happening.*

David Gibbs received his PhD in Political Science from MIT and is an associate professor of history and political science at the University of Arizona. He is the author of The Political Economics of Third World Intervention *and numerous chapters/articles on topics relating to social science propaganda and the historical imperialism of U.S. policies.*

***

> *They came to you under the guise and pretense of friendship and*
> *by the use of base flattery and hypocrisy gained your confidence,*
> *only to lead you into the crooked path of ruin and destruction.*

—KEOKUK (SAUK), 1832

A major theme of this volume has been that the victors have been writing the history (and the social science as well) with regard to the experience of Indigenous People. There is a clear if often unstated bias in much of U.S. social science that implicitly celebrates and apologizes for the onward march of colonialism and neocolonialism, while it slights the perspective of its numerous victims in North America and elsewhere. The history of the American Indian is, obviously, a part of this history of colonial conquest, and the present volume's focus on presenting the Indian perspective is a most welcome corrective.

In this chapter, I will explore some of the causes for the unstated biases—the procolonial "hegemony" that forms a major theme of the book—and will argue that at least one cause has been the close connections between the U.S. intelligence services and academia since 1945. This chapter will not focus on the issue of American Indian politics, but will instead serve as a case study in how academia can be co-opted to serve the interests of the powerful.

The close collaboration between academia and U.S. foreign policy had its origins during the First World War, when numerous academics worked for the Committee on Public Information, which disseminated propaganda in favor of the war. Such ties also were established during World War II, with the creation of the Army's Office of Special Services, whose staff included some of the most distinguished academics and intellectuals of the era. With the coming of the Cold War and the creation of the CIA in 1947, the alliance between academics and U.S. expansionism became a permanent feature of university life. During the 1950s, the CIA and military intelligence were among the main sources of funding for the social sciences, having supported such institutions as Columbia's Russian Research Institute, Harvard's Russian Research Center, and MIT's Center for International Studies. Outside the campus setting, major research foundations, including the Ford Foundation and the Asia Foundation, were closely integrated with the Agency. The field of political communications was transformed during the early Cold War by large-scale U.S. government funding, in which leading academics helped intelligence agencies to develop modern techniques of propaganda and psychological warfare. Fields across the social sciences and humanities were affected by this collaboration.

Major figures in such fields as history, political science, communications, sociology, and anthropology were closely integrated into the struggle against communism.[2] Some of the resulting activities strained the limits of academic propriety. Noam Chomsky provides the following recollection of his experiences at MIT:

> Around 1960, the Political Science Department separated off from the Economics Department. And at that time it was openly funded by the CIA; it was not even a secret ... In the mid-1960s, it stopped being publicly funded by the Central Intelligence Agency, but it was still directly involved in activities that were scandalous. The Political Science Department was so far as I know the only department on campus which had closed, secret seminars. I was once invited to talk to one, which is how I learned about it. They had a villa in Saigon where students were working on pacification projects for their doctoral dissertations.[3]

In a carrot and stick strategy, these activities were combined with rigorous scrutiny of dissident professors and, in the words of historian Bruce Cumings, "It is only a bit of an exaggeration to say that for those scholars studying enemy countries, either they consulted with the government or they risked being investigated by the FBI."[4]

The CIA also developed remarkably close ties to journalism and, during the period 1947–77, some four hundred American journalists "secretly carried out assignments" for the Agency, according to a classic investigative study by Carl Bernstein. Some two hundred of these journalists signed secrecy agreements or employment contracts with the CIA.[5] The recruitment of journalists was directed by longtime CIA officer Frank Wisner, who managed "respected members of the *New York Times, Newsweek,* CBS, and other communications vehicles, plus stringers." Wisner often commented on how easy it is to buy a journalist, and for not more than a couple of hundred dollars a month.[6] Overseas, U.S. intelligence officers funded academics and writers through a series of front organizations and publications, coordinated by the CIA-controlled Congress for Cultural Freedom.[7]

CIA influence extended to book publication, and a long series of books were Agency supported. According to a U.S. Senate report, "Well over a thousand books were produced, subsidized, or sponsored by the CIA before the end of 1967." The Central Intelligence Agency sometimes simply provided financial support toward a book's publication. In some cases, this was done without the author's knowledge; in others, Agency personnel worked directly with the author and influenced the actual content of the book. In the latter cases, the CIA sought to control the author to a considerable degree. According to one intelligence officer, the CIA wished to "make sure the actual manuscript will correspond with our operational and propagandistic intentions."[8] The CIA has never released a title list of the one thousand (or more) books it helped to publish in the course of its elaborate propaganda efforts. However, there can be no doubt that academics participated in some of these clandestine publishing activities. In addition, there is the problem of self-censorship: during the 1950s, a common practice at MIT's Center for International Studies was for researchers to write a classified study on a specific topic and then to publish a "sanitized" version of the same study as a regular academic book for public use.[9] To the best of my knowledge, the book publications that resulted from this process never acknowledged government support, nor did they acknowledge that the publication had omitted information.

Particularly troubling is the CIA's use of "black" propaganda, a common intelligence practice in which deliberately false information is released, and the true origin of the disinformation is obscured. One example of black propaganda is *The Penkovsky Papers*, a 1965 book that purported to be the published diary of a Soviet military officer. The book portrayed the Soviet system in general and the Soviet intelligence services in particular in a most unflattering light. As it turns out, the CIA actually wrote the book. Former officer Victor Marchetti wrote: "*The Penkovsky Papers* was a phony story. We wrote the book in the CIA."[10] More recently, the Agency helped coordinate a massive black propaganda operation to influence U.S. and world opinion against Nicaragua's Sandinista government and other adversaries in Central America.[11]

During the 1970s, academic-intelligence ties suffered a blow in the context of the general atmosphere of skepticism toward establishment policy associated with the Vietnam War and the massive student-led opposition to that war. A special U.S. Senate committee, chaired by Senator Frank Church, also damaged the Agency's image during its hearings in 1975. The "Church Committee," as it was known, revealed extensive CIA misdeeds, including secret interventions against democratic regimes, attempted assassinations against foreign leaders, and surveillance of American citizens. For a brief period during the late 1960s and early 1970s, some U.S. academics adopted critical views of official policy and distanced themselves from the intelligence agencies.

This situation caused consternation among policy elites; these elites, in turn, contemplated ways to regain influence in the academy. To illustrate this point, I attach below a discussion among Henry Kissinger, President Gerald Ford, and Shah Mohammad Pahlevi of Iran, which took place in 1975. The context of the conversation concerned a coup in Portugal in which a pro-U.S. dictator was deposed. The transcript, recently declassified, reads as follows:

> *Shah:* . . . Portugal could be an eye opener. Are the intellectuals for democracy? [This is surely an ironic comment, coming from the Shah.]
> *Kissinger:* Not really. They just can't have an enemy on the left . . .
> *Shah:* The intellectuals will destroy the world without knowing how to replace it. They don't have a plan. They would be street cleaners in a communist regime.
> *Kissinger: The West could buy off the intellectuals* [emphasis added]. Their pay is poor but they are expected to be upper middle class. But as it is, they resent the system rather than support it.
> *Shah:* That is true. It would be easy have a professor on the board of directors.
> *President [Ford]:* There is a trend here. The President of the University of Michigan is on several.
> *Kissinger:* It has to reach the professors. Because it is the ones who write who put out the poison.[12]

It is clear from this transcript that official circles were concerned about the trends on U.S. campuses, where previously compliant faculty now were becoming too independent and too critical of established policy. And there is explicit discussion by Kissinger and others about the need to co-opt intellectuals and to undercut their independence.

Kissinger's proposal to influence academia was gradually implemented. In reality, academic collaboration with the intelligence services never really ceased, even during the 1960s and 1970s. It proceeded on a more discreet basis, gradually picking up in intensity after the election of Ronald Reagan, which led to the initiation of a new round of CIA interventions in the Third World through the "Reagan Doctrine." And with the end of the Cold War, academic-intelligence ties have increased still further. During the late 1990s (even before the attacks on the World Trade Center and the Pentagon), the CIA made a special effort to augment its influence. A November 2000 article in *Lingua Franca* states that since 1996, the CIA has made public outreach a "top priority and targets academia in particular. According to experts on U.S. intelligence, the strategy has worked." The article notes that highly regarded academics—including Columbia's Robert Jervis, recent president of the American Political Science Association, and Harvard's Joseph S. Nye— worked for the CIA. Yale's H. Bradford Westerfield also states: "There's a great deal of actually open consultation and there's a lot more semi-open, broadly acknowledged consultation." [13] The pace of collaboration accelerated considerably after September 11, 2001. In a 2002 interview with the *Wall Street Journal*, CIA officer John Phillips openly discussed his efforts to recruit academics. His choice of words is revealing: "We don't want to turn [academics] into spies . . . We want to capture them intellectually." [14] The possibility that academics have been intellectually captured by an espionage agency is disconcerting.

An obvious question: Why is the CIA (and U.S. government agencies more generally) so interested in collaborating with academia? One reason is that officials seek to benefit from the expertise that academics possess. Indeed, academics have been useful in perfecting overseas propaganda techniques and psychological operations which have been used by the CIA and military intelligence to influence foreign audiences. [15] And there is a second and more disturbing motive: government officials have sought to influence the content of academia itself and to help ensure that perspectives critical of U.S. expansionism will be excluded from discussion, or at least minimized. We have already seen that some officials, notably Kissinger, have openly discussed the need to "buy off" potentially troublesome academics.

THE EFFECTS OF CO-OPTATION

It seems understandable that the U.S. government has sought to co-opt academics and to enlist their support in presenting a more sanitized version of external interventions, since the government has much to hide in this area. The simple fact is that U.S. policy has often used covert operations involving "dirty" methods which are inherently difficult to justify in public. Because of the widespread use of these methods, it seems natural that policy makers would seek to enlist the support of historians, social scientists, and journalists, who would be useful after the fact in whitewashing this history.

Let us briefly consider some of these covert operations. During the early 1960s, U.S. government agencies led by the CIA made extensive efforts to remove Fidel Castro from power. The CIA collaborated with elements of the Mafia and organized crime in repeated efforts to assassinate Castro. There were numerous attacks against economic targets in

Cuba. In 1962, the Joint Chiefs of Staff sought even more provocative actions and unanimously recommended an "Operations Northwoods," which aimed to "justify" a U.S. invasion. The JCS document describing Northwoods, recently declassified, reads as follows:

> The Joint Chiefs of Staff are to indicate brief but precise description of pretexts . . . for U.S. military intervention in Cuba . . . "Remember the Maine" incident could be arranged in several forms. We could blow up a U.S. ship in Guantanamo Bay and blame Cuba . . . We could develop a Communist Cuban terror campaign in the Miami area, in other Florida cities, and even in Washington . . . We could sink a boatload of [refugee] Cubans en route to Florida (real or simulated). We could foster attempts on the lives of Cuban refugees in the United States even to the extent of wounding in instances to be widely publicized. Exploding a few plastic bombs in carefully chosen spots, the arrest of Cuban agents, and the release of prepared documents substantiating Cuban involvement also would be helpful.[16]

Note that this operation was not in fact approved or implemented—President Kennedy rejected it. But the fact that it was recommended unanimously by the nation's top military officers is surely noteworthy.

Some of the covert operations involved mass killings. One well-documented example was the 1965 coup in Indonesia, in which the CIA helped overthrow a left-leaning, neutralist government, led by Sukarno, a major figure in the nonaligned movement of Third World states. During and shortly after this coup, there was a reign of terror against the Indonesian Communist Party, left-wing organizations, and the families and friends of leftist figures. Estimates of the death toll have ranged from 250,000 to 1 million. In 1984, long after the events took place, former CIA officer Ralph McGehee stated:

> The CIA prepared a study of the 1965 Indonesian operation that described what the Agency did there. I happened to have been custodian of that study for a time, and I know the specific steps the Agency took to create the conditions that led to the massacre of at least half a million Indonesians.[17]

More recent information, published in 1990, reveals that CIA and U.S. embassy officials in Jakarta helped draw up a "hit list" of Indonesians targeted for elimination, and passed on this information to the Indonesian military, a point that former U.S. officials have openly admitted. One U.S. diplomat associated with the covert program said the hit list was necessary during the Cold War: "I probably have a lot of blood on my hands, but that's not all bad."[18]

Many other operations have been well documented. Indeed, the (now overthrown) regime of Saddam Hussein was the result of past U.S. covert operations which helped Hussein and his Baath party to gain power. Former National Security Council staffer Roger Morris also notes CIA complicity in the Baath Party's earliest acts of violence in 1963: "Using lists of suspected Communists and other leftists provided by the CIA, the Baathists systematically murdered untold numbers." In Afghanistan, the Taliban and Al Qaeda grew out of Islamic fundamentalist groups backed by the CIA during the war against the Soviets in the 1980s.[19] While space will not permit a full account here, suffice it to say that covert operations have been undertaken in numerous countries, on every continent.[20]

Now, let us look at how academics have analyzed covert operations. I will focus on the analyses from my own field of political science. By and large political scientists have ignored the issue and have acted as though U.S. covert operations simply do not exist. I surveyed the five top journals in political science that specialize in international relations during the period 1991–2000.[21] I did not find a single article in any of these journals that focused on CIA covert operations. Mentions of these operations were very rare and, when they occurred at all, they were confined to a few sentences or a footnote. In effect, an entire category of international conduct has been expunged from the record, as if it never occurred.

Political science's neglect of covert operations is also evident in many of the datasets that are used as the raw material for research. Consider for example the Militarized Interstate Disputes (MIDs) dataset, which compiles quantitative information on international conflicts throughout recent history and is one of the most widely used datasets in political science. The MIDs dataset contains an exhaustive catalogue of conventional wars and military conflicts (many of which were relatively minor). Yet there is virtually no mention of covert operations. True, the MIDs database defines conflict in a way that rules out most covert operations.[22] This would not in itself be a problem, if there were some other standard dataset that did include a significant number of covert operations. The problem is that such a dataset does not exist (or if such a dataset does exist, it has elicited no notice in the top journals). The resulting scholarship can be summarized as an extended exercise in selection bias, because it omits covert operations, which constitute a major category of international conflict. This selection bias is far from innocuous; it virtually guarantees that U.S. actions will appear in a more favorable light.[23]

There are of course counterarguments to be considered. One objection, offered by Robert Jervis, is that political science has avoided covert operations because there is so little public information on the topic.[24] This is not a valid objection. The Indonesia and Iraq operations have been admitted by former U.S. officials in public statements. Numerous operations have been documented by the most reliable sources of information, such as Senate hearings. Political science's neglect of this topic is certainly not the result of a lack of source material. The problem is that political scientists have ignored source material pertaining to covert operations.

It is amusing to note that, in recent years, politicians have criticized academics for being excessively left wing and critical of official policy.[25] This claim has little merit. In fact social scientists have often acted as apologists for U.S. expansionism, ignoring its most ugly features. The resulting scholarship involves a measure of official propaganda. Some have gone so far as to advocate openly that academics *should* act as propagandists. Consider the case of Professor Conyers Reed, who served as president of the American Historical Association. In his 1949 presidential address, Professor Reed made the following statements:

> Discipline is the essential prerequisite of every effective army whether it marches under the Stars and Stripes or under the Hammer and Sickle . . . Total war, whether it be hot or cold, enlists everyone and calls upon everyone to assume his part. The historian is no freer from this obligation than the physicist . . . This sounds like the advocacy of one form of social control as against another. In short, it is.[26]

Few academics have had the sense of self-confidence to make such frank statements. While Reed's comments were made over half a century ago, I believe that his views hold some relevance for contemporary academic life.

Some qualifications must be noted: the CIA is not always successful in its efforts to gain scholarly support for official policy. A number of academics with intelligence consulting backgrounds—Chalmers Johnson, for example—have become highly critical of U.S. foreign policy. Despite these exceptions, it seems reasonable to conclude that the intelligence community's efforts to influence academia have met with success. This was implicitly recognized by Dwight D. Eisenhower (who, it should be remembered, served as president of Columbia University). In his 1961 Farewell Address, Eisenhower noted: "The prospect of domination of the nation's scholars by Federal employment, project allocations, and the power of money is ever present—and is gravely to be regarded."[27] Unfortunately, Eisenhower's warning had little impact.

Overall, the history of academic involvement with U.S. government agencies, especially with the CIA, has not been a particularly happy one. The relationship has reduced the sense of objectivity and intellectual independence that should be at the core of social science. The story of academic involvement with the intelligence services is only one example of the various ways that powerful interests can influence scholarship. One could just as easily look at the role of other government services or large corporate interests, and the way that these organizations have affected scholarship in various areas. The role of military funding in the physical sciences, pharmaceutical companies in the biomedical sciences, and multinational investment firms in economics no doubt would constitute other examples of external influence on scholarship. The intelligence connections discussed here surely represent just the tip of the iceberg. In short, academic research often entails a measure of partisanship which celebrates the rich and powerful while it slights the grievances of the victims.

NOTES

The epigraph to this chapter is taken from Perry A. Armstrong and H. W. Rocker, *The Sauks and the Black Hawk War* (Springfield, Ill.: 1887), 48.

1. Organic Consumers Association, "Monsanto's Dirty Tricks Campaign against Fired Berkeley Professor Ignacio Chapela," http://www.organicconsumers .org/monsanto/ignacio121604.cfm. Accessed December 16, 2004.

2. Christopher Simpson, ed., *Universities and Empire* (New York: New Press, 1998); and Christopher Simpson, *Science of Coercion* (New York: Oxford University Press, 1994).

3. Noam Chomsky, "The Cold War and the University," in *The Cold War and the University*, ed. David Montgomery (New York: New Press, 1997), 181. Note that Chomsky adds: "Certainly, nothing like that is true now [regarding the MIT Political Science Department]; it is a much more open department."

4. Bruce Cumings, "Boundary Displacement: Area Studies and International Studies during and after the Cold War," *Bulletin of Concerned Asian Scholars* 29.1 (1997): 14.

5. Carl Bernstein, "The CIA and the Media," *Rolling Stone* (October 20, 1977): 65–67.

6. Deborah Davis, *Katharine the Great: Katharine Graham and Her Washington Post Empire* (New York: Sheridan Square Press, 1991), 130–131.

7. Frances Stoner Saunders, *Who Paid the Piper? The CIA and the Cultural Cold War* (New York: Granta, 1999).

WHITEWASHING AMERICAN HISTORY AND SOCIAL SCIENCE ‖ 217

8. Both quotes from U.S. Senate, *Foreign and Military Intelligence*, Book 1 (Washington, D.C.: U.S. Government Printing Office, 1976), 193.

9. Simpson, *Science of Coercion*, 82.

10. Quoted from "An Ex-CIA Official Speaks Out: An Interview with Victor Marchetti by Greg Kaza," 1986, www.skepticfiles.org/conspire/cia_jfk.html . I telephoned Marchetti and confirmed the authenticity of this interview. See also discussion in Victor Marchetti and John D. Marks, *The CIA and the Cult of Intelligence* (New York: Dell, 1980), 161–162.

11. Robert Parry and Peter Kornbluh, "Reagan's Pro-Contra Propaganda Machine," *Washington Post*, September 4, 1988.

12. White House, "Memorandum of Conversation," May 15, 1975. From Declassified Documents Online, http://www.lib.utexas.edu/government/ declassified.html.

13. Chris Mooney, "For Your Eyes Only: The CIA Will Let You See Classified Documents—But at What Price?" *Lingua Franca* (November 2000). The full text of this article and many of the other citations are available on my website: www .gened.arizona.edu/dgibbs/CIA.htm.

14. Quoted in Daniel Golden, "After Sept. 11 CIA Becomes a Growing Force on Campus," *Wall Street Journal*, October 4, 2002, http://www.mindfully .org/Reform/2002/CIA-Growing-On-Campus4oct02.htm. Phillips' comments referred to academics in the "hard" sciences, but there is no reason to assume that the Agency's objectives are any different in the social sciences.

15. See Simpson, *Science of Coercion*.

16. "Justification for U.S. Military Intervention in Cuba," March 13, 1962. Transmitted to the Secretary of Defense from General L. L. Lemnitzer, the JCS chairman. The document was marked "Top Secret Special Handling Noforn [no foreign government dissemination]." It is available from the National Security Archive, www.gwu.edu/~nsarchiv/news/20010430/. The operation is also described in James Bamford, *Body of Secrets: Anatomy of the Ultra-Secret National Security Agency* (New York: Doubleday, 2001), 82–91.

17. Quoted in "Should the CIA Fight Secret Wars?" *Harper's* (September 1984): 33.

18. Quoted in Christopher Reed, "U.S. Agents 'Drew up Indonesian Hit List,'" *Guardian* (London), May 22, 1990.

19. On Iraq, see Roger Morris, "A Tyrant 40 Years in the Making," *New York Times*, March 14, 2003. On Afghanistan, see David N. Gibbs, "Forgotten Coverage of Afghan 'Freedom Fighters': The Villains of Today's News Were Heroes in the '80s," *Extra*, January/February 2002. Note that Hussein himself did not seize full power until 1979. The earlier CIA-supported coups in 1963 and 1968 did, however, aid Hussein's gradual assent.

20. Probably the best general account of covert operations is in William Blum, *Killing Hope: U.S. Military and CIA Interventions since World War II* (Monroe, Maine: Common Courage Press, 1995).

21. The five journals are *World Politics, International Organization, International Security, Journal of Conflict Resolution,* and *International Studies Quarterly.*

22. Daniel Jones, Stuart Bremer, and J. David Singer, "Militarized Interstate Disputes, 1816–1992: Rationale, Coding Rules, and Empirical Patterns," *Conflict Management and Peace Science* 15.2 (1996): 169–170.

23. For further discussion of this problem see David N. Gibbs, "Social Science as Propaganda? International Relations and the Question of Political Bias," *International Studies Perspectives* 2.4 (2001): 159–177. See also Peter Monaghan, "Does International Relations Scholarship Reflect a Bias toward the U.S.?" *Chronicle of Higher Education* (September 24, 1999).

24. This Jervis statement was made in a radio debate on the program *Democracy Now,* November 13, 2002. For audio see www.democracynow.org/article .pl?sid=03/04/07/0312250.

25. See Jerry L. Martin and Ann D. Neal, *Defending Civilization: How Our Universities Are Failing America and What Can Be Done about It* (Washington, D.C.: Defense of Civilization Fund, American Council of Trustees and Alumni, 2002), www.goacta.org/publications/Reports/defciv.pdf.

26. Conyers Reed, "The Social Obligations of the Historian," *American Historical Review* 55.2 (1950): 283–285. There is no specific evidence that Conyers actually consulted for the military or the CIA. However, the opinions expressed in the narrative do elucidate the general phenomenon of the "captured" intellectual.

27. Dwight D. Eisenhower, "Farewell Address," January 17, 1961, mcadams .posc.mu.edu/ike.htm.

BEFORE PREDATOR CAME:
A PLEA FOR EXPANDING FIRST
NATIONS SCHOLARSHIP AS EUROPEAN
SHADOW WORK
David Gabbard

Chapter 14

As difficult as it may be for non-Indian people to realize the corruption of American institutions, such as universities, or to acknowledge the hypnotic effect of propaganda and hegemony, it may be far more difficult for them to mitigate the shadow side of their own cultural histories. In this chapter a non-Indian scholar stresses how vital it is to do so nonetheless, for until a true realization occurs, the United States of America will likely continue its cultural genocide against Indigenous People, as well as continuing its similar intrusions of colonialism in other parts of the world and on other people. He points out that for this realization to take place, we must recognize First Nations scholarship as a set of practices aimed at helping everyone remember *themselves and that efforts to discredit that scholarship and the worldviews that it attempts to recover can keep us in a cycle of genocide that will ultimately consume us.*

David Gabbard holds the rank of Professor in the Department of Curriculum and Instruction at East Carolina University in Greenville, North Carolina. He is the editor of Knowledge and Power in the Global Economy: Politics and the Rhetoric of School Reform, *and co-editor (with Kenneth J. Saltman) of* Education as Enforcement: The Militarization and Corporatization of Schools. *He has also edited a volume in E. Wayne Ross'* Defending Public Schools *series entitled* Education under the Security State.

***

In his latest contribution to First Nations scholarship, *Kill the Indian, Save the Man,*[1] the controversial scholar Ward Churchill strives to correct some of the shortcomings of his earlier work, *A Little Matter of Genocide: Holocaust and Denial in the Americas, 1492 to the Present.*[2] Primarily, he explains, that the earlier work exhibited "too great a concentration upon the raw physicality of killing rather than the more insidious cultural dimensions of the genocide suffered by the peoples indigenous to this hemisphere."[3] To rectify those shortcomings, Churchill turns directly to the work of Raphaël Lemkin, who coined the term "genocide" in 1944 to designate "*any* policy undertaken with the intent of bringing about the dissolution and ultimate disappearance of a targeted human group, *as such*."[4] Lemkin would later head a committee of experts on behalf of the United Nations to draft international laws to help define, prevent, and punish genocide. In what would become the Secretariat's Draft of the present-day Genocide Convention, Lemkin's committee sought to protect any "racial, national, linguistic, religious, and political groups" threatened by policies aimed at destroying such groups or preventing their preservation and development. Such policies, the committee determined, could seek to achieve their ends through one or more of three means.

First, such policies could reflect the patterns of *physical genocide*, which would include the familiar practices of immediate extermination associated with the holocaust in Nazi Germany as well as "slow death measures" such as subjecting a people

> to conditions of life which, owing to lack of proper housing, clothing, food, hygiene, and medical care or excessive work or physical exertion are likely to result in the debilitation [and] death of individuals; mutilations and biological experiments imposed for other than curative purposes; deprivation of [the] means of livelihood by confiscation, looting, curtailment of work, and the denial of housing and of supplies otherwise available to the other inhabitants of the territory concerned.[5]

Biological genocide represented the second category of means identified by Lemkin's committee, which includes involuntary "sterilization, compulsory abortion, segregation of the sexes and obstacles to marriage."[6]

Finally, in the original Secretariat's Draft, Lemkin's committee identified *cultural genocide* as the third means by which one group could seek to eliminate another. As Churchill explains, cultural genocide includes all policies aimed at destroying the specific characteristics by which a target group is defined, or defines itself, thereby forcing them to become something else. Among the acts specified in the original draft are the "forced transfer of children . . . forced and systematic exile of individuals representing the culture of the group . . . prohibition of the use of the national language . . . systematic destruction of books printed in the national language, or religious works, or the prohibition of new publications . . . systematic destruction of national or religious monuments, or their diversion to alien uses [and] destruction or dispersion of objects of historical, artistic, or religious value and of objects used in religious worship."[7]

Churchill points out that Lemkin attached no hierarchy to these classifications because he believed that "the crux of what others would later call 'the genocidal mentality' resides squarely in the cultural domain, and because he understood that there is ultimately no way of segregating the effects of cultural genocide from its physical and biological counterparts."[8]

> A culture's destruction is not a trifling matter. A healthy culture is all-encompassing of human life, even to the point to determining their time and space orientation. If a people suddenly lose their "prime symbol," the basis of culture, their lives lose meaning. They become disoriented, with no hope. As social disorganization often follows such loss, they are often unable to ensure their own survival ... The loss and human suffering for those whose culture has been healthy and is suddenly attacked and disintegrated are incalculable.[9]

In other words, there is no difference between *ethnocide* and *genocide*. In fact, as Churchill points out, Lemkin also originated the term "ethnocide," using it as a synonym for genocide.

Sadly, though not surprisingly, the United States' delegate who chaired the seven-member UN panel charged with reviewing the Secretariat's Draft led the way toward eliminating the entire category of *cultural genocide* from the final Convention on Prevention and Punishment of the Crime of Genocide.[10] Hence, the historic pattern of genocide by cultural destruction has continued virtually unabated. Churchill traces a significant portion of this history through his illumination of the atrocities committed in and around the residential school movement in the United States and Canada.

As described by U.S. Indian Commissioner Francis Leupp, these schools established "a mighty pulverizing machine for breaking up [the last vestiges of] the tribal mass."[11] Given the deliberateness of this process and other atrocities described by Churchill, it should not surprise us that the United States would have failed to fully ratify the UN Convention, even in its diluted form, until 1996. Even when the United States finally submitted its ratification with the UN in 1998, it used a perverse form of self-proclaimed, international executive privilege known as the "Sovereignty Package" to effectively exempt itself from compliance. In other words, the U.S. government will hold others responsible for complying with the Convention, when convenient for *its* interests, but because the U.S. Constitution occupies higher status than international law, no one may hold the U.S. government to the same, or any, standard.

In the final section of *Kill the Indian, Save the Man*, Churchill identifies genocide as an integral aspect of colonialism. From this, as he asserts,

> it follows that the antidote will be found in *decolonization*. To be consciously anti-genocidal, one must be actively anti-imperialist, and vice versa. To be in any way an apologist for colonialism is to be an active proponent of genocide.[12]

It is in this light that we can best understand what Four Arrows (Don Trent Jacobs) has sought to address through this present volume; namely, the "third wave of killing the indigenous" via academic assaults against Indigenous People's philosophies, worldviews, and histories.

If the various modes of genocide originally described by Raphaël Lemkin (*physical, biological,* and *cultural*) represent different methods for *dismembering* people and peoples, then we must recognize First Nations scholarship as a set of practices aimed at helping those people *remember* themselves. Efforts to discredit that scholarship and the worldviews that it attempts to recover, and in many cases preserve, contribute toward perpetuating colonialism's genocidal acts of *dismemberment*. While it may be difficult to prove an author's intent in such cases, it should be enough to recognize how anti-Indigenous writings reflect the worldview and values underlying the persistent patterns of imperialism and colonialism that we see in the world today. In reflecting those values and that worldview, then, such authors participate in the hegemony of "the genocidal mentality" characteristic of imperialism and colonialism, rationalizing and legitimating past, present, and future atrocities by assigning inferior cultural status to victimized groups.

As acts of *remembrance*, First Nations scholarship constitutes an important element of any project for decolonization. Not only does First Nations scholarship forestall cultural genocide in the sense that it helps maintain an Indigenous culture's collective memory, but it also sustains their sense of being *members* of an interdependent life-world characterized by an underlying harmony. The challenge of being human, as defined by most primal cultures, entails living a life that is synchronous with that harmony. *Remembering*, then, entails reconnecting one's self to those to whom one belongs as a co-member of a larger shared universe of meaning, including a collective memory, as well as reconnecting to one's intuitive feelings of relatedness to the natural world.

Decolonization, as Churchill acknowledges, presents a daunting task. It

> will be painful, unavoidably and exceedingly so, and it will not be over in a hurry. While its form will no doubt be decisively different, both

its duration and the deprivations experienced by participants will likely surpass those evidenced in China during the Long March.[13]

In spite of the hardships that will unavoidably follow from the process of decolonization, he claims that those hardships could be minimized if "significant sectors of the colonizing populace joined hands with the colonized before the fact, eliminating colonialism in a common project."[14]

For Americans of European descent, embracing such a project will require a unique process of healing. In the process of healing the wounds left by the sins of our fathers on the backs of Indigenous People across the planet, we must simultaneously heal our own wounded spirits. Left unhealed, as most recently witnessed in the invasion of Iraq, where the genocidal patterns of colonialism have resurfaced, those wounds condemn us to perpetuate those same sins generation after generation.

THE PSYCHOLOGY OF DECOLONIZATION

In the terminology developed by Carl Jung, our dominant institutions have manipulated many of us into participating in a very dangerous, collective habit of *ego inflation*, an exaggerated sense of who we are and what we know about ourselves. Like Narcissus, who sat admiring his own reflection in the still pool of water, Americans have learned to fall in love with their collective persona as "Americans." For Jung, an individual's persona consists of what we want to be and how we wish to be seen by the world. Through the hypnotic powers of manipulation marshaled over us by our dominant institutions, particularly the state and corporations, Americans have learned to ground their own personas in the persona projected by these forces. Hence, to be American is to be like our perceptions of the American government—unique in the history of the world in its (and, therefore, *our*) commitment to equality, freedom, justice, honesty, and other values associated with democracy. Domestically, we learn to believe, our government and our society adhere to these values above all others. Internationally, when we *do* intervene in the affairs of other nations, we do so *only* to defend or advance those same values. The decision of the United States to invoke the "Sovereignty Package"—to place itself above compliance with the UN's Convention on Prevention and Punishment of the Crime of Genocide when it was finally ratified—serves as a perfect example of this ego inflation at an institutional level. The Bush II administration's decision to place itself above the codes of the Geneva Convention in order to "legally" subject prisoners at Guantanamo Bay and in Iraq to torture, as well as the U.S. government's refusal to subject itself to the authority of the International Criminal Court, provides us with two more recent examples of how our inflated ego plays itself out on the world stage. A more simple term for it is "arrogance."

This collective ego inflation, purposefully cultivated by our institutions, occurs through the suppression of another vital element of our individual and collective psyches, which Jung referred to as our shadow. Jungian analyst Robert A. Johnson describes the shadow as "that part of us we fail to see or know . . . that which has not entered adequately into conscious- ness . . . the despised part of our being."[15] We should add an element to his definition of "shadow": that part of us we *refuse* to see or know.

We *say* that we believe in equality, and yet, as Thomas Kostigen of CBS.MarketWatch.com reports, "The Congressional Budget Office says the income gap in the United States is now the widest in 75 years."[16] According to a report sponsored by United for a Fair Economy in 1999, "At the dawn of the 21st century, the distribution of wealth has regressed to the perilous inequality of the 1920s. The top 1 percent of households has more wealth than the entire bottom 95 percent combined."[17]

We *say* that we believe in freedom, but many people, teachers in particular, are inhibited from speaking out on workplace issues (salaries, policies, working conditions, etc.) for fear of losing their jobs. In the wake of the September 11, 2001, terrorist attacks, the vice president's wife, Lynn Cheney, and Democratic Senator Joe Lieberman issued a "white paper" to numerous university alumni organizations requesting them to pressure colleges and universities to fire, or otherwise censure, any professors who might dare criticize the Bush administration's War on Terror.

These do not represent minor inconsistencies. They constitute symptoms of a larger failure or refusal of Americans and their institutions to confront their own shadow. While we tell ourselves that our alleg- edly democratic government defines our individual and national char- acter, this delusion rests on the false assumption that the state functions as our society's dominant institution. Hence, because the government is democratic and possessed of high-minded ideals and values, it *must* also define us and our national character. In truth, however, as I have argued elsewhere, "The market functions as our dominant institution, while the state's central role has always been to provide the security needed by the market to maintain its dominance and to enforce the social and politi- cal conditions that the market demands at home as well as abroad."[18] Hence, the dominant values of our society reflect a greater commitment to greed, dishonesty, and materialistic consumption than to anything remotely associated with democratic values or any set of values conducive to sustainable social and ecological relationships.

Though we may despise those aspects of ourselves, and particularly those aspects of our dominant institutions (including the state in its role in securing and expanding a market society), when we deny their reality, we push them into our shadow. Instead of acknowledging these aspects of who we are and who we have been, we deny them. This does not mean that they disappear. They only, as Johnson says, "collect in the dark corners of our personality. When they have been hidden long enough, they take on a life of their own — the shadow life."[19] The shadow

> often has an energy potential nearly as great as that of our ego. If it accumulates more energy than our ego, it erupts as an overpowering rage ... The shadow gone autonomous is a terrible monster in our psychic house.[20]

The neoconservative push to create an American global empire, as articulated in the Project for the New American Century now mirrored in the Bush II administration's "national security" policies, may be a manifestation of this shadow life reaping its vengeance on us for our collective failure to recognize and deal with our historic patterns of colonialism and genocide.

The same holds true for the terrorist attacks on September 11, 2001. On that morning after learning of the perversely poetic attacks on the World Trade Center (a symbol of America's efforts at global economic domination) and the Pentagon (the center of the American military force used to enforce and expand that domination), I was optimistic that those horrifying events would provide the catalyst for pushing us to finally deal with our shadow. However naively, I held some hope that we could take a serious inventory of our values and evaluate our actions in the world that could trigger such a violent response. I had hoped that we might have finally learned our lesson. Instead, we brought out the flags. We brought out the arrogant persona. Instead of seriously asking "why would anyone do this to us?" we responded with a collective "how *dare* someone do this to us?" "If they hate us," we told ourselves, "they hate us because we are free, because we love freedom, justice, equality, and democracy."

One of the certain manifestations of our refusal to deal with our shadow concerns the purpose of this book. Those Euro-American authors attacking First Nations scholars are guilty of projecting their shadow, those things we secretly don't like about ourselves, onto others. First Nations scholarship frequently shines a light on the dark elements of our past, illuminating those areas of our collective psyche that Euro-Americans would prefer to repress, ignore, or deny. When First Nations scholars point out the genocidal patterns of what we innocently portray to children as "westward expansion," for example, they threaten to burst our overinflated ego. Having pushed the record of that genocide into our collective shadow, some of us seek to project that same shadow onto Indigenous People by engaging in a hunt to find instances of genocidal activity among them. Psychologically, finding such instances among Indigenous People would let the Euro-American psyche "off the hook," allowing Euro-Americans to say to themselves, "See! They're really no better than we are!"

Not only do such academic attacks on First Nations scholarship help keep the history of imperialism, colonialism, and genocide relegated to the shadow of the Euro-American psyche, they also enable the perpetuation of those same patterns through further instances of projection. Just as the early perpetrators of imperial genocide labeled the Indigenous Peoples of North America as "savages" in order to rationalize the savagery that imperialism intended to commit against them, so today's imperialists project the image of the "terrorist" onto those populations whom they intend to terrorize. One of the U.S. government's own army manuals defines "terrorism" as "the calculated use of violence or threat of violence to attain goals that are political, religious, or ideological in nature . . . through intimidation, coercion, or instilling fear."[21] Protecting the inflated ego of the imperial psyche prohibits the use of this word to characterize the means by which it seeks to attain its goals. It may only be applied to those who interfere with the ambitions of empire, reminding us that Crazy Horse and Sitting Bull, Cochise and Geronimo would have been labeled "terrorists" had the word been in circulation during the nineteenth century.

As Marie-Louise von Franz once wrote,

> The shadow plunges man into the immediacy of situations here and now, and thus creates the real biography of the human being, who is always inclined to assume he is only what he thinks he is. It is the biography created by the shadow that counts.[22]

The same principle applies to a people and its collective "biography"—its history. If there is any hope at all for humanity, as Jung once observed, it rests in the willingness of enough of us to do our inner work. Much of this work is individual, as we all strive to contend with our own personal shadows. It also possesses a collective dimension, a form of historical inner work to help us *uncover* those elements of our collective shadow that continue to fuel the genocidal patterns of our dominant institutions and our complicity with them. Again, Johnson explains that

> to refuse the dark side of one's nature is to store up or accumulate the darkness . . . We are presently dealing with the accumulation of a whole society that has worshipped its light side and refused the dark, and this residue appears as war, economic chaos, strikes, racial intolerance. The front page of any newspaper hurls the collective shadow at us. We must be whole whether we like it or not; the only choice is whether we incorporate the shadow consciously or do it through some neurotic behavior.[23]

THE COLONIZATION OF EUROPE

Understanding imperialism, colonialism, and genocide as patterns of neurotic behavior stemming from Western society's ongoing refusal to deal with the destructive elements of its own shadow, we can begin that conscious shadow work at the collective level by reframing the title of one of Churchill's earlier works, *Since Predator Came*.[24] There he describes how "the 'Columbian Encounter' . . . unleashed a predatory, five-century-long cycle of European conquest, genocide, and colonization in 'the New World,' a process which changed the face of Native America beyond all recognition."[25] From his perspective, as a First Nations scholar writing from the vantage point of a Native American, we see nothing unconventional here. After all, Churchill, a Creek and enrolled Keetoowah Band Cherokee, understandably concerns himself most with the atrocities committed "*since* predator came" to North America. However, in limiting our identification of predator as "colonialism"—an easily discernible pattern of conquest and genocide committed by Europeans against non-Europeans—we ignore the history of that same pattern of conquest and genocide as it occurred in Europe "*before* predator came" to the Americas, Africa, Asia, and Australia. Moreover, while it is perfectly understandable for non-Europeans to equate predator with colonialism, we need a deeper analysis of colonialism to avoid associating it exclusively with the patterns of post-Columbian conquest.

The history of colonialism begins with Rome during the sixth century BCE. The Romans established settlements known as *colonia*, initially as a line of defense and later as a means for extending their imperial reach. The name of the German city of Cologne, one of the later Roman

colonia, reminds us of this history. The colonists who populated these
settlements frequently volunteered, but many were forced recruits. After
133 BCE, the role of the colonia expanded beyond military domination
to become a means for dealing with urban homelessness and unemploy-
ment within Roman cities. Surplus members of the urban population
were forced to become farmers in the rural colonia, but their presence
continued to aid the empire in "Romanizing" the occupied territory,
subjecting the indigenous peoples of those lands, known to the Romans
as "barbarians" (anyone who was not a Roman citizen), to physical and
cultural genocide.

> During the empire, colonies were showcases of Roman culture and
> examples of the Roman way of life. *The native population of the prov-
> inces could see how they were expected to live.* Because of this function,
> the promotion of a town to the status of colonia civium Romanorum
> implied that all citizens received full citizen rights and dedicated
> a temple to the so-called Capitoline triad: Jupiter, Juno, and Minerva,
> the deities venerated in the temple of Jupiter Best and Biggest on the
> Capitol in Rome.[26] (Emphasis added)

This Romanization of Europe, facilitated through the formation of
these colonia, would set the stage for its later "Christianization." Though
Christianity became the official state religion of the Roman Empire during
the reign of Theodosius I (379–395 CE)—when the practice of all other
religions was formally outlawed—the Christianization of Northern and
Western Europe did not begin in earnest until the fifth and sixth centuries.
While space prohibits a full account of their significance, the history of
these two processes—Romanization and Christianization—marks a crucial starting point from which to begin expanding First Nations scholarship so that it includes an examination of how these processes play out
in the conquest of European Indigenous cultures. This expansion of First
Nations scholarship would also include efforts to improve our understanding of the Indigenous, pre-Roman, pre-Christian cultures of Europe. Only
in this manner can we begin to establish the bonds of solidarity necessary
for creating a *decolonization* movement that is truly inclusive.

If only because of the scope and scale of the five-hundred-plus years
of imperialism and colonialism, it *must* involve "significant sectors" of
what Churchill characterizes as the "colonizing populace." However,
participating in *decolonization,* for them, must not be conducted *for* the
colonized. Rather, it must be conducted *with* them. Decolonization, for

the "colonizing populace" as well as for the "colonized," must begin with *remembering* themselves, for they, too, have been colonized—*dismembered* from their own Indigenous cultures. By expanding the range of First Nations scholarship, we honor Paulo Freire's insight that "as the oppressors dehumanize others and violate their rights, they themselves also become dehumanized."[27] While First Nations scholarship by the Indigenous Peoples of the Americas, Australia, Africa, and Asia—grounded in the desire to pursue the right to be human—"removes the oppressors' power to dominate and suppress, they restore to the oppressors the humanity that they had lost in the exercise of oppression. It is only the oppressed who, by freeing themselves, can free their oppressors (from their own dehumanized and dehumanizing oppressor consciousness)."[28]

Churchill could not be more correct in his assessment that decolonization will not be easy. For those of us who belong to that category of "colonizers," the task is made more difficult by the fact that we have been *dismembered* from own Indigenous cultures for such a long period of time. I find myself feeling somewhat envious of those people recognized as members of Indigenous cultures, for many of them *do* remember. Unlike my kind, Europeans—cultural orphans from their Indigenous wisdom traditions—they have not been totally *dis-membered* from "much that once was." Many Indigenous peoples *do* remember; some of them never forgot, and they understand *re-membering* themselves and their cultures as prerequisite for averting a market-induced, ecological holocaust.

CONCLUSION

Turning to the second of the two epigrams that I included in this chapter: Europeans and Euro-Americans who insist on running away from the destructive elements of our collective shadow unconsciously feed the power of predator. As its power accumulates, so too does its destructive potential. At the beginning of the twenty-first century, that destructive potential threatens every living creature on this planet. Defusing that potential for global annihilation requires all of us, especially Euro-Americans, to begin a highly conscious and deliberate process of collective shadow work crucial to the process of *remembrance* requisite to the creation of any truly inclusive project of *decolonization*. While space renders it impossible for me to provide a full accounting of the history of the genocidal forces responsible for virtually eliminating the Indigenous cultures of Europe, I hope that the limited portion of the story told here can awaken a new interest among Europeans and

European Americans in their Indigenous past and its destruction by the forces of internal colonization.

For European Americans in particular, we need to inquire into the history of our ancestors' journeys across the Atlantic. Did they really leave Europe to escape religious persecution, or were the majority of our ancestors deemed elements of a surplus population whose deportation could help facilitate predator's virulent spread to other corners of the earth? Did the enclosure movement and the subsequent deportation of the unemployed and "criminal" elements to the Americas, Africa, and Australia constitute our own "Trail of Tears"? Was it a forerunner to the reservation system imposed on the Indigenous People that predator would later establish? These and other questions abound. Seeking their answers is vital for the sake of *remembering* ourselves. First Nations scholars from the Indigenous Peoples of North America and elsewhere have shown us the door; it is up to us to walk through it. It's the only path home.

NOTES

1. Ward Churchill, *Kill the Indian, Save the Man: The Genocidal Impact of American Indian Residential Schools* (San Francisco: City Lights Books, 2004), 72–73.

2. Ibid., 74.

3. Ibid., xiv.

4. Ibid., 3.

5. Robert Davis and Mark Zannis, *The Genocide Machine in Canada: The Pacification of the North* (Montreal: Black Rose Books, 1973), 19–20. Yitzak Arad, Shuel Krakowski and Shmuel Spector, eds., *The Einsatzgruppen Reports: Selections from the Nazi Death Squads' Campaign against the Jews in Occupied Territories of the Soviet Union, July 1941–January 1943* (New York: Holocaust Library, 1989), cited in Churchill, *Kill the Indian, Save the Man*, 6.

6. Davis and Zannis, *The Genocide Machine*, 20, cited in Churchill, *Kill the Indian, Save the Man*, 6.

7. Churchill, *Kill the Indian, Save the Man*, 6.

8. Ibid.

9. Davis and Zannis, *The Genocide Machine*, 20, cited in Churchill, *Kill the Indian, Save the Man*, 6–7.

10. See Churchill's *Kill the Indian, Save the Man* (7–11) for a full accounting of the dilution of that document and the slow history of its ratification by member nations.

11. Francis E. Leupp, *The Indian and His Problem* (New York: Scribner's, 1910), 93, cited in Churchill, *Kill the Indian, Save the Man*, 12.

12. Ibid., 79.

13. Ibid., 81.

14. Ibid., 82.

15. Robert A. Johnson, *Owning Your Own Shadow: Understanding the Dark Side of the Psyche* (San Francisco: Harper, 1991), 4.

16. Thomas Kostigen, "Rich-Poor Gulf Widens: 'Inequality Matters' Conference Puts Nations on Alert," CBS MarketWatch.com (June 1, 2004), http://cbs.marketwatch.com/news/story.asp?guid={4299A2CD-D4D1-4B81-89A8-63B872F2E626}&siteid=mktw&dist=&archive=true.

17. Chuck Collins, Chris Hartman, and Holly Sklar, *Divided Decade: Economic Disparity at the Century's Turn* (Boston: United for a Fair Economy, 1999), http://www.faireconomy.org/press/archive/1999/Divided_Decade/DivDec.pdf.

18. David Gabbard, "Introduction 'Defending Public Education from the Public'" in *Defending Public Schools: Education under the Security State*, ed. David Gabbard and E. Wayne Ross (New York: Praeger Press, 2004), xxv–xxxv.

19. Johnson, *Owning Your Own Shadow*, 4.

20. Ibid., 4–5.

21. *US Army Operational Concept for Terrorism Counteraction* (TRADOC Pamphlet No. 525–537, 1984), cited in Noam Chomsky, "International Terrorism: Image and Reality," in *Western State Terrorism*, ed. Alexander George (New York: Routledge, 1991), 41.

22. Marie-Louise von Franz, cited in D. Patrick Miller, "What the Shadow Knows: An Interview with John Sanford," in *Meeting the Shadow: The Hidden Power of the Dark Side of Human Nature*, ed. Connie Zweig and Jeremiah Abrams (New York: Jeremy P. Tarcher/Perigee Books 1991), 21.

23. Johnson, *Owning Your Own Shadow*, 26–27.

24. Ward Churchill, *Since Predator Came: Notes from the Struggle for American Indian Liberation* (Littleton, Colo.: Aigis Publications, 1995).

25. Ibid., 28.

26. Jona Lendering, "Colonia," *Livius: Articles on Ancient History*, http://www.livius.org/cn-cs/colonia/colonia.html.

27. Paulo Freire, *Pedagogy of the Oppressed* (1970; New York: Continuum, 1993), 56.

28. Ibid.

Chapter 15

ROY ROGERS, TWIN HEROES, AND THE
CHRISTIAN DOCTRINE OF EXCLUSIVE
SALVATION

Four Arrows

In the previous chapter, David Gabbard asserted that we must examine how "Christianization" played an important role in the conquest of European Indigenous cultures as well as in the colonization of Indigenous Peoples of the Americas. Christian fundamentalism has continued to inform the language of conquest against Indigenous People, and it is often embraced "unknowingly" by Indigenous People themselves in ways that contribute to the ethnocide Gabbard describes.

In this chapter, I address several issues relevant to Christian fundamentalist hegemony: the absence of American Indian heroes, the doctrine of exclusive salvation, and the loss of Indigenous twin hero myths, the latter of which allow for an authentic partnership between American Indian spiritual philosophies and teachings attributed to Jesus. I also present a hypothesis suggesting that traditional Indigenous spirituality might reconcile opposing views that have served to divide Christians for thousands of years.

Wahinkpe Topa-Four Arrows, aka Don Trent Jacobs, is of Creek, Cherokee, Scottish, and Irish ancestry. Formerly the Dean of Education at Oglala Lakota College on the Pine Ridge Indian Reservation, he is currently an associate professor in Educational Leadership at Northern Arizona University and a professor at Fielding Graduate University. The 2004 recipient of the Martin-Springer Institute's award for moral courage, he has been an activist for more truthful ways of viewing reality since his awakenings to the falsehoods surrounding the Vietnam War, during which time he served as an officer in the U.S. Marine Corps. Among his numerous publications are The Bum's Rush: The Selling of Environmental Backlash *(1994);* Primal Awareness: A True Story of Survival, Awakening and Transformation with the Raramuri Shamans of Mexico *(1998);* Teaching Virtues: Building Character across the Curriculum (An American Indian Approach to Character Education) *(co-authored with Jessica Jacobs-Spencer, 2002); and* American Assassination: The Strange Death of Senator Paul Wellstone *(co-authored with Jim Fetzer, 2004). (More information is available at www.teachingvirtues.net.)*

***

CHILDHOOD HEROES?

In my early childhood, raised to disparage my Indigenous heritage and weaned on early television episodes of white heroes shooting red villains, I saw no clear line between heroes and horses. Hopalong Cassidy and Topper were embroidered on my bedspread and a portrait of Gene Autry and his horse Champion hung on my wall. I do not think I missed an episode of the Roy Rogers and Dale Evans television show on our small, black-and-white TV. Images of the rearing palomino, Trigger, and the words and melody of the program's closing song, "Happy trails to you, until we meet again," still resonate in my mind.

But as I approach my sixtieth birthday, I am amazed to say that only recently did I learn that Roy Rogers had American Indian ancestry! Of course I did know that he was Christian. He was well known for being the "Christian cowboy." He spoke at Billy Graham revivals, sang Christian songs regularly on a Christian cable network, and referred often to "the Lord" in public appearances. But I did not know he was part Choctaw. Moreover, as I have also now learned, he was not too ashamed of this fact, at least not at the peak of his success. In fact, in 1967 he was named outstanding Indian citizen of the year by a group of western tribes. Although he played it down a little, claiming he was mostly Dutch upon receiving the award, he was pleased to accept the recognition according to some reports.[1] This might explain why he and Dale had adopted an American Indian child, which I also did not know, and produced the first TV series, *Brave Heart*, to feature an American Indian as the lead character, though of course a non-Indian played the role and it ran only twenty-six episodes.

How knowing all of this when I was young would have changed my life! My mother encouraged me to ignore our Native heritage, one that I would not begin to embrace until after my stint in the Marine Corps. Perhaps her misguided efforts to protect me from the dominant culture's anti-Indianism would not have created confusion about my own identity had I known that Roy Rogers was also part Indian.

I only learned about Rogers recently because a dear friend, Tony, came to visit me. Tony is an eighty-five-year-old Dutchman who lived six years in the Dutch underground as an officer (and former cavalryman!) in the Dutch army during Hitler's occupation of Holland. During his amazing life he has served as a technical adviser for noted feature film producer and director George Stevens, specifically for *The Diary of Ann Frank* (1959) and *The Greatest Story Ever Told* (1965). For the latter, Tony

2 3 4 FOUR ARROWS

had a significant budget to spend four years researching the life of Jesus of Nazareth for Stevens.

Tony told me that Stevens, considered one of the greatest American filmmakers of all time, was also a mixed blood. He was nominated as best director for both of these movies, and won the coveted Academy Award for *Shane*, a story about a cowboy with a mysterious past who stood for justice; for *Giant*, a story that exposed the swagger and racial bigotry of Texas oil tycoons; and for *A Place in the Sun*, a movie about the self-destructive pursuit of wealth and status. (Tony also told me that the screenwriter for this latter film, Michael Wilson, was Indian and Irish, defied Joseph McCarthy, and was blacklisted in Hollywood for a remarkable fourteen years.) Stevens himself was Comanche, though unlike Roy Rogers, he was loath to ever admit it publicly. Interestingly, however, the anti-establishment themes of his movies challenged some of those things in the dominant culture that continue to influence anti-Indianism in America. Still, what might it have meant for Indigenous Americans to at least have known that this Academy Award–winning cinematographer was a brother at a time when authentic Indian heroes were few and far between?

Although Tony, working closely with Carl Sandberg, offered four years of research on Christian history for "The Greatest Story Ever Told," Stevens used only his information about costumes, customs, and architecture, and not the historically accurate information about Jesus himself. Owing to pressures from the Christian fundamentalist community, who became aware of Stevens' position that Jesus was an enlightened man, not a deity, Stevens did not challenge fundamentalist Christian ideas by telling the truth about the history of Jesus as a revolutionary man who departed from traditional Jewish ideas to talk about love and nonviolence for all humans.

Carl Sandberg's fascinating initial script, supported by Tony's four years of research, described Jesus as a socialist and working-class carpenter who worked and preached throughout the land, as was common for many during these times. The script, along with Tony's collaborating research, revealed the background of mythologies regarding the ideas of physical resurrection and virgin birth, both of which were common in Roman mythologies and in many tribal creation stories. Tony and Sandberg knew that most of the stories about Jesus that are now accepted by fundamentalists the world over as "truth" resulted from the process by which Constantine "legalized" the Christian religion, which involved the incorporation of Roman Mithraism and other religions to create a strong church that would emerge as a new, practical, powerful political structure that would support the subsequent genocide of Indigenous People.

THE RAPTURE INDEX

Joe Bageant, in an article entitled "The Covert Kingdom, Thy Will be Done, On Earth as It Is in Texas," recently wrote that it is impossible to understand American politics without understanding Christian fundamentalism. "For liberals to examine the current fundamentalist phenomenon in America is to accept some hard truths," he says.[2] Similarly, Bill Moyers, in his acceptance speech for Harvard Medical School's Global Environmental Citizen Award, remarked on the pervading perversion of fundamentalism and its influence on the body politic:

> Remember James Watt, President Reagan's first Secretary of the Interior? He told the U.S. Congress that protecting natural resources was unimportant in light of the imminent return of Jesus Christ. Beltway elites snickered. But James Watt was serious. So were his compatriots out across the country. They are the people who believe the Bible is literally true—one third of the American electorate, if a recent Gallup poll is accurate. In this past election several million good and decent citizens went to the polls believing in the rapture index. That's right, the rapture index . . . I'm not making this up. I've reported on these people, following some of them from Texas to the West Bank. They are sincere, serious, and polite as they tell you they feel called to help bring the rapture on as fulfillment of biblical prophecy. That's why they have declared solidarity with Israel and the Jewish settlements and backed up their support with money and volunteers. It's why the invasion of Iraq for them was a warm-up act, predicted in the Book of Revelation . . . A war with Islam in the Middle East is not something to be feared but welcomed—an essential conflagration on the road to redemption.[3]

Moyers explains that a 2002 Time/CNN poll found that 59 percent of Americans believe that prophecies found in the Book of Revelation are going to come true. Nearly one quarter think the Bible predicted the 9/11 attacks. He quotes from a high school history book that refers to secular people as socialists who have a limited-resources mentality, as opposed to Christians, who know that there is no shortage of resources in God's earth. He speaks of the lack of any challenge to these ideas because of the influence of the Christian right on politics and media.

His point, and mine, is that until Western culture reckons with the influence of Christian fundamentalism on the present and past and how it has contributed to the annihilation of opposing Indigenous perspectives, the language of conquest will remain the language of our world.

THE DOCTRINE OF EXCLUSIVE SALVATION

At the heart of Christian fundamentalism is the doctrine of exclusive salvation, which says that only by believing in Jesus Christ as the only son of God will one have eternal life and not "burn in hell." It is this aspect of fundamentalism in any religion that may be responsible for unimaginable atrocities and wars throughout history, including the genocide of American Indians supported by the papal bulls.[4] Columbus relied upon these bulls, yet in spite of his atrocities (or perhaps because of them?), "Columbus Day" has been an officially recognized public holiday since 1971; all federal offices are closed on this day—one of eight federally recognized holidays. Why? The title of Michael Berliner's article, "On Columbus Day, Celebrate Western Civilization, Not Multiculturalism," offers one answer—one that once again reveals the influence of Christian fundamentalism.[5] The Wikipedia Encyclopedia offers a more specific reason, stating, "The casting of Columbus as a figure of 'good' or of 'evil' often depends on people's perspectives as to whether the arrival of Europeans to the New World and the introduction of Christianity or the Roman Catholic faith is seen as positive or negative."[6] In my view, it is ultimately belief in the doctrine of exclusive salvation that makes Christian fundamentalism a religion rather than a political ideology.

It is probably true that many Americans continue to honor Christopher Columbus, ignoring his responsibility in the genocide of American Indians, simply because "he was a deeply committed Christian whose own writings prove that his desire to carry the message of Jesus Christ to faraway lands was the primary motivation of his historic voyage to the New World."[7] Starting in 1417, Columbus's homeland of Portugal had resumed the Christian Crusades of the previous century. By 1492, "The Portuguese were in a position to resume Christendom's long struggle against the Muslims," and Christian Spain had conquered Muslim Granada.[8] This "Crusade" mentality helped determine the actions of Columbus and his men against the Indigenous Peoples of the "New World." Columbus' own writings show that he believed that the Bible was the infallible word of God and that his voyage was a crusade to fulfill the prophesies of the Book of Isaiah; to convert the natives he encountered, and to provide gold that could be used to finance the efforts to regain Jerusalem.[9]

As Moyers pointed out, this "mentality" and blind acceptance of biblical inerrancy, which contributed to the genocide of American Indians during Columbus' time, has, in many ways, continued and continues to inform U.S. foreign policy, including its dealings with its own sovereign Indian nations. The doctrine of exclusive salvation is an important aspect of this fundamentalist perspective. Even in 2004, unquestioned, widespread acceptance of this doctrine underscores the cultural hegemony that has supported the policies of President Bush, whose Christian beliefs led him to believe that God appointed him to be president and that he is serving the "Lord's will."[10]

Since exclusive salvationists believe, literally, that the only way to eternal life is to profess that Jesus Christ was resurrected and that he is the only true representative of "God" and the only way to eternal life, it follows that anyone who does not profess this will suffer unending punishment in Hell. They further believe that people are admitted into "heaven" by this affirmation via God's grace and not by how they live their life on earth. There are several places in the Bible that are used to support this doctrine, but the one most often quoted is John 14:6. "Jesus said to him, I am the way, and the truth, and the life; no one comes to the Father, but by me."

Although there are numerous Christian books that promote and rationalize the doctrine of exclusive salvation, Archbishop George Hay's book, *The Sincere Christian*, first published in 1787, is often used to explain its "truth." The book received an "imprimi potest," stating officially that the book was free from doctrinal or moral errors. An extraction from this book explains the "truth" of exclusive salvation:[11]

> Q: What is to be said of all those Turks (Muslems), Jews, and heathens, who having never heard of Jesus Christ or of His Religion, are, therefore, invincibly ignorant of both; can they be saved, if they live and die in that state?
>
> A: The plain answer to this is, that they cannot be saved, that not one of these *"can enter the kingdom of God."* Now all those we hear speak of are in the state of original sin, *"aliens from God, and children of wrath,"* as the scripture calls all such, and unbaptized; and it is a constant article of the Christian Faith, that, except original sin be washed away by the grace of baptism, there is no salvation; for Christ Himself expressly declares, *"Amen, amen, I say to thee."* Except a man be born again of even

the children of Christian parents, who die without baptism, cannot go to heaven, how much less can those go there, who, besides being never baptized, are supposed, in the present case, to live and die in ignorance of the True God, or of Jesus Christ and His Faith, and, on that account, must also be supposed to have committed many actual sins themselves. Nay, to suppose that heathens, Turks, or Jews who live and die in that state, can be saved, is to suppose that worshippers of idols, and of Mohammed, and blasphemers of Christ, can be saved in the guilt of original sin, as well as all of those actual crimes by their ignorance, which is putting them upon a better footing, by far, than even Christians themselves and their Children. The fate of all such the scripture decides as follows: *"The Lord Jesus shall be revealed from heaven, with the angel of his power, in a flame of fire, yielding vengeance to those who know not God and who obey not the Gospel of Our Lord Jesus Christ, who shall suffer eternal punishment in destruction, from the face of the Lord and from the Glory of His Power"* (2. Thess. i 7) This is precise, indeed, and a clear and decisive answer to the present question.

Such a doctrine led to the 1248 decree of Pope Innocent IV during the medieval Crusades, proclaiming that Europeans had a divine mandate to protect the spiritual life of nonbelieving infidels and giving Christians the right to conquer and assume sovereignty over non-Christians throughout the world. It may also have supported Pope Alexander IV's "Right of Discovery" in 1492, claiming that any Christian European discovery of territory held by nonbelievers gave Christians title to the land. And now, at some level of the American psyche, this doctrine may continue to rationalize globalism and other oppressive aspects of capitalism, perhaps including invasions of sovereign nations, such as Iraq.

Until relatively recent times, all or most Christians believed in the idea of exclusive salvation, perhaps with the exception of Universalists, Gnostics, or those who have studied the biblical interpretations of Thomas Aquinas. Today a number of churches have modified their position, allowing that those who do not know about Jesus Christ still have a chance for life ever after. Nonetheless, many Americans sincerely believe those not in the fold are doomed to eternal damnation. For example, a recent Gallup poll showed that 48 percent of Americans believe in creationism.[12] An ABC poll found that of the 83 percent of Americans that profess to be Christians, about 40 percent claim to be evangelical.[13] Moreover, Christian fundamentalism is gaining momentum throughout the world. Professor Philip Jenkins, a professor of history and religious studies at Pennsylvania State University, explains in his book *The Next*

Christendom: The Coming of Global Christianity that Christianity is rapidly expanding south into Africa, Asia, and Latin America and that Christian fundamentalism may lead to a new age of Christian crusades and Muslim jihads.[14]

For every effort to reform the doctrine of exclusive salvation, there seems to be a countereffort. For example, Alan Morrison's paper, "Saving That Which Is Lost: The Challenge to Christian Mission and Evangelism at the Close of the 20th Century," strongly appeals to the reader for a return to this fundamentalist doctrine:

> But as relativism, sentiment and psychobabble have become the dominant influences in the life of the Church, many are no longer willing to be guided by the plain teaching of the Bible concerning eternal salvation and eternal condemnation, but instead they have substituted either what they "feel" to be correct or whatever harmonizes with the prevailing trends of the day ... At the heart of this process is the Hegelian notion that all religions essentially worship the same God and are merely different pathways to ultimate truth and perfection. This notion challenges the uniqueness and exclusiveness of the Christian message concerning the Lord Jesus Christ and the need for the Gospel to be preached to all nations. It is part of a dark, universal process by which the very fabric of the body of truth we call Christianity is being torn apart.[15]

Part of this resurgent requirement for exclusive salvation involves a call to patriotism alongside a revisionist view of America's founding. There seems to be an effort to convince people that this fundamentalist movement is simply an effort to return our nation to what the founding fathers intended, though it is *not* what they intended. In addition to assertions that none of America's ideals were based on the Iroquois Confederacy, a number of people have been led to believe that the founding fathers were Christian. However, the short time period immediate before, during, and after the American Revolution saw a rejection of the doctrine of exclusive salvation and all that came with it. Perhaps this is because the founding fathers (and, perhaps, their wives) understood the oppressive nature of such assumptions. This desire is underscored in Article 11 of the Treaty with Tripoli, written during George Washington's administration, which declared in part that "the government of the United States is not in any sense founded on the Christian religion . . ."[16]

In fact, many of America's revolutionary leaders were deists who blatantly rejected Christian doctrine, even when "swearing an oath" on a

Christian Bible, a holdover from previous times. The Bible Washington swore on was a Masonic Bible, essentially the same text but symbolizing significant deviations in belief. Deists did not believe in the virgin birth, divinity, the resurrection of Jesus, or the divine inspiration of the Bible. They certainly did not believe in the doctrine of exclusive salvation.

Not only the leaders of the American Revolution, but also many of the earliest colonial settlers tended to shy away from religious orthodoxy. Historian Richard Hofstadter says that "mid-eighteenth century America had a smaller proportion of church members than any other nation in Christendom."[17] Historian James MacGregor Burns concurs, noting that it had been a "very wintry season for religion everywhere in America after the Revolution."[18]

Such ideas were powerfully articulated by Thomas Paine, another founding father, in his famous *Age of Reason*, a book that would in his lifetime anger his contemporaries as Christianity regained a foothold in America. Paine states:

> Of all the systems of religion that ever were invented, there is no more derogatory to the Almighty, more unedifying to man, more repugnant to reason, and more contradictory to itself than this thing called Christianity. Too absurd for belief, too impossible to convince, and too inconsistent for practice, it renders the heart torpid or produces only atheists or fanatics. As an engine of power, it serves the purpose of despotism, and as a means of wealth, the avarice of priests, but so far as respects the good of man in general it leads to nothing here or hereafter . . . The most detestable wickedness, the most horrid cruelties, and the greatest miseries that have afflicted the human race have had their origin in this thing called revelation, or revealed religion. It has been the most destructive to the peace of man since man began to exist. Among the most detestable villains in history, you could not find one worse than Moses, who gave an order to butcher the boys, to massacre the mothers and then rape the daughters. One of the most horrible atrocities found in the literature of any nation.[19]

Referring to the exclusive salvation concept in another of his writings, he stated, "We must be compelled to hold this doctrine to be false, and the old and new law called the Old and New Testament, to be impositions, fables and forgeries."[20] Paine saw in such impositions an unnatural rationale for the oppressive politics that caused the injustices of European life and that would continue to be perpetrated on the American Indians. Furthermore, he contrasted the European worldview with the life and worldviews of the Indigenous People he observed. "Among the Indians," he wrote, "There are not any of those spectacles of misery that poverty and want present to our eyes in the towns and streets of Europe."[21] He truly admired what little he understood of the Indians' way of life and thinking, especially their relatively equal distribution of property, but he thought it would not be possible for Europeans "to go from the civilized to the natural state."[22]

Vine Deloria Jr. tends to agree with Paine's concern. He argues in his classic *God is Red* that a polarity exists between Native religiosity and Christianity in large part because of Christianity's relative disregard for the sacredness of "place."[23] I also argue that Christianity is essentially incompatible with Indigenous worldviews *insofar as the religion is generally practiced in the United States* and as such practice reflects the political/historical aspects of Christianity. Sadly, many Indigenous People have succumbed to the lure and authority of Christian fundamentalism, many losing their own vital worldview in the process.

TWIN HEROES AND A NEW PARTNERSHIP

In an effort to "solve" the problems that such fundamentalism has brought to silencing the voice of Indigenous People and its contribution to world health, I wish to introduce here a new consideration that might reconcile Christianity to both itself and to Indigenous wisdom. In brief, my hypothesis is this: original Christian thought, based on the purported teachings of Jesus of Nazareth, represented an understanding of both the physical and the spiritual in balance. However, political structures put into place less than one hundred years after the death of Jesus established an authoritarian version of Christianity, one based on the "physical" aspects of his teachings, which better fit the exclusive hierarchical power needs of those "designated" to be authorities. At the same time, an opposing understanding of the teachings of Jesus asserted a more "spiritual" aspect of the teachings. Those in opposition believed Jesus opposed outside authority in favor of that which comes from personal reflection leading to transcendence. This group was branded by the other as heretical and remained so for thousands of years.

In *The Gnostic Gospels*, Elaine Pagels discusses the contents of the buried scrolls discovered in Nag Hammadi in 1945. These documents, as old as the Dead Sea Scrolls and now often referred to as the "Gnostic Gospels," offer strikingly different interpretations of the biblical Gospels than have guided Christian thinking through the ages, and include additional

Gospels as well. These texts were banned as heresy within one hundred years after the death of Jesus. "For example, some of these Gnostic texts question whether all suffering, labor, and death derive from human sin." "Others speak of the feminine element in the divine, celebrating God as Father *and* Mother. Still others suggest that Christ's resurrection is to be understood symbolically, not literally."[24]

Pagels shows how the disciples of Jesus were divided as to whether they saw Jesus return from the dead as a spirit or as a physical person. In the Gospel of Mary, Mary Magdalene sees Jesus in a vision where Jesus speaks of perceiving through the mind. The Apocalypse of Peter explains that Peter, while in trance, saw Christ, who explained that he was "intellectual spirit."[25] The Gospel of Philip, in expressing the belief that Christ's resurrection should not be taken literally, says that Jesus meant for the resurrection to be about spiritual transformation in one's life.

The point is that the Gnostic interpretations which were advocated by early followers of Jesus but were seen as heresy by those that established the organized religion in many ways conform to the Indigenous world-view, which sees authority only in personal, spiritual reflection, embraces the feminine, rejects the doctrine of sin, and so on. Pagels refers to scholars who have proposed that Gnosticism in fact originated from the "universal experience of the self that lends itself to a particular world view."[26]

Thus even Christian orthodoxy is not completely alien to Indigenous spirituality, although one has to read against the grain of literalism. The assertion that Jesus arose from the dead and appointed authority to others before leaving again was of course politically expedient for the architects of the church; at the same time, however, as Jurgen Moltmann points out, the orthodox version of the resurrection, if read symbolically, expresses "the conviction that human life is inseparable from bodily experience: even if a man comes back to life from the dead, he must come back physically."[27] This recognition of the significance of the physical life experience is also reflected in Indigenous thinking, and this emphasis on physicality contrasts with Eastern philosophies, which tend to see the body merely as a vessel for a spirit focused almost exclusively on transcending the body to a "higher consciousness."

Thus, the Indigenous view would seem to challenge *both* Christian perspectives, the orthodox and the Gnostic, at different levels, while at the same time joining them in a more complete understanding not only of the teachings of Jesus but also the Christian elements of the virgin birth and the resurrection.

Another way to look at this is to consider the phenomenon of "twin" motifs throughout mythology. Every culture has stories of twin heroes, with the twins reflecting the complementarity of body and spirit; of solar and lunar; of male and female principles. For example, the Navajo stories about the twins Monster Slayer and Child Born of the Water show how important it is for these opposing energies to work together in harmony. In fact, most American Indian cultures have similar stories about twins; one is direct and "solar" and the other is indirect and "lunar," and they work together to fight the monsters that reside within. However, many of the twin stories from Western cultural myths have evolved in such a way as to have the twins fighting one another with the solar twin dominating, for example, Cain slew Abel, Romulus overshadowed Remus; Hercules became more honored than his half brother, Iphicles.

Thus, playing out the myths of the separated twins, Christianity has emerged primarily as the "solar" twin: active, heroic, intent on mastery. Adherents must believe in the *physical* resurrection; only Jesus and belief in his physical reality can bring eternal salvation. This "religion of the sun" prevails over Gnostic Christianity—the spiritual "twin" that reveals "God" in all things and accepts the spiritual mystery at the heart of creation. Native spirituality may be the force that can reunite these twins!

According to Pagels, "the titles of the Gospel of Thomas and the Book of Thomas the Contender (attributed to Jesus' 'twin brother') may suggest that 'you, the reader, are Jesus' twin brother.' Whoever comes to understand these books discovers, like Thomas, that Jesus is his twin," his spiritual "other self."[28] In other words, Jesus as the solar, physical energy has been separated from his twin, the spiritual realization of God that is also inside all other life forms, a truth supported by his early Gnostic followers, who were attacked as heretics. The dominant, assertive "above Nature" cultures, under the banner of Christian fundamentalism (and perhaps its related Islamic and Jewish versions), may be the "twin" of the more reflective, creative Indigenous spiritual traditions of interconnections with Nature. This is the spirituality of the people of the water, the people who

1. see reflection on lived experience, on intuitive spiritual awareness, and on cultural traditions that "make sense" for the greater good as the only true authority in life;
2. believe that animals are fellow creatures, not lowly things;
3. put the community above selfish individualism or ambition and hold that cooperation, not competition, is the natural dynamic in life;

4. maintain an even balance of power between men and women;
5. respect the development of children, who are considered sacred, with a higher degree of permissiveness and positive peer pressure;
6. recognize and respect the significance of everyone in the community;
7. view criminals as people out of balance who need to be brought back into the community, rather than as villains;
8. value self-sacrifice, generosity, and courage as ideals for adulthood;
9. believe that honesty and integrity are too important to allow for deception;
10. understand that the spirit life—good heart, love of neighbor as your brother, sister, mother, father, grandparents—is at the heart of spiritual practices;
11. assert that generosity is the greatest virtue and the highest expression of courage; and
12. recognize the interconnectivity between humans and Nature as the ultimate reality.

Or maybe this theory of the twin relationships is no more than a wistful hope for a partnership between the dominant religion of the United States and the Indigenous spiritual philosophies of the land. In his article "Canaanites, Cowboys, and Indians," published in *Christianity and Crisis*, Robert Allen Warrior, a member of the Osage Nation, tends to agree that the Bible will always be incompatible with authentic Indigenous ways of seeing the world. He says that the Bible

> is part of the heritage and thus the consciousness of people in the United States. Whatever dangers we identify in the text and the god represented there will remain as long as the text remains. These dangers only grow as the emphasis upon catechetical (Lindbeck), narrative (Hauerwas), canonical (Childs) and Bible-centered Christian base communities (Gutierrez) grows. The peasants of Solentiname bring a wisdom and experience previously unknown to Christian theology, but I do not see what mechanism guarantees that they—or any other people who seek to be shaped and molded by reading the text—will differentiate between the liberating god and the god of conquest. But we, the wretched of the earth, may be well advised this time not to listen to outsiders with their promises of liberation and deliverance. We will perhaps do better to look elsewhere for our vision of justice, peace, and political sanity—a vision through which we escape not only our oppressors but our oppression as well. Maybe, for once, we will just have to listen to ourselves, leaving the gods of this continent's *real* strangers to do battle among themselves.[29]

All I know for sure is that it took me almost sixty years to learn that one of my childhood heroes, Roy Rogers—an icon for the Christian population, many of whom believe in the destructive doctrine of exclusive salvation—was also an American Indian. As well as George Stevens and Michael Wilson and who knows how many others, both by virtue of blood and, it would seem, by virtue of their attempts to challenge a worldview that does not understand how we are all related. My late-in-coming realization that my "cowboy" hero was really an "Indian" seems a small thing, especially in the face of the overwhelming influence of Christian fundamentalism on policies of genocide, war, and environmental calamity. Yet my mind is still reeling about how the language of conquest contributed to a young boy's suppression of his own identity, and how its subtle power continues to suppress a worldview that may be our only real "salvation."

NOTES

1. Richard Severo, "Roy Rogers, America's Favorite Cowboy Dies at 86," http://elvispelvis.com/royrogers.htm. Accessed August 22, 2004.

2. Joe Bageant, "The Covert Kingdom, Thy Will be Done, On Earth as It Is in Texas," *Counterppunch* (May 25, 2003), http://www.counterpunch.org/bageanto5252004.html. Accessed December 17, 2004.

3. Bill Moyers, "On Receiving Harvard Med's Global Environmental Citizen Award," *Truthout*, http://www.truthout.org/docs_04/120504G.shtml. Accessed December 17, 2004.

4. Bartolomé de las Casas, *The Devastation of the Indies: A Brief Account*, trans. Herma Briffault (Baltimore: Johns Hopkins University Press, 1992). See also Hans Koning, *The Conquest of America: How the Indian Nations Lost Their Continent* (New York: Monthly Review Press, 1993).

5. Michael Berliner, "On Columbus Day, Celebrate Western Civilization, Not Multiculturalism," http://www.aynrand.org/medialink/columbus.html. Accessed November 7, 2004.

6. See http://en.wikipedia.org/wiki/Christopher_Columbus. Accessed November 14, 2004.

7. Phyllis Schlafly radio script, October 14, 2002, http://www.eagleforum.org/educate/columbus/columbus.shtml. Accessed November 14, 2004.

8. Thomas C. Tirado, Encarta Encyclopedia, 2000, http://muweb.millersville.edu/~columbus/columbus.html. Accessed November 4, 2004.

9. Paul Boyer, "Apocalypticism Explained," http://www.pbs.org/wgbh/pages/frontline/shows/apocalypse/explanation/columbus. Accessed November 2, 2004.

10. John le Carré, "The United States of America Has Gone Mad," London *Times*, January 15, 2003. Also at http://www.commondreams.org/views03/0115-01.htm. Accessed December 2, 2005.

11. George Hay, "Questions and Answers on Salvation regarding the Doctrine of Exclusive Salvation," http://www.franciscan-archive.org/apologetica/extra .html. Accessed November 4, 2004. See entire text at www.catholictradition.org/ salvation.htm.

12. "Evolution and the Polls," http://www.pathlights.com/ce_encyclopedia/ 22scho2.htm. Accessed November 3, 2004.

13. Gary Langer, "Poll: Most Americans Say They're Christian. Varies Greatly from the World at Large," http://abcnews.go.com/sections/us/DailyNews/ beliefnet_poll_010718.html. Accessed December 1, 2004. See also Dennis L. Cuddy, "Mental Health, Education and Social Control" (October 7, 2004), http://www.newswithviews.com/Cuddy/dennis18.htm. Accessed November 4, 2004.

14. Philip Jenkins, *The Next Christendom: The Coming of Global Christianity* (New York: Oxford University Press, 2002).

15. Alan Morrison, "Saving That Which Is Lost," Interim Paper No. 3, September 1999, http://www.diakrisis.org/challenge_to_cm_.htm. Accessed November 4, 2004.

16. Hunter Miller, ed., *Treaties and Other International Acts of the United States*, vol. 2 (Washington, D.C.: U.S. Government Printing Office, 1931), 365.

17. Richard Hofstadter, *Anti-Intellectualism in American Life* (New York: Knopf, 1974), 89.

18. James MacGregor Burns, *The American Experiment: Vineyard of Liberty* (New York: Vintage Books, 1983), 493.

19. Thomas Paine, *Thomas Paine: Life and Works* (New York: Routledge, 1996), 134.

20. Ibid., 282.

21. Eric Foner, ed., *Paine: Collected Writings*, vol. 1. (New York: Library of America, 1995), 610.

22. Moncure Daniel Conway, ed., *The Writings of Thomas Paine* (New York: G. P. Putnam's Sons, 1894), 70.

23. Vine Deloria, *God is Red* (Golden, Colo.: North American Press, 1992).

24. Elaine Pagels, *The Gnostic Gospels* (New York: Random House, 1979), xxxv.

25. Ibid., 12.

26. Ibid., xxiii.

27. Ibid., 26, quoting Jurgen Moltmann.

28. Ibid., 18.

29. Robert Allen Warrior, "Canaanites, Cowboys, and Indians: Deliverance, Conquest, and Liberation Theology Today," *Christianity and Crisis* 49 (1989): 263.

If Indigenous People and the larger society are to prevent the problems associated with religious fundamentalism described in the previous chapter, both may have to make a commitment to deeper reflection on the great teachings of Christianity, those that go beyond that which is proffered under the heading of "biblical inerrancy." The same reflection must be applied to other spiritual traditions, especially those of Indigenous People, which have been overshadowed by the language of conquest.

In this chapter, Greg Cajete offers a new rationale for such reflection on the traditions, stories, ceremonies, and creative understanding of the world that are found in traditional Indigenous cultures, where art, music, dance, and other creative expressions are woven into the fabric of everyday existence. He shows us how such understanding is beginning to be "validated" by quantum physics. Perhaps his insights may motivate a number of people, perhaps those with a more scientific bent, to initiate this deeper reflection. Greg shows us how the new physics is starting to "prove" Indigenous wisdom and how we must begin to reassess the totality of Western science, which seems to have lost its creative energy. In light of ancient Indigenous understandings about life, this loss of creativity will have serious consequences. Greg suggests that we vitally need an inclusive foundation for a new cosmology in the coming years.

Gregory A. Cajete, PhD, a Tewa from Santa Clara Pueblo, is the Director of the University of New Mexico Native American Studies Program and also an Associate Professor in the Department of Language, Literacy, and Sociocultural Studies in the UNM College of Education. Before serving on the faculty of the University of New Mexico, he was a teacher for twenty-one years at the Institute of American Indian Arts in Santa Fe, New Mexico. While at the Institute he also served as Dean of the Center for Research and Cultural Exchange and Chair of Cultural Studies. He is the editor of A People's Ecology: Explorations in Sustainable Living, *and* Native Science: Natural Laws of Interdependence; *he is also the author of* Look to the Mountain: An Ecology of Indigenous Education; Ignite the Sparkle: An Indigenous Science Education Model; *and* Spirit of the Game: Wellspring of Indigenous Education.

***

As we approach the second decade of a new millennium, Native and Western cultures, with their seemingly irreconcilably different ways of knowing and relating to the natural world, must search for common ground and a basis for dialogue. The images for relating to the natural world originating from the modern mechanist paradigm will not work for us in the twenty-first century. Indigenous wisdom might work, if only we could stop dismissing it as being "of another time." Thomas Berry talks about the importance of renewing our faith in the possibility of a sustainable future in tune with the truth of nature's primal laws; our images of the future, he points out, are self-fulfilling. The images we create, the languages we speak, the economics we manifest, the learning systems we espouse, and the spiritual, political, and social order we profess must all reflect and honor interdependence and sustainability.[1] If we live the images of despair that are growing in the minds and hearts of too many people; if all that matters is "me, mine, now;" then we will bring about realities that are despairing! Reading the signs of the times in broader ways and allowing the pain of the dysfunction they cause to come into us rather than running away and shielding ourselves are ways to begin to manifest a sustainable future.

Given the dawning of such realizations, the mechanistic, Cartesian model reveals itself as wholly inadequate and inappropriate for founding the kinds of institutions that are inclusive and multidimensional enough to sustain us in the twenty-first century and beyond. The question is, what will a new cosmology include? The new cosmology and philosophy must encompass the realization that the earth is in essence a superbeing in a universe of superbeings and supercommunities. It must incorporate the understanding of human beings as dynamic bodies intimately cradled in the body of the world.

Native science evolved from a different creative journey and a different cultural history from that of Western science. Native science is not quantum physics or environmental science, but it has come to similar understandings about the workings of natural laws through experience and participation with the natural world. The groundwork for a fruitful dialogue and exchange of knowledge is being created. But it must be a dialogue in which Native cultures have the opportunity to gain as much as they share about their understanding of the natural world.

The word "science" is derived from the Greek word for "knowledge." In this chapter, "science" is used in terms of the most inclusive of its meanings, that is, as *a story of the world and a practiced way of living it.* "Native science" is used as a metaphor for Native knowledge and creative participation with the natural world in both thought and practice. This chapter celebrates and acknowledges the Native contribution to an evolving contemporary philosophy of science as well as ecological awareness. This is not a work about Native religion; in fact, religion will be discussed only as a reflection of environmental philosophy. The essence of Native spirituality is not religion in the Western sense of the word, but rather a set of core beliefs in the sanctity of personal and community relationships to the natural world, which are creatively acted upon and expressed at both the personal and communal levels.[2]

Native science reflects the unfolding story of a creative universe in which human beings are active and creative participants. When viewed from this perspective, science is evolutionary—its expression unfolds through the general scheme of the creative process of first insight, immersion, creation, and reflection. Native science is a reflection of the metaphoric mind and is embedded in creative participation with nature. It reflects the sensual capacities of humans. It is tied to spirit, and is both ecological and integrative.

An understanding of the nature of creativity is important for gaining insight. Native science embraces the inherent creativity of nature as the foundation for both knowledge and action in an ever-evolving and creative process of "seeking life." Seeking life is the most basic of human motivations since it is connected to our natural instinct for survival and self-preservation. The linguistic metaphors of "seeking life," "to find our life," and "for life's sake" are reminders of this essential motivation and the proper context of expression in human interaction with our natural sources of life. Ultimately, the universe is a creative expression at a magnitude beyond human recognition. Human life at all levels is wholly a creative activity and may be said to be an expression of the nature within us. We are, after all, a microcosm of the macrocosm. We are a part of a greater generative order of life that is ever evolving. It is from this creative generative center of human life that central principles of Native science emanate. Native people relate all things in myth by virtue of being born of this creative center.

Creativity is both the universe's ordering principle and its process. Creativity in all forms is part of the flow of a greater, all-encompassing dynamic in nature. Creativity flows from an "implicate order" or inherent potential of the universe, and whatever it produces becomes a part of the "explicate order" of material or energetic expressions. These expressions range from entire galaxies to the quarks and leptons of the subatomic world.[3] Human creativity is located in this immense continuum.

In this chapter I want to briefly discuss two basic concepts that are related to creativity. One has to do with "chaos theory" and the other with "participation and creative sensibilities." These concepts lend themselves specifically to the way in which Native peoples envision the process of science. They also form a conceptual bridge between Native and Western science, although Native science refers to them differently through particular cultural representations in story, art, and ways of community. These theories and their connections to quantum physics have brought Western science closer to understanding nature as Native peoples have always understood it: nature is not simply a collection of objects, but rather a dynamic, ever-flowing river of creation inseparable from our own perceptions. Nature is the creative center from which we and everything else have come and to which we always return.

CHAOS THEORY

Chaos is both movement and evolution. It is the process through which everything in the universe becomes manifest and then returns to the chaos field. The flux, or ebb and flow, of chaos appears in everything and envelops us at all times and in all places. From the evolving universe to the mountain to the human brain, chaos is the field from which all things come into being. No wonder Native science envisions the spirit of the natural world as alive, with disorder becoming order and all the mystery of mirrored relationships.

Today, with the creative influence of chaos theory and quantum physics, a new scientific cultural metaphor has begun to take hold. The insights of this new science parallel the vision of the world long held in Indigenous spiritual traditions. Because of this parallel, Indigenous thought has the potential to inform a contemporary understanding of chaos. Such understanding allows modern consciousness to encompass the primal wisdom of Indigenous thought and with this to understand the fallacy of scientific and societal control. The modern obsession with being in control and the dream of eliminating uncertainty through control of nature, which is the underlying philosophical premise of Western science, must give way to the reality of moving creatively with the flow of events, which is the true reality of the universe.

Western science is committed to increasing human mastery over nature, to go on conquering until everything natural is under absolute human control. In this vision, when we have fusion power, when we farm the oceans, when we can turn weather on and off, when all things natural can be controlled, everything will be just fine. Western science and technology are viewed as the great panacea and as the ultimate means for human survival.

Chaos theory, derived from the cutting edge of Western scientific research itself, implies that systems are beyond the ability of scientists to predict or control except at the most superficial levels, and that all of nature is a chaotic system. Rather than seeking to control natural reality, Native science focuses its attention upon subtle, inner natures wherein lie the rich textures and nuances of life. This is exactly what chaos theory shows us: small, apparently insignificant things play major roles in the way a process unfolds. Indeed, Native science may be said to be the "science of the subtle."

In the mythology of all ancient cultures, chaos plays a central role in the creation of the universe, the earth, humankind, and other major elements of the world. Chaos and its offspring, creativity, are the generative forces of the universe. In Mayan cosmology, for example, the first sun-fire beings, Tepeu and Gucumatz, arose out of the dark turbulent waters of the void. In Egyptian mythology, Ra, the sun, rose out of the chaos of Nun, the great floodwaters of the universe. Another example is in expansion and contraction, the primordial yin and yang, which flow from the primal soul of the Great Tao. In Chinese mythology, creativity is associated with nine dragons that arise from the vortex of heaven and whose heavenly presence guides creative order. As in Chinese mythology, the theory of chaos represents nature in its creative activity. The role of chaos also appears in mythology throughout the world in stories of the trickster—the sacred fool whose antics remind us of the essential role of disorder in the creation of order. Chaos theory describes the way nature makes new forms and structures out of the potential of the great void. It also represents the unpredictability and relative randomness of the creative process.

There is an ordering or self-organizing process that results from chaos, called "order for free." A simple example may be found in the boiling of water. As water is heated, the water at the bottom of a saucepan starts to rise to the top while cooler water at the top moves to the bottom. This movement causes a turbulence which takes the form of boiling water, or as a chaos theorist might describe it, the water in the pan exercises its "maximum degree of freedom." In other words, the water in the closed system of the saucepan is exercising the maximum range of behavior available to it. However, if the water is brought slowly to the point just before boiling, something interesting and characteristic of chaotic systems occurs. The

water self-organizes into a pattern of vortices. This is called the "bifurcation point," the point just before the system transforms itself, in this
case, to boiling water. The bifurcation point is the direct result of the
interaction of "positive feedback," which amplifies the transformation to
boil, and "negative feedback," which dampens the transformation. These
tendencies interact to create a stable pattern of vortices. In nature, all
systems of energy transformation exhibit a similar kind of behavior. The
survival of any self-organizing system depends upon its ability to keep
itself open to the flow of energy and matter through it.

Then there is the notion of subtle influences, or the "butterfly effect,"
in chaos theory. In chaotic systems, even small things turn out to have
large-scale effects over a period of time. For example, if we look at
weather, we see a recurring climatic pattern over a long period of time.
However, if we examine details we see that weather is in constant flux due
to the bifurcating and amplifying activity of a host of subtle effects. In a
weather system, everything is interconnected. Positive and negative feedback loops are in constant motion, and somewhere in the system, a "butterfly" loop may cause slight changes. Sooner or later, one of these loops
is amplified, and we see a dramatic and unpredictable shift in the pattern.
The butterfly effect may be called chance, but it is really the cumulative
influence of a small change in a system. It may be an increase or decrease
of temperature in a weather pattern, an individual such as Gandhi taking
a stand against oppression, or a Native prayer, song, dance, or ritual to
bring rain to a parched land. In the world of chaos, anything is possible.

Chaos theory shows that everything is related, everything has an
effect, and that even small things have an influence. In a postmodern
society ruled by an obsession with control, we as individuals may feel
powerless, but each of us may subtly influence the course of any system,
including those that seem to be the most intractable. Human "butterfly
power" resides in our ability to create.

Chaos theory offers insight into human creativity. Chaos is embodied
in the human mind and body, allowing humans the ability to creatively
respond to constant changes in the environment. Our instinctual
ability to "flow" with the stream of chaos and creativity leads us meta-
phorically to the "vortices" of individual and collective truth. What is
true from this viewpoint is the experience of the moment of balance
inherent in chaos, like that point at which water, not quite boiling, forms
vortices.

This moment when a truth comes to be intuitively known is like the
still point in the eye of a hurricane; it is that point when a connection is

made to a natural principle manifesting itself in the unfolding of a natural process. Like the birth of a child or a bolt of lightning connecting sky and earth for a moment in time, these are the infinite moments of both chaos and order. This is a precept of Native science, for truth is not a fixed point, but rather an ever-evolving point of balance, perpetually created and perpetually new.

Native science at its highest levels of expression is a system of pathways for reaching this perpetually moving truth or "spirit." This understanding of the creative nature of the world and of human beings is reflected in the core beliefs of Native thought, life, and tradition. The quality and nature of human life are the result of human consciousness, or the influences of our experiences, perceptions, language, and society. Human consciousness is inherently an open system, and is "created," in that this system is constantly being influenced by the forces of chaos expressed through us and by us at the individual and collective levels. Herein lies the true power of individual and collective creativity and its subtle power to influence the entire world. This is the basis of the precept of Native science that a single individual's vision may transform a society, or that a rain dance done properly, with one mind, can bring rain. Hence, Native science is a reflection of creative participation, a dance with chaos and her child, the creative spirit.[4]

PARTICIPATION AND CREATIVE SENSIBILITIES

The primacy of a lived and creative relationship with the natural world cannot be underestimated in Native science. Native science acts to mediate between the human community and the larger natural community upon which humans depend for life and meaning. In the few remaining Indigenous communities, Native science is practiced, and its practitioners from child to elder to specialist continually engage the entities and natural processes of their environments as "participants" in the greater order of nature. This intimate and creative participation heightens awareness of the subtle qualities of a place.

Nature is reality, and worthy of awe in the perceptions of the person who practices a culturally conditioned "tuning in" of the natural world. He or she sees, hears, smells, and tastes the natural world with greater acuity. The body feels the subtle forces of nature with a heightened sensitivity. The mind perceives the subtle qualities of a creative natural world with great breadth and awareness. In spite of anthropologists' cultural bias and misinterpretations, which continue to influence views of the

Indigenous experience, none of this sensual participation with nature is "supernatural" or "extraordinary." Rather, it is the result of an ancient and naturally conditioned response to nature.

The Indigenous "physicist" not only observes nature, but also participates in it with all his or her sensual being. Humans and all other entities of nature experience at their own levels of sensate reality. The Indigenous experience is evidenced not only through collective cultural expressions of art, story, ritual, and technology, but also through the more subtle and intimate expressions of individual acts of respect, care, words, and feelings that are continually extended to the land and its many beings. *As we experience the world, so we are also experienced by the world.* Maintaining relationships through continual participation with the natural creative process of nature is the hallmark of Native science. This practiced ability to enter into a heightened sense of awareness of the natural world allows the Indigenous physicist intimate understanding of the processes of nature, and forms the foundation for respecting the compacts of mutual reciprocal responsibility shared with other inhabitants of one's environment.

Through this way of participation, Indigenous peoples receive gifts of information from nature. In Native science, there is then an inclusive definition of "being alive." Everything is viewed as having energy and its own unique intelligence and creative process, not only obviously animate entities, such as plants, animals, and microorganisms, but also rocks, mountains, rivers, and places large and small. Everything in nature has something to teach humans. This is the Indigenous view of "animism," the anthropologically defined, superficially understood, and ethnocentrically biased term used to categorize the Indigenous way of knowing the world.

Creative participation with the living earth extends from birth to death and beyond. At birth, humans come new yet recycled through the elegant cycles of metamorphosis, transformation, and regeneration that form the basis for all life on earth. Indigenous peoples view the body as an expression of the sensual manifestation of mind and spirit. Death and the body's ultimate decomposition into the primal elements of earth, wind, fire, air, and water mark the transformation of one's relatives and ancestors into living landscape, its plants, animals, waters, soils, clouds, and air. This is a literal biological truth as well as a metaphoric one—hence the meaning in Chief Seattle's statement, "I cannot sell the body, the blood and bones of my people." Life and death are transformations of energy into new forms, the material and energetic fuel of nature's creativity. Death is understood as a metamorphosis, wherein the spirit of the deceased does not disappear, but becomes part of the animating and creative forces of nature.

Becoming open to the natural world with all of one's senses, body, mind, and spirit is the goal of the practice of Native science. The Kogi of Colombia have a way of creating a *mama*, or spiritual leader, who personifies the honing of the initiate to become fully sensitive to the detail and subtle nuances of the natural world. At birth a child who has been chosen to become a mama is taken from the mother and sequestered for the first nine years in a dark cave called the Womb of the Earth Mother. The child's experience of the outer world is limited to only the sounds and environmental qualities of the cave. Other mamas, including the child's birth mother and relatives, constantly keep the child company.

The mamas teach the child the Kogi language, stories, prayers, and ritual philosophy. The mamas also describe the natural world in detail. But the child never really sees, hears, or feels the natural world directly until the long initiation is completed. During the ninth year the child emerges from the "Womb" for the first time and is introduced to the Earth Mother. This is an experience that cannot be described in words; it so influences such children that it indelibly guides their perception of the natural world throughout their lives. Because of their perceptual conditioning and extensive training in Kogi science, they are able to participate in the world with all of their being. As a result of their long and sustained *relationship* to the natural world, they are able to identify the stresses between the human community and the natural landscape, and therefore advise on ways to restore the harmony of relationship. Understanding, maintaining, and restoring harmonious relationship is another foundation of Native science.[5]

The tragedy of modern society is that people fall into the trap of abstraction. The host of modern technologies that only mirror ourselves to ourselves hypnotizes perception and attention. While our bodies have been tuned to the sounds of birds and the changing qualities of natural environments, our socialization makes us oblivious to our natural sensibilities.

In many people, such sensibilities quickly atrophy. We are no longer able to participate with nature with our whole being—we cannot hear its subtle voices or speak the language of nature. Herein lies the disregard modern people feel for nature—when something no longer exists in your perceptual memory, it no longer matters.

The blindness of modern perception with regard to nature prevails throughout postmodern technocratic society. Western science and society continue to deny the spirit and intelligence of nature. Enclosed in a technologically mediated world, people rarely encounter nature in any significant or creative way. Nature may be the topic of the latest *National Geographic* special or the focus of the newest Walt Disney theme park, but direct experiences with nonhuman nature, if they happen at all, are limited to pets, zoos, parks, and farms. What most people know about animals and nature comes from television. While moderns may have technical knowledge of nature, few have knowledge of the nonhuman world gained directly from personal experience.

Native science is an echo of a premodern affinity for participation with the nonhuman world. As a way of knowing the world, it exists at the margins of modern society as an unconscious memory, a myth, a dream, a longing, and as the lived experience of the few Indigenous societies that have not yet been totally displaced by the modern technologically mediated world.

Creative participation in nature provides a glimpse of the human nature that has grounded our sensual experience. Before we developed modern perceptual habits and linguistic prejudices, this experience was common. The perceptual process upon which Native science rests remains a mystery for most moderns. It is certainly not the "real world" of jobs, school, the mall, and television. Yet, if we learn once again to feel, see, hear, smell, and taste the world as our ancestors did, we may remember something truly wonderful about nature in humans.

This does not mean that we should or even can return to the premodern, hunter-gatherer existence of our ancestors, but only that we must carry their perceptual wisdom and way of participation into the twenty-first century, where the environmental challenges we face will require a totally different way of living in nature. The French phenomenologist Maurice Merleau-Ponty makes the following observation: "We begin by reawakening the basic experience of the world, of which science is the second-order expression . . . To return to things themselves is the return to that world which precedes knowledge, of which knowledge always speaks, and in relation to which every scientific schematization is an abstract and derivative sign language."[6]

Native science embodies the central premises of phenomenology (the philosophical study of phenomena) by rooting the entire tree of knowledge in the soil of direct physical and perceptual experience of the earth. In other words, to know yourself you must first know the earth. This process of intersubjectivity is based on the notion that there is a primal affinity between the human body and the other bodies of the natural world.

According to Edmund Husserl, the conceptual father of phenomenology, there is a kind of "associative empathy" between humans and other living things, which is grounded in the physical nature of bodies.[7]

Husserl believed that lived experience, or the "life-world," was the ultimate source of human knowledge and meaning. The life-world evolves through our experience before we rationalize it into categories of facts and apply scientific principles. Our life-world evolves through our experience from birth to death and forms the basis for our explanation of reality. In other words, it is subjective experience that forms the basis for the objective explanation of the world.

The Western science view and method for exploring the world starts with a detached "objective" view to create a factual blueprint, a map of the world. Yet, that blueprint is not the world. In its very design and methodology, Western science estranges direct human experience in favor of a detached view. It should be no surprise that the knowledge it produces requires extensive recontextualizing within the lived experience in modern society. This methodological estrangement, while producing amazing technology, also threatens the very modern life-world that supports it.

The life-world that Husserl describes is culturally relative. It is diverse and different for each culture and each person because it is based on the experienced world of distinct peoples who evolved in distinct places and described themselves and their surroundings in distinct languages. Yet, there is a unity in such diversity, derived from the fact that humans share a species-specific experience and knowledge of nature. Humans also share an experience of nature with all other living things, although our perceptions are different from those of other species due to our unique physical biology. This is the basis of the life-world, a vast ocean of direct human experience that lies below all cultural mediation. This consciousness of the life-world forms another foundation of Native science. Current cultural concepts of time, space, relationships, and linguistic forms are rooted in this precultural biological awareness.

From a phenomenological viewpoint, all sciences are Earth-based. Western science must acknowledge this common foundation, this rootedness in the same physical world as Native science, and for its continued evolution, it must integrate and apply the collective lived experience of human participation with nature. In David Abram's words, "Every theoretical and scientific practice grows out of and remains supported by the forgotten ground of our directly felt and lived experience, and has value and meaning only in reference to this primordial and open realm."[8]

Of course, the physical body is an essential aspect of lived experience. The body, as the source of thinking, sensing, acting, and being, and as the basis of relationship, is a central consideration of Native science. This is why the metaphor of the body is used so often by tribes to describe themselves, as well as their communities, social organization, and important relationships in the world. Tribal use of the metaphor describes not just the physical body, but the mind-body that experiences and participates in the world. Indeed, humans and the natural world interpenetrate one another at many levels, including the air we breathe, the carbon dioxide we contribute to the food we transform, and the chemical energy we transmute at every moment of our lives from birth to death.

Phenomenology parallels the approach of Native science in that it provides a viewpoint based on our innate human experience within nature. Native science strives to understand and apply the knowledge gained from participation in the here and now, and emphasizes our role as one of nature's members rather than striving to be in control of it. "Ultimately, to acknowledge the life of the body, and affirm our solidarity with this physical form, is to acknowledge our existence as one of earth's animals, and so to remember and rejuvenate the organic basis of our thoughts and our intelligence."[9]

The creative body and all that comprises it—mind, body, and spirit—are the creative, moving center of Native science. Although this may seem commonsense, modern thinking abstracts the mind from the human body and the body of the world. This modern orientation, in turn, frequently disconnects Western science from the lived and experienced world of nature. The disassociation becomes most pronounced at the level of perception, because our perceptions orient us in the most elemental way to our surroundings. Ultimately, our innate receptivity to our surroundings, combined with our individual creativity and mediated by our cultural conditioning, characterizes our perception.

In reality, orientation, receptivity, creativity, perception, and imagination are integrated through participation with nature. This is why participation is a key strategy of Native science; it can take many forms and can be individual as well as collective. In Native contexts, creative participation may result in a story, song, dance, new technology, or even a vision, ritual, or ceremony.

We cannot help but participate with the world. Whether we acknowledge and are creatively open to the perceptions that will result, or remain oblivious to its influence and creative possibilities toward deeper understanding, is our decision. This is the perpetual trap of Western science and the perpetual dilemma of Western society: all humans are in constant interaction with the physical reality. Western science and society perpetuate the illusion of "objective" detachment and psychological disassociation. Anti-"Indian" hegemony maintains this illusion, an illusion the world cannot afford to serve any longer.

NOTES

1. Thomas Berry, *Dawn over the Earth: Our Way into the Future*, tape recording (Boulder, Colo.: Sounds True Recordings, 1991).

2. Gregory A. Cajete, *Native Science: Natural Laws of Interdependence* (Santa Fe: Clear Light, 2000), 13–14.

3. Ibid., 21–22.

4. David Briggs and F. David Peat, *Seven Life Lessons of Chaos: Spiritual Wisdom from the Science of Change* (New York: HarperCollins, 1999), 28–30.

5. Ibid., 5–22.

6. Maurice Merleau-Ponty, *Phenomenology of Perception*, trans. Colin Smith (London: Routledge and Kegan Paul, 1962), viii–ix, cited in David Abram, *The Spell of the Sensuous: Perception and Language in a More-Than-Human World* (New York: Pantheon Books, 1996), 36.

7. Edmund Husserl, *Cartesian Meditations: An Introduction to Phenomenology*, trans. Dorion Cairns (The Hague: Martinus Nijhoff Publishers, 1960), cited in Abram, *The Spell of the Sensuous*, 35–44.

8. Abram, *The Spell of the Sensuous*, 43.

9. Ibid., 47.

Chapter 17

ON THE VERY IDEA OF

"A WORLDVIEW" AND

OF "ALTERNATIVE WORLDVIEWS"

Bruce Wilshire

Cornel D. Pewewardy, a First Nations educator who specializes in "Indian education," has suggested that an eighth intelligence called "Indigenous Worldview" be added to Howard Gardner's famous "multiple intelligences." (The other seven are linguistic, logical-mathematical, bodily kinesthetic, spatial-visual, intrapersonal, interpersonal, and musical.)[1] Such an idea seems to speak to the naturalness, the uniqueness, and the significance of this way of viewing the world, yet it does not discount in any way the importance of "multiple intelligences." In fact, one aspect of the Indigenous worldview is that it takes a thousand voices to tell a story. The Native Hawaiians say, "A'ohe pau ka 'ike I ka halau ho'okahi," which translates, "Not all knowledge comes from the same school."

All of this is meant to convey the idea that it is not the intention of this text to imply that only the Indigenous worldview has value. Moreover, speaking of a singular Indigenous worldview is itself not without risk of contradicting such a worldview. Too much emphasis on human ways of merely seeing the world or on human wisdom alone may keep us from remembering and embracing animal wisdom, or intuitive knowledge, or it may prevent us from honoring traditions that emerged from Nature that may be compromised by too much analysis. Too much cognitive thinking or too much emphasis on the limited idea that we "see" the world can limit our "multiple intelligences."

Nonetheless, in spite of the problems associated with talking about a worldview, a challenge to the Western worldview seems necessary at this point in time, for as Bruce Wilson tells us in this chapter, despite the considerable achievements of Western development, the Western worldview has indeed created "a one-sided evolution, the price for which, we now understand, may be terrible." And, as we have tried throughout this text to release the Indigenous understanding of the world from the oppressive shadow of the language of conquest, it may be wise to end our conversation with Bruce's cautions.

Bruce Wilshire is Senior Professor of Philosophy at Rutgers University. For most of his career he has taught there, although he has also held positions at Purdue University and at New York University. He has served as Visiting Professor at Oberlin College, Colorado College, and at Texas A & M University. As a scholar of

connections between Anglo-American and American Indian thought and practice,
he has written such books as The Primal Roots of American Philosophy:
Pragmatism, Phenomenology and Native American Thought, *and* Get
'Em All, Kill 'Em!: Genocide, Terrorism, Righteous Communities.

***

> *Everything on the earth has a purpose, every disease an herb to*
> *cure, every person a mission. This is the Indian way of seeing the*
> *world.*

—MOURNING DOVE-SALISH, CIRCA 1915

The first thing to be pointed out is that "worldview" is a European idea,
specifically German (*Weltanschauung* = world looked-at [also ideology]).
So we must recognize initially that in speaking of an Indigenous worldview we may have already generated an egregiously distorted account,
determined in advance by a European bias that gives priority to seeing
and vision.

Much of European-Western theory of knowledge and reality occurs
under the aegis of a tacit or explicit visual-optical metaphor. To know or
grasp something is to "see the point." But for the human organism, seeing and vision is the distancing and detaching sense par excellence: the
sense in which we are least involved as whole bodies, least involved emotionally and existentially in whole environments over the long term (thus,
for example, the perversion of voyeurism). This approach may be appropriate within the sixteenth- and seventeenth-century Western scientific
project of narrowing down to particular cogs within "the world machine"
(for example, Newton's "celestial mechanics"). But the price paid is that
knowers must mask out the whole emotional and cosmical context within
which knowing and living occur. If this is not recognized initially, the
masking-out will be paved over and forgotten. The habitual boring and
focusing, the "normal" partializing and fracturing, will be concealed, the
initial assumptions concealed, and the concealing concealed. We will be
oblivious of the possibility of other "worldviews," other ways of grasping,
living, and behaving in the world. "There is only one right way."

This is no mere matter for the philosophy classroom. Because of contemporary clashes between cultures animated by very different "worldviews," and because of current weapons and communications technologies widely spread, we face the possible or probable extinction of life on
our planet. If we can, we must grasp the bias and limitation of the West's
worldview, which powers, focuses, tunnels United States power aiming

at hegemony, all oblivious of other worldviews and visions, for instance Native American or Islamic.

As already suggested, the bias and limitation of the contemporary North American worldview is from the start built into the European notion of worldview itself: that is, the world as viewed, as the seen, the visual (and the visual-ideological). This deeply masks out the fact that fundamental components of a culture's way of thinking and being in the world are not visual at all, not accessible to vision at any moment or through any sequence of moments (*Augenblick* in German: blink of the eye).

As William James wrote in Lecture II of the *Varieties of Religious Experience:*

> Religion, whatever it is, is a man's total reaction upon life, so why not say that any total reaction upon life is a religion? Total reactions are different from casual reactions, and total attitudes are different from usual or professional attitudes. To get at them you must go behind the foreground of existence and reach down to that curious sense of the whole residual cosmos as an everlasting presence, intimate or alien, terrible or amusing, lovable or odious, which in some degree every one possesses. This sense of the world's presence . . . involuntary and inarticulate and often half unconscious as it is, is the completest of all our answers to the question, "What is the character of the universe in which we dwell?"[2]

The "whole push and pressure of the residual cosmos"—as he sometimes puts it (other times it's "circumpressure")—is not an exclusively visual matter, not by a long shot. It's an experience of being always already carried along in a tide of events funded from the past and flowing obscurely and powerfully into the present and future. It is a people's living traditions of being, knowing, doing, and cannot be framed in a visual snapshot or glimpse, or any series of snapshots or glimpses, no matter how vivid. It is built into the whole bodies of the culture's members as they are carried along in their habitual perceptual stances, practices, rites, interrelationships. This is infinitely more than "seeing no matter how many points" intellectually and in an emotionally detached way.

Black Elk's healing visions cannot be understood only visually. They may occur in a coma. Funded and mobilized in the healer's body are the practices of his people over countless generations. For example, in what John Neihardt transcribes as Black Elk's first cure, the healer places the sick boy at the northeastern sector of the inside of the teepee, the direction

from which comes "the cold wind of the north that teaches endurance"—
which has taught this to his Lakota people from time immemorial. The
climactic moment of the cure is emphatically nonvisual: Black Elk places
his mouth on the boy's abdomen and "sucks the cold wind that teaches
endurance" through his body. When Black Elk repeatedly exhorts his
people to "follow the good red road," he enjoins them to *walk* it, not just
to look at it, or to form accurate propositions about it "in their minds."[3]

Insofar as indigenous North American philosophies regard Nature
as sacred, they can be compared to Islam. For the latter's scientific and
mathematical accomplishments did not take it through what we in Europe
and the West in the sixteenth and following centuries traversed and were
formed by: the desacralization of Nature. Islamic mathematics did not
entail the reduction of the essential properties of things to the measurable only. The Eternal—God, Allah—still manifests through countless
aspects of an unfallen Nature (though not exclusively there): in the cry
of the eagle, the sound of the call to prayer, the murmurs of streams, the
waters and fruit trees of oases, and so on. When, for example, Israeli bull-
dozers level a grove of fruit trees in the land Palestinians believe to have
been promised to them as children of Abraham, they experience this not
only as aggression and destruction, but as blasphemous to the Eternal.

President George W. Bush and his tight circle of advisers are locked
into the North American worldview so totally that they have no idea,
apparently, that they are locked in, and, of course, no idea of what they
are locked away from grasping: other cultures' ways of being, believing,
living, finding the good life. So suffocating is this parochialism, as I will
attempt to show below, that our nation can't now discern even what is to
our *own* immediate advantage in dealing with these "backward peoples."

What we facilely call worldview would be better described as the way
a people erotically appropriate an environment as their own. Over many
generations, they have learned to embrace and savor their land and sky
and waters in a certain right and appropriate way. If the home group is
shaky for any reason, a foreign culture's ways of living and thinking are
simply wrong—wrong and dangerous. If not shaky, the foreign culture's
ways tend to be regarded as quaint and retrograde or as weird and ridiculous. These patterns of behavior are ingrained in habituated nervous
systems and muscles culturally conditioned. To attribute these ways to
patterns of *looking at* the world in certain ways is a pitiful constriction and
reduction of the meaning and the reality of what is going on. Even if cultures should try to do so, no culture can excavate, exhibit, and articulate
all the assumptions involved in its primal ways of appropriating, living,

reacting, celebrating, creating, producing, and procreating in the world. Concisely put, no culture can exhibit perspicuously all the assumptions involved in "constructing" for itself the world as it experiences it—its world-experienced. Nor, of course, can it exhibit all the assumptions involved in another culture's "construction" of its world-experienced: it just seems *wrong* to the home group.

About twelve years ago I began a course in American philosophy at Rutgers University by asking, How shall we begin this course? Where and when in our history should we begin? I knew that without asking these questions we would be making assumptions without being aware of what they were, and that once we had begun the course these assumptions would get buried deeper and deeper: until after awhile it would be nearly impossible to excavate and acknowledge them. Should we begin in what would be a usual way, given the highly professionalized and technical nature of academic philosophy today, that is, with the more or less technical philosophers of the nineteenth and early twentieth centuries— Charles Peirce, William James, Josiah Royce, and John Dewey, say? Or why not begin with the founding fathers before them, those who thought out the Revolution and the legal documents that undergird our government? Or why not with Native Americans? After all, these people had or do have now basic, philosophical "views," what I would have said at the time unblinkingly were worldviews, and they greatly antedated the occupying Europeans in the sixteenth century and later.

I asked the latter question to try to goad us into reflection. Much to my surprise, a student asked, Why not start with the Indians? I had never really considered this. I evaded the question somehow, but I was determined never to be put in that position again, and began cramming in some research. It was one of the great surprises of my adult life. Particularly with *Black Elk Speaks* in one hand and Thoreau or Emerson in the other, I was thunderstruck by the affinities. The Euro-Americans were descendants of families who had lived for generations on this continent, under this sky, lured by the frontiers of the time, and in fairly close proximity to these Indigenous Peoples.

I began for the first time to see the extent of the cleavages that divided these Euro-American thinkers from their strictly European ancestor-thinkers. The manifest affinities to Native American views goaded me into recognizing, for example, just how radically William James's radical empiricism diverged from both the empiricisms and the rationalisms of Europe. The course of my career as an academic "Americanist" was abruptly shifted and has remained shifted—and has deepened.

The endemic distancing and detaching of paradigmatically European thinking of the past twenty-five hundred years was no longer entrancedly taken for granted by me, but leapt into thematic focus. When Native Americans live, breathe, and know in the world, it is not a Nature "out there," but truly a Mother Nature that empowers, enlivens, nurtures, and guides them instant by instant. Nature irradiates them and circulates through them. They know things without knowing exactly how they know them. Suddenly I got the gravity and punch of what Thoreau writes in his *Journals:*

> I hear the sound of Heywood's Brook falling into Fair Haven Pond— inexpressibly refreshing to my senses—it seems to flow through my very bones—I hear with insatiable thirst—it allays some sandy heat in me—it affects my circulations—methinks my arteries have sympathy with it. What is it I hear but the pure water falls within me, in the circulation of my blood—the streams that fall into my heart.[4]

Black Elk's "The Great Hoop of the World" and Emerson's "Nature" leapt into embrace. The whole universe irradiates and energizes us, if we are only open and allowing of it. Holy, it is healing. Black Elk:

> Then I was standing on the highest mountain, and round about beneath me was the whole hoop of the world . . . And I saw that the sacred hoop of my people was one of many hoops that made one circle, wide as daylight and starlight, and in the center was one mighty flowering tree to shelter all the children of one mother and one father. And I saw that it was holy.[5]

Emerson in "Nature" on the horizon:

> Miller owns this field, Locke that, and Manning the woodland beyond. But none of them owns the landscape. There is a property in the horizon which no man has but he whose eye can integrate all the parts . . . This is the best part of these men's farms, yet to this their warranty-deeds give no title.[6]

The horizon seems to be Emerson's version of Black Elk's "the whole hoop of the world," of the cosmos, extending "as far as starlight." For when we attend closely to horizons (and they needn't be visual ones—but can be auditory, kinesthetic, tactile), don't we grasp that they are double-faced: pointing inward to all that we might directly perceive and outward toward *everything else?* Don't we sense that we can't imagine all the sorts of things that might be going on at any place and time in the cosmos?

Don't we sense *the mysterious*, and that this is "somewhat as beautiful as our own nature"?

But touching on the mysterious, we sense a certain hesitation in Emerson. And we recall James' later struggles in *The Varieties of Religious Experience* to flesh out his very broadly religious notion of the whole residual cosmos in its immediately felt circumpressure. Is it holy? Is it mysterious? In what way does it release "salvific powers"? In the end, James can only call it, with certainty, "the More."

Powerfully influenced by Native Americans as they doubtless were, nevertheless these Euro-American philosophers exhibit a certain tell-tale hesitancy and constriction not found in the Indigenous ones. Through his nearly incredible powers of insight and honesty, Emerson himself best reveals this. In his essay "History," he claims that we do understand the past, and this is so because we identify with those who created past events. We share their motivations: to escape oppression, to achieve and be glorified, to eat and sleep, to make merry, to exact revenge, to understand, and so on. He feels at home in the centers of Western civilization: Athens, Rome, Constantinople, Paris, from which centers we inherit the very idea of understanding, of finding reasons, of making sense.

Then in the last page of the essay, a terrible second thought stops him in his tracks. It's as if an evil wind strikes him in the face:

> Is there somewhat overweening in this claim? Then I reject all I have written, for what is the use of pretending to know what we know not? But it is the fault of our rhetoric that we cannot strongly state one fact without seeming to belie some other. I hold our actual knowledge very cheap. Hear the rats in the wall, see the lizard on the fence . . . As old as Caucasian man—perhaps older—these creatures have kept their counsel beside him, and there is no record of any word or sign that has passed from one to the other . . . What a shallow village tale our so-called History is. How many times must we say Rome and Paris and Constantinople? What does Rome know of rat and lizard? What are Olympiads and Consulates to these neighboring systems of being?[7]

Emerson confronts a hitherto unsuspected vista. He sees that our inherited idea of making sense, of understanding, is undermined, is not fundamental. That we are not enclosed and at home in "the family of man," but that we are neighbors to, in fact kin to, the rats in the wall, the lizard on the fence, primitive forms of scurrying life.

With this stunning about-face, Emerson delineates a—or the—salient feature of European-Western thought. The West's primal erotic bite into the surround (it is hardly a tender kiss) magnifies ourselves—we, the fierce, self-involved biters. In our impulsiveness and narcissism, we become the measure of all things: we believe that we are the universal consciousness. Nonhuman animals resemble us generically, but they are deviant, inferior. In sharpest contrast stands the Native American erotic appropriation of Nature: their reveling in the boundless variety, the multifold differences between things. Nonhuman animals are different from us in some ways, but they have their own nobility, their own teaching for us, and should be respected. Though neither Native American development nor Islam's desacralized Nature, it is difficult to imagine any of the three great Western religions seconding Black Elk's insight that the roundness of teepees corresponds to the roundness of birds' nests: "Birds build their nests in circles for theirs is the same religion as ours." For all three Western religions, this blasphemes a supposedly transcendent Deity.

From this primal origin point emanate salient features of the West's "worldview." It is hierarchical, dualistic, exclusivist, and divisive: humans over animals; male over female; mind over matter; light or white over darkness or dark; transcendent over immanent; rational over nonrational; West over East; active over passive; etc., etc.

Nevertheless, the West also breeds an apparent universalism and egalitarianism. This is vividly evident in Hegel, to take but one example. Both the physical sun and the intelligible Sun arise in the East and aim toward and progress through the West. Roughly, in the Orient only one is free, the despot; in Greece some are free; only in Europe, with constitutional guarantees, are all free, and are so just because they are human. Hegel binds all this together with a Christian theodicy. God integrates the divine and the human in Jesus Christ, the God-man. Even for the deistic, heterodox framers of the United States constitution, we (or some of us) are endowed by our Creator with certain privileges and inalienable rights.

The space allotted for this essay does not permit the kind of complex analysis and evaluation that should come at this point. Suffice to say, perhaps, that some have benefited mightily from these Western conceptions of freedom. I myself have benefited: coming from a less than munificent background, I have been given countless opportunities and safeguards for my development.

I wish to emphasize here that the West has built up a worldview as world-picture so bright and dazzling that it completely eclipses its costs, limitations, lacunae, even its one-sidedness. It is the West's one-sidedness that is the most difficult of its features for Westerners to recognize, given our pretensions to universality. Caught up in the rushing and leaping movement of empire and dominion westward, we clutch at a few of this movement's most easily recognized features. These have become abstractions monumentalized and valorized: Freedom!, say, or Enlightenment! The actual concrete consequences of this movement's coursing over the planet, the actual conditions in which people must try to live together day by day, in ours and in other cultures, tend to be masked off and overlooked.

Despite the considerable achievements of Western development, it has been a one-sided evolution, the price for which, we now understand, may be terrible. Our arrogance and ignorance may cost the life of this planet as we know it. Although it will likely reemerge some day through the devastation, there may be no "seventh generation" to be a part of it. We have eccentrically emphasized the distinctively human at the expense of the animal, the rational-calculable at the expense of the nonrational-incalculable, the grand project and bright vision at the expense of the daily and the earthy, the "advanced" nations at the expense of the "backward," the brightly focused individual thing of the moment at the expense of vast contexts and long-term developments.

Perhaps the recent American and British initial conquest of Iraq epitomizes in some ways the development of the West? Leap-frogging from place-overrun to place-overrun and plummeting into Baghdad, the places leapt over and scantily observed breed smoldering problems, hatreds, and resentful members plot revenge. Will the West have its way in Iraq and the Muslim Near East? There are far too many unknowns to calculate an answer. Untold numbers of the forgotten of the earth, wriggling into crannies in the West's corporate body, armed with some of the West's own marvelous high-tech weaponry, may put an end to the West's glory—and beyond that, the earth's. The chickens have come home to roost.

The fact is, we are animal organisms—strange ones to be sure—evolved out of earlier forms of animal organisms that survived and procreated, because they adapted and took shape as hunter-gatherers over hundreds of thousands of years in wilderness environments. And the fact is, even today we live in physical environments, despite cunningly produced, artificially lighted and heated subenvironments. We must live moment by moment in a world that registers all that we have done to it, and are doing to it, adding up and funding every exploitation and desecration of it. Quick fix nitrogen-bristling chemical fertilizers wash into the

Mississippi and create a monstrous dead zone in the Gulf of Mexico the size of several states. Or, huge, quick-yield agribusiness farming creates a spirit-numbing, body-numbing monotony that breeds an insatiable craving for variety, highs, ecstasy—all too often counterfeit ecstasies and miserable addictions.[8]

"Worldviews" generate over centuries the deepest habits and inertias, whether good or bad. For example, we have depended on modern technology for so long now that we find it nearly impossible to believe that much of our marvelous weapons technology is in fact obsolete. Without the continuities of regenerative rites and rituals and times of rest, we decay and fall to pieces. With degenerative fixations on the false goods of ease and comfort and the crudest pleasures, we fall to pieces. Julian Simon, tireless champion of "a better life through chemistry," writes,

> This is my long-run forecast in brief:
>
> The material conditions of life will continue to get better for most people, in most countries, most of the time, indefinitely. Within a century or two, all nations and most of humanity will be at or above today's Western living standards.[9]

I also speculate, however, that many people will continue to *think and say* that the conditions of life are getting worse.

In fact, we face the possibility that the "material conditions of life" will be utterly destroyed. But beyond that, if they do improve, as Simon predicts, one sentence from any wise teacher should dash us into wakefulness. Say, Jesus Christ: "Man does not live by bread alone." Or Black Elk, speaking of maniacal miners seeking the universal solvent: "Gold, the metal that drives them crazy." The Western worldview embodied in today's U.S. leadership is so thick and tunneling that it cannot or will not grasp such nonmaterialistic perspectives. Perhaps this is why it does not bother with exploring elements in the Koranic tradition of Islam itself that encourage truly democratic practices that could legitimate the Middle Eastern governments in their own way. (Perhaps in the same way that truly democratic practices would be encouraged in the U.S. by exploring Indigenous traditions?—ed.) Such attitudes of U.S. leadership seem to assert that the main problem of the West today is that important sectors of the society no longer believe in the West's superiority, and that we have overreacted to defeat in Vietnam. The solution? To exercise brawny power, and to assert unabashedly, without any reservation, the correctness of rightist ideology.

Hamlet observed, "The times are out of joint," as many today can agree about our own time. Everything hurried up by electronic communication, the grossest hedonism and avarice jostles cheek by jowl with lunges for stability in Old Time Christian Religion. Cultures are slammed together electronically and militarily. These groups with their differently "constructed" worlds abrade against each other and provoke raging temper tantrums and fear (an audiotape from Osama bin Laden electrifies and mobilizes the world).

Even through the thick peach haze of sentimentalizing, and countless sorts of misunderstanding, our own American Indian cultures hold promise of helping us to stabilize ourselves. Oddly, the glories of the Western "worldview" appear together with the grave inadequacies of that view. The penetration to laws of physical nature, the awesome assemblages of these laws in the physical sciences, reveal a disturbing gap: these laws and their applications in technologies cannot be sufficient for us to live as whole, healthy, ecstatic human beings moment by moment, day by day, generation by generation. There is much more going on around us and in us than we can imagine to look for and perhaps discover. We are over our heads in jarring contingencies, and in momentary bright baubles of sensations communicated electronically, and we grope for continuity and spiritual fuel (call it that), trying to put our fingers on the thread that would lead us home.

Perhaps one example will illustrate the point I am trying to make. An astronomer, say, may relinquish her use of a telescope on Thursday night, not to regain it until Sunday night. Her calculations and tabulations of the behavior of stars begin on Sunday night just where they left off on Thursday night. Yet her life as an astronomer probably supports her only marginally in her encounter with her mother-in-law, say, on Sunday noon.

One major assistance that Indigenous thought and practice can afford us now is to nudge us toward a cohesive experiential matrix that supports and guides us from situation to situation, moment by moment through time. Fellow nonhuman beings will then not be merely objects to be studied and tabulated by some special science, but fellow subjects, regenerative presences moment by moment, place into place, on this planet. There exists a Curtis photo from 1908 of a Mandan tribesman offering a Bison skull in thanksgiving to the dawn.[10] To live vitally we must celebrate and memorialize somehow every new dawn. Or, Indigenous People who still practice their ancient tracking skills might initiate us into them: on tiptoe perhaps, the margins of consciousness quiveringly alert, the hunter is alive to everything on every hand. With hunters' "splatter vision" we are held in the universe moment by moment. We might recover from withering isolation and loneliness. Or, the Indigenous American artificer's artistry and patience glows in worked-up matter—jewelry, sand, wood, ceremonial clothing. A turquoise is not a gem, in the Western sense, but a bit of sky that made its home in the earth. The cosmos is not just "out there," measurable in billions of light years, but lodges us within itself as tiny but vital members of it.

There were warning signals from the very beginning of the West's "worldview." For example, the Sophocles' play *Oedipus Rex* formalizes an immemorial myth: the sightless prophet who "sees" what the brilliant and sighted cannot. Or the bard of bards, Homer, was understood to be blind. Or, again, the so-called romantic thinkers and artists of the nineteenth century were drawn to indigenous peoples, because they knew that fellow Enlightenment Europeans saw only what they saw, saw only one-sidedly, did not bother to guess that there was that which they did not know that they did not know. Abysmal ignorance and arrogance. But these warning signals did not then, and do not now, have much effect, apparently.

But perhaps we still have a little time. *Possibly* we will not destroy ourselves. Forced against the wall, possibility may become numinous and compelling. We might finally begin to learn from the "primitive" people, learn together with them, and, perhaps, regain our balance.

NOTES

1. Cornel D. Pewewardy, "The Holistic Medicine Wheel: An Indigenous Model of Teaching and Learning," *Winds of Change* 14.4 (1998): 28–31.

2. William James, *The Varieties of Religious Experience* (New York: Library of America, 1988), xi.

3. John G. Neihardt, *Black Elk Speaks: Being the Life Story of a Holy Man of the Oglala Sioux* (London: Bison Books, 2004), 199.

4. Henry David Thoreau, *The Journal of Henry David Thoreau*, vol. 7 (Salt Lake City: Peregrine Smith Books, 1984), 340.

5. Neihardt, *Black Elk Speaks*, 98.

6. Ralph Waldo Emerson, "Nature," in *Ralph Waldo Emerson: Essays and Lectures*, ed. Joel Porte (New York: Library of America, 1983), 4.

7. Ralph Waldo Emerson, "History," in *Ralph Waldo Emerson: Essays and Lectures*, 26–27.

8. For more on addiction, see my *Wild Hunger: The Primal Roots of Modern Addiction* (Lanham, Md.: Rowman and Littlefield, 1998).

9. Julian Simon, quoted in the epigraph to Bjorn Lomborg, *The Skeptical*

Environmentalist: Measuring the Real State of the World (New York: Cambridge University Press, 2001). A measure of the power of the neoconservative movement.

10. A reproduction in miniature of the Curtis photo of the Mandan tribesman can be found on the cover of my *The Primal Roots of American Thought: Pragmatism, Phenomenology, Native American Thought* (College Park: Penn State University Press, 2000).

EPILOGUE

Four Arrows

How smooth must be the language of the whites, when they can make right look like wrong and wrong look like right.

—BLACK HAWK-SAUK

In his book *A Time Before Deception: Truth in Communication, Culture and Ethics*, Thomas W. Cooper, a Harvard-educated communications professor at Emerson College, defines "Indigenous People," with the simplest of words, like "authentic" and "genuine," and "natural." Indeed, many Indigenous People refer to the precolonial period as "the time before the lies."

If we can point to anything that might be construed as a source for the troubled times of our world today, it may well be the deceit, propaganda, and the cultural hegemony that inform our collective decisions. Although a part of the American social/political phenomenon for two centuries or more, it seems that this deception has reached new heights in recent years. For example, an enormous factual database now exists that documents the deceptions of the Bush administration alone, including a number of books, many of them scholarly, with titles such as *The Lies of George W. Bush: Mastering the Politics of Deception; The Bush Betrayal; Fraud: The Strategy behind the Bush Lies and Why the Media Didn't Tell You; The Book on Bush: How George W. Misleads America; Worse than Watergate: The Secret Presidency of George W. Bush; All the President's Spin: George W. Bush, the Media and the Truth; The Immaculate Deception: The Bush Crime Family Exposed; American Dynasty: Aristocracy, Fortune and the Politics of Deceit in the House of Bush; Weapons of Mass Deception: The Uses of Propaganda in Bush's War on Iraq; The Five Biggest Lies Bush Told Us about Iraq; How Mr. Bush Got His War: Deceptions, Double-Standards and Disinformation; Big Bush Lies: The 20 Most Telling Lies of President George W. Bush*, and so on. Yet it seems that the larger and more consequential the lie, the more likely it goes unchallenged.

This text has been an effort to reciprocate the vast, hurtful deceptions that have been perpetrated against Indigenous People, as well as against the great and necessary wisdom of their various and varied cultures, not just because Indigenous People deserve a truthful portrayal at long last, but because such a portrayal may be vital for all of us if we are to survive.

The language of conquest ignores the Indigenous idea that we are all related and thus, to lie to one another is to lie to ourselves. Communication is a sacred release of power. Words can literally sing things into existence. A language of conquest has the power to bring about destruction. A language of truth has the power to renew. The contributing authors of this volume pray that their words will somehow ultimately bring back joyfulness intended for all creatures, in the same way that the Navajo Blessing Way ceremony restores happiness to a sick patient.

In a version of Chief Seattle's speech, he concludes, "At night when the streets of your cities and villages are silent and you think them deserted, they will throng with the returning hosts that once filled them and still love this beautiful land." We pray that we will not have to wait for such a silence before we can all once again live with such love in our hearts, a love that comes not from a language of conquest, but from a language of truth.

ESSAYS FROM *The Encyclopedia of* *American Indian History* || **Appendix**

Four Arrows

I requested and received permission to publish my three submissions for the *Encyclopedia of American Indian History* (2006) as an appendix to this volume. The first essay, "The Myth of the Noble Savage," will hopefully deflect allegations that our text overly glorifies Indigenous perspectives in the same way that Rousseau and others romanticized them.

The second piece, on social control, is offered to emphasize the seemingly intentional role of public education in the language of conquest, a topic not sufficiently addressed in this text and deserving of a book unto itself. This snapshot illustrates how the language of conquest is woven into schools.

The third submission is a brief overview of what the concept of Indigenous worldview means. Throughout this text we have challenged the forces that have tried to suppress it, but only marginally have actually defined it. Ending with this essay may inspire the next step in the right direction, now that the reader understands that such worldview concepts have been suppressed for centuries.

All pieces are reprinted with permission from *The Encyclopedia of American Indian History*, ABC-CLIO, 2006.

THE MYTH OF THE NOBLE SAVAGE

One of the most enduring, ironic and perhaps damaging of the concepts used to describe American Indians is represented both by the idea of a "noble savage" and by the phrase, "myth of the noble savage." In the first instance, the oxymoronic pairing of words and the myth that has surrounded them puts First Nations People in an untenable social position. In the second instance, the "myth" idea has been used to dismiss legitimate contributions, worldviews, and qualities of Indigenous People.

Christopher Columbus may have started the concept of the noble savage with his first reports about the islanders he "discovered" in the new world. He described them as being generous, innocent, peaceful, and easy to make servile while rationalizing his treatment of them because they were nonetheless "savages." Throughout European and American literature, poetry, paintings and film, the noble savage was painted as being totally innocent, physically perfect, always fearless, highly instinctive (without thinking or emotional skills), peaceful, free of social restraints, and a part of nature that is extremely brutish when provoked. In literature, such attributes made for good fantasy. They also played to European audiences as they set the stage for showing how the stronger, more realistic characteristics of Europeans could be used to conquer the weaker, "outdated" primitives. Historically and politically, such images of Indigenous People may have helped rationalize genocidal atrocities on the one hand, and assuage guilt for such crimes on the other.

Although the phrase, "noble savage," was first used to describe the Natives of Mexico in the fictional writings of John Dryden around 1672, Jean-Jacque Rousseau and others gave significance to the idea in political discourse. Rousseau used it to criticize dominant European political and educational assumptions, and as a backdrop for his own political agenda in the mid-1700s. In so doing, he mentioned authentic ideas about Indigenous approaches to democracy and equality that would later be used by the founding fathers of the United States to develop its constitution. However, like Thomas Hobbes and John Locke, he also dehumanized and disenfranchised the American Indians by placing them in a state of evolution to which "civilized" humans could not return. These writers wrongly promoted the idea that Indigenous People merely wandered freely in nature and did not have social institutions that might otherwise cause them to be less equitable in their lifestyles and culture.

The Jesuit missionaries also contributed to the noble savage myth. Wanting to achieve martyrdom, they described the danger and savagery of the Indigenous People. Wanting to rationalize their Christian missions, they also had to convey that the People were nonetheless children of God and deserving of being saved by their missionary agenda. Thus, they gave them the noble attributes of innocent children, as were favored in the noble savage myth, simultaneously with those of the brute savage with whom they took great risks for God's work.

After the conquest and submission of American Indians, many people subscribed to the ideas about their nobility and strengths to legitimize their own right to the land and to challenge new immigrant "invaders." The settlers could claim to be a native of the land themselves now. By so doing they could rationalize their right to resist the migration of new settlers who brought their foreign, ignorant and threatening ways with them. Later, in the 1800s, American pioneers may have used similar appropriations about Indigenous virtues in their stories about such "heroes" as Red Cloud, Sitting Bull, and Crazy Horse to convey their own strength and their own claims to the land.

The myth of the noble savage has been but one of the European ideas that served to colonize and oppress American Indians. Even in contemporary times, the media has made American Indians appear as anything but who they really are: a perfect sidekick for a white hero; a dangerous foil for the military might of other white heroes; or as a romantic artifact of the past.

Throughout history, this ironic phrase has been used to rationalize physical and cultural genocide against Indigenous People. It supported manifest destiny.

Scholars employed the concept in discussions about human nature and social progress. Politicians refer to it as a way to promote Eurocentric superiority. And it continues to be used to dismiss legitimate potential contributions that might offer a proven challenge to the worldview, policies and practices of the dominant Western culture.

INDIAN EDUCATION AND SOCIAL CONTROL

Federal control of "Indian Education" in the United States began as and largely has continued to be a way for the dominant social interests of the U.S. government to control American Indian cultures and prevent their various unique philosophical perspectives from being re-established. Beginning with the earliest tribal treaties in the late 1700s up until the last ones in 1871, the government agreed to provide vocational training in return for land and peace settlements. In truth, the educational provisions were designed to assimilate Indians. In fact, for the most part such education was contracted out to religious groups whose main purpose was to convert Indian people.

Conflict between U.S. troops and American Indians continued throughout the 1800s by those Nations that did not want to sign treaties or by those reacting to broken treaties, and in 1897, boarding schools were established by Congress as an alternative to shooting Indians. Army officer Richard H. Pratt convinced legislators that it would cost less money to "kill the Indian and save the man" than to use bullets. Children were forced into boarding schools where all aspects of Indian culture were forbidden. Indian families that would not send their children to the schools would be imprisoned and those on reservations were denied rations.

Federal treaties continued to guide the U.S. inclination to provide education for American Indians, but beginning in 1917 more and more responsibility was transferred to state public schools. In 1928, the Meriam Report, which harshly criticized the boarding schools, enhanced this transfer to the states, although the federal government continued to finance the programs. Education was now administered largely through the newly established Bureau of Indian Affairs, but public schools receiving funds for Indian Education still did not involve tribes in the education process and assimilation remained the goal.

The 1965 Elementary and Secondary Education Act, the 1972 Indian Education Act, the 1975 Indian Self-Determination and Education Assistance Act, the 1978 Tribally Controlled Community College Assistance Act, and the 1990 Native American Language Act attempted to reduce school problems, illiteracy and dropout rates in Indian schools, enhance educational opportunities for Indian students and replace U.S. control of Indian education with more tribally controlled policy and curriculum decisions. Problems continued however and in 1998 an executive order entitled, "American Indian and Alaska Native Education" stated a commitment to improve academic performance and reduce drop out rates of the half a million or so elementary and secondary tribal students who attend state public schools.

Funding for the 1965 Elementary and Secondary Education Act was reauthorized in 1994 as Title IX and in 2001, funding for the 1972 Indian Education Act was reauthorized as Title VII, Part A, in the No Child Left Behind Act. Both reauthorizations specifically recognize that American Indians have unique, educational and culturally relative academic needs and distinct language and cultural needs. Title VII, entitled "Indian, Native Hawaiian, and Alaska Native Education" allows for grants to school districts that focus on culturally related activities and Native-specific curriculum content. Unfortunately, a stipulation requires that such activities and curriculum must be "consistent with state standards." As a result, the forced assimilation of boarding school approaches to Indian Education has, in significant ways, merely been replaced by another, more subtle approach to assimilation goals in that state standards and the process identified by NCLB for implementing compliance to them often contradict the very goals of cultural relevance intended by Title VII.

This more subtle hegemony in modern education may be the most effective method of social control of all those employed against American Indians under the guise of education policy. Indian education systems are still shaped by non-Indian social, cultural and economic purposes that differ from those of traditional Indian people. The majority of teachers in Indian schools are non-Indian and those who are Indian have been certified in teaching through teacher education programs that emphasize dominant cultural values. Not only curriculum, but the form of most education programs for Indian children opposes that which reflects the values of various First Nations. For example, learning goals more in line with traditional American Indian philosophies relate to specific roles for males and females in society; to a strong experience of democratic ideals and freedom at an early age; to a concept of authority that does not recognize position but instead honors wisdom or ability; to a teaching style that is indirect; and to learning styles that are about observation, imitation and acceptance of responsibility. Labeling, punishment, the concept of a delinquent child, social stigma emphasizing incompetence, materialism, competition, irrelevant and fragmented curriculum, a de-emphasis on creative expression, the absence of spirituality, and alienation from Nature are all aspects of American education that violate Indigenous approaches to education.

A number of American Indian scholars are claiming that "anti-Indianism" is a major challenge to education in America and that it is rampant and largely unrecognized in television programming, Hollywood films, popular and academic literature and textbooks, radio talk shows, magazines and newspapers. As the purpose of education for all Americans moves more and more toward the goals of global competition and less and less toward creating good people and a healthy world, the loss of and continual suppression of American Indian cultural assumptions for education should be a major concern for all of us.

AMERICAN INDIAN WORLDVIEWS AND VALUES

American Indians enjoyed a rich diversity of worldviews, values, philosophies, spiritual concepts, mythologies and ceremonies, both as individuals and as

Nations. However, there are certain characteristic ideas that American Indian cultures had and have in common. Indeed, recognition of an "Indigenous World-view" as a philosophical system is gaining momentum in academic circles, though it is still in its infancy as a field outside the boundaries of traditional anthropology or "new age" literature. Such generalized values and ways of experiencing the world offer positive alternatives to contemporary Western assumptions. Unlike the "myth of the noble savage," the following concepts deserve serious study as an opportunity to restore the health and balance in all living systems.

Perhaps the most obvious consideration that runs through all or most Indigenous worldviews is a strong sense of relatedness. The idea of interconnectedness between animals, rocks, rivers, people, etc., informs many of the values and ways of thinking and being in the world that are typical to American Indian People. It naturally leads to avoiding dualistic thinking. It tends to prevent looking at the world as a detached observer. It emphasizes cooperative engagement over competition. It focuses on living in harmony with Nature rather than attempting to conquer it. It underlies the basic American Indian regard for reciprocity as a cornerstone for decision-making and relationships of all sorts.

Dovetailing also from the concept of relatedness are four other typically American Indian values: the acceptance of mystery; the honoring of alternative paths; an authentic sense of humility; and the belief that the highest form of courage is in the expression of generosity. These four concepts underscore American Indian spirituality, which might be defined as a life that gives sacred significance to all things. Perhaps an understanding that everything is related and significant, coupled with a learning style that emphasizes keen observation, has led cultures that maintained a close relationship with the Earth toward realizing that humans cannot possibly have all of the answers to the complex mysteries regarding life.

Although Indigenous cultures are unique in their widespread adherence to such realizations about life, philosophers from all cultures have expressed similar ideas and values throughout time. Interestingly, however, many of these seem to refer to their own Indigenous traditions. A prime example is found in the worldview of Gandhi, which parallels American Indian thinking. Gandhi often referred to the "primordial traditions" of India in describing this worldview that he called, "swaraj," and which might be interpreted as "fearless action and self-less suffering." Swaraj included selfless action in behalf of community welfare; complete individual freedom to seek truth in light of a deep understanding of relatedness with other; a non-anthropocentric understanding of self in relation to Nature; sustainable lifestyles; shared wealth; fearlessness in pursuit of truth; and an understanding of pain and suffering in terms of a healing, integrative force for social welfare.

When such ideas are organic manifestations of the lived life of an entire community, rather than an idealism advocated or practiced by a few, a number of perspectives tend to emerge as behaviors in a culture that seem to oppose Western assumptions and behaviors. For example, taking care of others, not just self, guides all action. Enjoying the present becomes more important than preparing for the future, as long as actions do not create harm for "the seventh generation." Place becomes more important than time. Age is honored for its wisdom more than youth and beauty are honored for their virtues. Patience is more easily accommodated than is aggression. Listening becomes more prevalent than speaking up. Giving and sharing are a priority over taking and saving. Intuition is trusted as much or more than logic. Humility and modesty overshadow arrogance and ego. Aesthetics and creativity outshine the idea of a work ethic. And women are seen as equal to or even superior in their ability to contribute to society than are men.

Finally, the Indigenous worldview includes an approach to conflict resolution that may explain why American Indian people were/are less war-like than those with more Indo-European worldviews. Peace making is rooted in transformative theory rather than retributive, hierarchical, adversarial, punitive or codified assumptions. Responsibility is emphasized over rights, and when parties reach consensus for restoration and accountability, opposing parties are seen as being back in good relationship with one another, seeing the world more with their hearts than with their heads.

Recommended Reading

Cajete, Gregory. *Look to the Mountain: An Ecology of Indigenous Education*. Durango, Colo.: Kivaki Press, 1993.

Grim, John, ed. *Indigenous Traditions and Ecology: The Interbeing of Cosmology and Community*. Cambridge: Harvard University Press, 2001.

INDEX

Lightning Source UK Ltd.
Milton Keynes UK
UKHW011941160922
408955UK00011B/264

9 780292 713260